MW01130052

The

ASTROLOGY WORKBOOK

Explains the first principles of astrology, and presents the birth chart as a unique system of visualizing the complexities of our natures and lives.

'Ms Mansell should be congratulated on her thoughtful and wide-ranging attitude to the subject . . . I warmly recommend this book.' — Prediction

In the same series

THE ASTRAL PROJECTION WORKBOOK
J. H. Brennan

THE CHINESE ASTROLOGY WORKBOOK
Derek Walters

THE CRYSTAL WORKBOOK
Ursula Markham

THE DOWSER'S WORKBOOK
Tom Graves

THE DREAMER'S WORKBOOK
Nerys Dee

THE DREAMWORK MANUAL
Strephon Kaplan Williams

THE ESP WORKBOOK
Rodney Davies

THE FORTUNE-TELLER'S WORKBOOK
Sasha Fenton

THE GRAPHOLOGY WORKBOOK
Margaret Gullan-Whur

THE I CHING WORKBOOK
R. L. Wing

THE MEDITATOR'S MANUAL
Simon Court

THE NUMEROLOGY WORKBOOK
Julia Line

THE PALMISTRY WORKBOOK
Nathaniel Altman

THE PLAYING CARD WORKBOOK
Joanne Leslie

THE PSYCHIC ENERGY WORKBOOK
R. Michael Miller & Josephine M. Harper

THE REINCARNATION WORKBOOK
J. H. Brennan

THE RITUAL MAGIC WORKBOOK
Dolores Ashcroft-Nowicki

THE RUNIC WORKBOOK
Tony Willis

THE TAROT WORKBOOK
Emily Peach

The ASTROLOGY WORKBOOK

Understanding the Art of Natal Interpretation

CORDELIA MANSALL

THE AQUARIAN PRESS

First published August 1985

British Library Cataloguing in Publication Data

Mansall, Cordelia
The astrology workbook.
1. Astrology
I. Title
133.5 BF1708.1

ISBN 0-85030-343-5

The Aquarian Press is part of the Thorsons Publishing Group, Wellingborough, Northamptonshire, NN8 2RQ, England.

Printed in Great Britain by Woolnough Bookbinding Limited, Irthlingborough, Northamptonshire

7 9 11 13 15 14 12 10 8

The Astrology Workbook is
dedicated to my students past
and present, my son Raymond
and to you.

Acknowledgements

I would like to thank Mr Thomas L. Prothero who taught me to look at life with eyes wide open, Lee Phillips who has always kept faith, Frederick Davies through whom I learned that there was more to astrology than sun signs, Alice Back, my FAS tutor who allowed me space to grow, Jim White whose profound thoughts stimulated and inspired at just the right times, John Sugarman for his helpful healing, Maggie Linford and Hermione Raven for the peace of their home in which to think and write. It was Sheila O'Hara who said 'See the person in the chart, and listen to what they say!' I used her words as they are for this is the way it is. Most of all I wish to acknowledge my good fortune to have a mother who believes in the ready outward expression of feelings. Thank you to Geoffrey Dean, Mary Ann Ephgrave, Pat Harris, Sandra Levy, Tony Lewis, Val Mulligan and Alma Newnham who read, checked, criticized or generally gave practical help. Special thanks must go to Clare Hawley who generously gave time, energy, constructive criticism and support without whom this book would not have been written. And, of course, to my long-suffering family and my patient publisher, thank you.

Contents

Introduction

It is a satisfying surprise to find that the study of astrology is more fascinating than you could ever imagine. Most of us owe eternal gratitude to the popular **Sun signs** for our initial introduction to this subject. Whether in the newspaper or magazine columns, on radio, T.V. or anywhere else for that matter, there is no doubt about it, **Sun sign astrology** is fun! It is often extraordinary how revealing a simple birth date can be. Certainly the basic characteristics associated with the twelve Sun signs provide a useful working knowledge of human behaviour in any situation, at home, work or play. There comes the time, however, when you reach the conclusion that the Sun signs reflect the rather general personality traits that are most obvious, as if the face or mask that is presented to the world. In fact, they usually reveal *how others see us!* Once the mask has been recognized for what it is, glimpses of the character that lies behind it become increasingly more noticeable. The Sun signs have served their purpose very well: not only have they acted as an introduction to the further study of astrology but they have also sharpened your capacity to observe human nature and, perhaps most significantly, they have encouraged you to begin the lengthy process of opening You up to Yourself!

Since *astrology is the study of the mirror image of life upon this Earth with the patterning of the planets in our solar system,* all knowledge of human existence is reflected in that mirror. This means that the study of astrology must be endless. There are no 'experts' for no-one can possibly know all that there is to know of the variety of human expression, for new understanding is occurring all the time. In the same way, knowledge of the principles of astrology is forever unveiling. Apace with today's dramatic escalation towards an ever-heightening technological society, is the growing awareness that the exciting development of 'harmonics' by John Addey is enabling astrologers to gain insight into the workings and essence of astrology. We all have our part to play in this magical time for the way is open for you and I to make a contribution to greater human understanding. There is plenty of room for you should you wish to become a practising astrologer; to join with those already actively involved in research; to found research areas of your own to work upon, or to simply use astrology as a tool to gain greater appreciation of yourself in your daily life. At this point in time, my role is to provide you with a guide to understanding astrology in the light of modern thought and to try to give some insights into the *why* of the principles of astrology that are so often taken for granted. It is my belief that knowledge of the *why* facilitates a more flexible appreciation and usage of what is available. You will also find details concerning how to further your knowledge of astrology through the recognized astrological schools and organizations should you so wish, together with a list of recommended books. With a long and richly fascinating road ahead, remind yourself that there is no hurry; relax and enjoy discovering more about yourself and life in general.

The more knowledge we possess of life, the more tolerant we can become of our own nature and that of others. *Astrology is a way of understanding human expression.* While there are many ways of pursuing this knowledge, each having much to offer, astrology's uniqueness lies in its capacity to give *context and perspective* to that expression. Through its tenets we are privileged to actually witness the oft talked about *sense of wholeness*. The study of astrology can, and should, alter your conscious appraisal of life; a subtle shift in emphasis away from self to consider an individual life as part of the life of the universe inclines the astrological student to become more philosophical and compassionate towards himself and others. Life's problems and difficulties are also seen in a similar perspective, placed, as they are, in the context of patterns of existence, so that the manner in which they are tackled invariably becomes noticeably more positive. It is not simply a matter of knowing 'good' or 'bad' periods but of appreciating the rhythmic cycles of being in order to monitor human development and divine the potential to be more than we are.

In itself, astrology does not moralize or preach the domination of one code of behaviour over another; rather it draws upon the totality of our individual experience which is subject to our upbringing and education. The nature of astrology is such that it relates to life as it pulsates throughout the universe. The references to 'God' found in this book speak of that universal sense of 'Oneness' that is at the heart of all religions. The knowledge and insight that you will gain from using the cosmic language, astrology, will always be translated according to your own religious views and socio-ethnic considerations.

There is nothing that need worry anyone; astrology will not rule your life but it will assuredly open your eyes and heart to human understanding.

It is impossible to say all that should be said about astrology in one book. I can do no more than attempt to provide some explanations and insights into the first principles of astrology, for it is a firm grasp of these which will create a basis for any further work. It is fair to state that the natal or birth chart is the hub of all the astrologer's work. We are drawn like magnets to the fascinating techniques of *progressions* for they enable the unfoldment of the life-span to be seen; *transits* using the current positions of the planets to provide the detail; *mid-points* and the excitement of *harmonics*. It is easy to get out of one's depth, floundering in a sea of so much confusing new information. Without the ability to read a natal chart with confidence, any such techniques become meaningless.

You will find that in some areas of this book there is something of an imbalance, for I have devoted less time and space to those areas in astrology which are well served by the astrological community. Many books are now available that take areas such as the Sun signs or individual planets as their main theme. I have tended to give more space to those areas which, although forming the basis of the birth chart, have so far received little attention. The whole of Chapter 4 has been devoted to the *houses*, for example. The *aspects*, too, have their own chapter and are presented in accord with the principles of numerology (the meaning of numbers) forming an introduction to the harmonics of astrology.

To gain a good working knowledge of astrological principles and a full appraisal of the differing viewpoint among astrologers, you are urged to read as extensively as possible. At the back of this book, you will find a list recommending books according to the individual chapters.

I wish you joy and fulfilment.

CORDELIA MANSALL D.F. ASTROL. S.
London, 1985

Chapter 1
Growth and Development

Scientists and sceptics are very fond of deriding astrology on the premise that there seems to be little proof concerning *how* it works. Surprisingly, no-one ever seems to question *why* it should work. While a good deal of proof has and is being gathered, research and testing is invariably conducted by dedicated individuals at their own cost simply because they believe it important to examine the whole fabric of astrology fairly. Virtually all astrological research is funded by astrologers.

Possibly the most baffling feature to any newcomer is that there are differing opinions concerning *what* astrology is. While it is popularly believed that we are directly affected by the planets in our solar system, it comes as a surprise to many people that this is, in fact, a view held by only a small minority of astrologers. However, there may eventually be proof of an actual effect. Space probes are providing information that we are, as the Ancients maintained, comprised of the same matter as the rest of the universe. It is possible that there is an interlinking biochemical reaction between the cosmos and the trace elements in our bodily systems which are known to vary in quantity according to the individual. In the sixteenth century, Paracelsus, the most brilliant physician of his day, treated his patients' lassitude and 'poverty of Mars' with appropriate doses of iron. Today metallurgist, Nick Kollerstrom is investigating the disturbances of iron filings at the times of configurations involving the planet Mars, traditionally said to rule iron.

Atmospheric ionization may be found to be affected by the planets or sunspot activity. It is a known fact that people are affected differently according to the build-up of positive ions in the atmosphere; some being more noticeably 'weather sensitive' than others. There is evidence of the increase in the crime rate, for example, in areas such as Geneva at certain times of the year when there is a marked increase of positive ions in the atmosphere. Pollution, particularly that from lead from traffic fumes, may link with symptoms of stress and depression. Any astrologer will note that the reasons for a consultation are very often associated with Saturn, the planet said to traditionally rule lead: perhaps research will be able to link these occurrences together, perhaps not.

Electricity is a relatively recent discovery and, although we take its uses for granted, it is still not known precisely what it is. By the same token, who can deny the possibility of the discovery of another more subtle source of energy. Perhaps it is linked with gravity. Virtually three hundred years have elapsed since Newton's principle of universal gravitation was made known to the world yet scientists are no closer to understanding what it is.

The natural rhythms of existence cannot be refuted. We are all conscious of the fundamental axial rotation of this planet in each twenty-four hour period creating day and night but are, perhaps, unaware of the subtle daily changes in body temperature. Sequences of heightened sunspot activity occur in an apparent cycle of approximately eleven years and are recorded in the differences in the annual rings of trees and in the changes in the annual harvests which have been found to have a direct correlation with the rise and fall of wheat prices on the Stock Market. Unfortunately, these are cycles too numerous to describe for they are a study in themselves. There are also plenty of research opportunities for linking terrestrial cycles with celestial phenomena.

Many people become aware of a pattern emerging over a period of years. Depending upon the individual life pattern, three, four or seven year cycles, for instance, become apparent. Familiarity with the basic rhythms can enable us to cope more rationally with the highs and lows encountered through the course of normal living. Easiest to observe is the Sun's annual cycle. Each year our vitality follows a relatively predictable pattern traced by some discerning medical practitioners. During the four months immediately following on from the birthday, in normal health, energy flows freely with good vitality, by which time the habit may have been acquired of taking such energy for granted. During the following two months, a gradual slowing down is experienced until the point *exactly six months after the birthday* when we all encounter our lowest ebb. Precisely on that day, a general feeling of lassitude, depression and the complaint, 'why am I like this?' is often the norm. Be of good cheer, the cycle of vitality picks up again over the course of the next five months. 'Pre-birthday blues' are usually encountered in the four weeks preceding the birthday. Rather than giving way to negative thoughts of yet another year ticking by, you can make use of this period by planning the coming year in order to make more constructive use of the up-swing in vitality after your birthday. You can live more harmoniously with your cycle of vitality by organizing a healthful regime at least two months prior to your lowest ebb of the year. It is wise, too, to try to incorporate an annual holiday at some stage in that period. In this way you can help to mitigate any possible health problems that tend to occur more frequently when the vitality is lowered. It is a relatively simple matter to trace this and the many more complex cycles that are apparent in human nature and all life upon this planet, using the natural tool, astrology.

The nature of astrology is that it deals essentially with life, and the understanding that life is a series of relationships. What may appear to be a myriad complexity of

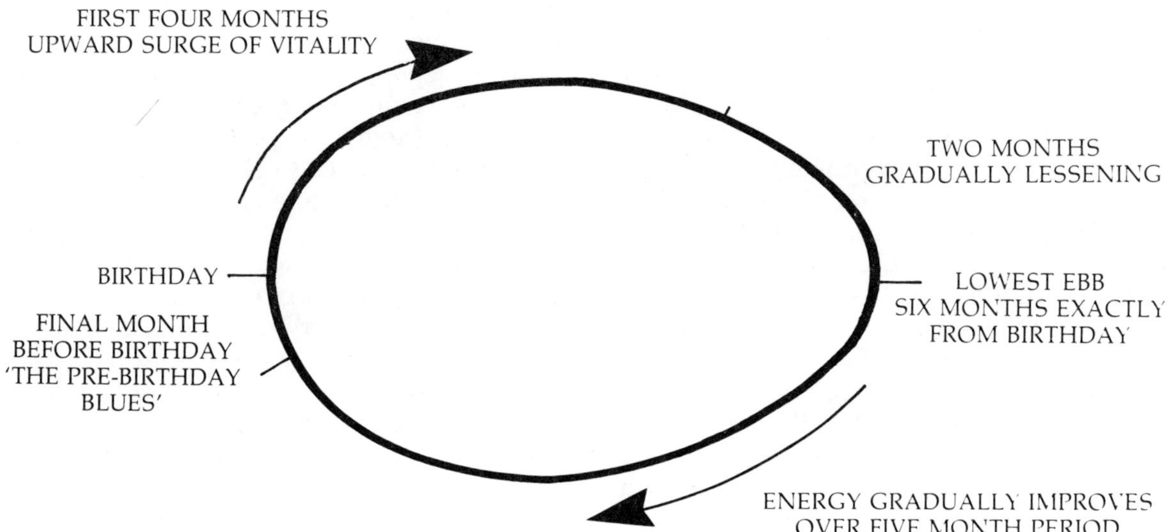

Figure 1 Annual vitality cycle

inter-relationships becomes utter simplicity when viewed via the framework of astrology. However, to examine life with such clarity means that you must know astrology intimately. It is a complex study since the more you study, the more understanding flows, opening up hitherto unsuspected channels and areas that need to be explored. The main channel that is used must be yourself. Thus, it is essential that you come to know yourself thoroughly.

The complexity of an individual's nature continues to perplex the most able psychologists, behaviourists, doctors, etc., and if we are using astrology to shed light upon the intricacies of the human personality, it follows that it too must be more complex than is often supposed. The biggest problem that scientists have when confronted with a true astrologer in action, is the system by which they intend to measure his work. Usually, just one feature of the birth chart is taken and analysed out of context of the whole, rather like a doctor attempting to diagnose a patient's ailment by only examining an elbow. With growing sophistication in the use of computers, it may be possible to devise a multi-variant analysis in which several features are examined simultaneously. Things to come!

By maintaining that we are directly influenced by the planets in our solar system, we effectively absolve ourselves from bearing the responsibility for our actions. Granted it is easier to believe in some kind of 'influence' causing us to be as we are, rather than accepting that the symbolism of the patterning of the heavens can reveal the true nature of being, so that we can come to know ourselves thoroughly and, by doing so, command our actions. According to the fundamental premise of astrology, mankind is capable of being greater than he is. Astrologers believe that everything in our universe is synchronized and linked together. One part does not function without another part.

Astrologers are in the privileged position of being able to *witness the cycles of nature occurring on Earth through the mirror image of the planets' cyclic motions.* These cycles are the *patterns of being* and are *symbolic* in concept. Why such a correlation should exist is not yet known. It is arguably theological. Some astrologers, including myself, believe that this correlation exists as 'God's guidelines', hence the meaning of the *signs* of the zodiac literally sign-posting the way to Knowledge, Wisdom and Enlightenment. Other astrologers are perfectly happy that it exists simply by chance (perhaps, like Mount Everest, because it is there!). Certainly it is healthy to question, to be sceptical, to duly study the subject and then to formulate your own opinion.

The popular image of astrology is that of a system of prediction. Because the mirror image of the planets' unceasing motion offers the advantage of viewing life upon Earth at will from the past, through to the present and into the future, time is seen as a continuous thread. It does not make sense to view the future as if a separate entity divorced from its rightful position as the natural outcome of the past and the present. Modern astrologers are reluctant to simply predict the possible happenings of the future for that reason. In preference, they seek to enlighten by examining the individual personality seen in the context of the whole life-span. It is possible to determine the nature and circumstances of the birth, the conditioning received during childhood and, indeed, the formation and development of the personality. It is not possible to determine the nationality of the individual nor that of the parents. However, it is interesting how national characteristics as such are often discernible in the personality. It is not possible to ascertain the time of death and thought unethical to make decisions of any kind. A client would be encouraged to exercise his or her own right to choose any course of action, but must certainly feel more confident to do so when able to understand the prevailing conditions more fully.

In terms of modern society, astrology is becoming more relevant than at any time in its history. As we become more aware of society's needs, so we can witness the crises that accompany the growth of the individual and collective man. The noteable times of crises during the life-span correspond with known planetary cycles. At the crisis ages of, for example, 29, 36, 42, 58 and so forth, certain configurations enable the astrologer to trace the *meaning* of the critical period for the individual, for it is that meaning which lends substance and reality to all of our actions and brings greater understanding. Thus, astrology is probably the single most valuable tool for self-understanding and invaluable in *counselling the individual or the family.* Planetary links between members of a family can be examined to give insight into problems that affect not just one member, but the whole family. Insight into the likely manner of development can enable parents to encourage the true potential of their children to emerge constructively. There are astrologers who are combining their qualifications as marriage guidance counsellors, to provide a deeper understanding of the problems encountered in *personal relationships*. In India, a Hindu couple would not risk marriage without first consulting an astrologer. A number of Australian *businesses* are successfully using astrology to deploy *personnel* into areas of work more suited to their personalities and capabilities. Astrology can be used in any area where career guidance is required: the school leaver; redundancy; the wish to try something more suitable; the rehabilitation of those who have been institutionalized in hospital or in prison, etc. *Financial* and *political* trends can also be monitored. However, in all instances, a firm grounding in the subject matter with which you wish to correlate astrological data is essential, otherwise the 'mirror image' can reflect only a limited picture.

In an extensive study carried out by a Czechoslovakian gynaecologist, the positioning of the Sun and the Moon in relation to individual fertility cycles have been proven to be 98 per cent reliable. The monitoring of such cycles provides an alternative method of contraception, or of determining the most propitious time for the creation of a family.

For countless centuries, the zodiac has been used to signify the differing parts of the body and until comparatively recently no diagnosis would be formulated without correlating it astrologically. Growing awareness of the astrological view that the physical body reflects and harbours the pain of the soul, can aid the body to heal itself. Nevertheless, *medical* astrology is as yet in its infancy. Although astrology clearly has much to offer modern medicine more medical practitioners are needed to do further research.

Probably most relevant to today's society is the use of astrology in any form of psychological counselling or therapy. Those involved in these fields often envy the astrologer the remarkable ability to examine the personality in great depth over long periods of time. The counsellor or therapist is invariably solely able to assess a patient's condition from the immediate circumstances or the remarks made by the patient. These can often be biased according to the state of mind of the patient. Astrology offers the 'over-view', so that the remarks may be seen in the context of the whole situation. Co-operation between astrologers and psychologists is occurring with more frequency and while a growing number of astrologers are seeking qualifications in varying fields of psychology, there are psychologists studying to become qualified to practise astrology. In spite of this, astrology is still rarely acknowledged for being such a vibrant tool for self-understanding. However, like astrology, times are changing!

The links between celestial phenomena and human activity have been recorded since 10,000 B.C. when hunters noted the phases of the Moon by carving notches on reindeer horns. Recognizable astrological records date back more than 5,000 years. Always tracing the growth of civilization, astrology has refined its tenets and developed to emerge in modern times as a sophisticated artifact able to examine and, often, to inspire the human condition. At the present time, astrology is undergoing its most vital renaissance. Traditional astrology is in the process of being revised, re-organized and re-assembled in the light of modern thought. Today's astrologers are the archaeologists of thought, peeling back the layers of knowledge assembled in the intervening years to re-examine the original theories of the Ancients. We are in the fortunate position, with computers at our disposal, and the opportunity to freely seek after truth in a truly scientific manner, to draw upon the legacy handed down to us from our ancestors. Such an undertaking was attempted earlier in our history by Johann Kepler (1571-1630) who wanted to synthesize the teachings of Pythagoras with the knowledge of his day. It is often thought that Kepler scorned his astrological work, but it seems that critics have ever been unaware of the difference between the popular almanacs that he published in order to feed his large family and the utterly pure astrology that was his love. He proclaimed that there was much to value in true astrological thought and urged that 'the baby not be thrown out with the bathwater'. An avowed Pythagorean, he sought to rationalize the ancient belief of the 'Harmony of the Spheres'. Pythagoras (fifth century B.C.) believed that the vibration of sound is subject to the laws of numbers causing a harmony which links the distances and dimensions of the universe in musical terms so that the heavenly bodies, the planets, must cause sounds as they move. Nature was visualized in terms of number, and music was thought to be the expression of number in terms of sound. Aristotle said, 'He supposes the whole heavens to be a harmonia and a number.'

By recognizing that the law of universal gravitation — 'every particle of matter in the universe attracts every other particle' — was the inevitable next step to the three laws of planetary motion, Isaac Newton effectively brought Kepler's scientific achievements to adulthood, but he was unable to do the same for Kepler's concurrent astrological achievements. Three hundred and fifty years later, quite independently, but in a manner that would have won Kepler's wholehearted admiration, John Addey (1920–1982) was to make that breakthrough with his invaluable contribution of the harmonics in astrology. In applying scientific theory to determine the validity of astrology, the truth forcibly emerged that the rhythms and sub-rhythms of cosmic cycles can be seen as being in harmony one with another. Addey's harmonics are the *visible expression* of the Pythagorean concept of number and the heavenly music of the spheres. He has provided the unifying factor that interlinks the meaning of cosmic periods (astrology) with the meaning of number (numerology) so that we can actually witness the vibration of the life force in man and all of man's endeavours. Addey's discovery is parallel to the giant leap that man has made this century to travel beyond the confines of this Earth to begin the exploration of space, for harmonics provides us with the key with which we can begin to unlock the mysterious meaning of life.

Chapter 2
The Tools

Long before it was realized that our Earth is but a member of a system of planets orbiting a rather ordinary star, that is one of countless millions of other stars comprising a galaxy, that is one of countless millions of galaxies, mankind viewed this Earth as the cradle of all being, as the centre of the universe. The planets, including the Sun and the Moon, seen moving through a fixed pathway that encircles the Earth, were understood to be one system that is part of a far greater mass. As a means of relating to that greater mass, our planetary system was taken to symbolize the universe.

Since man began to dominate this planet as its most intelligent creature, his progress has been sharply affected by his perception of Earth in relation to the rest of the universe. He is instinctively aware that it is expressive of his intimate relationship with God, and as such is the Prime Relationship containing the spirit of Oneness from which all emerges and to which all returns. Man's progress has undergone differing phases in which his developing knowledge of the relationship between this Earth and the rest of the universe has been accompanied by significant alterations to the manner in which he comprehends God, and in his attitude to himself.

With the advent of the telescope in 1609, making it possible to see the vastness of our universe, man's image and confidence in himself suffered a severe blow from which he has yet to fully recover. The universe had become too vast to contemplate. In an effort to reassert control over his existence, he turned his gaze away from the unfathomable unknown universe and directed his energies towards his own planet, for the Earth is tangible and can, therefore, be understood. The belief that a purely realistic view gives us control over our environment has become part of our daily lives. At the centre of our own private universe, our expectation is that we should be able to exert control over all that lies within our immediate compass. This is clearly apparent in the general pre-occupation with current experiences and problems which encourages us to endow them with a significance that may or may not be their due. Our expectation of life is amended by our discovery of what actually happens to us. This view has been compounded by the way in which we are taught from an early and impressionable age to view our planet as a small globe as if from somewhere out in space. By this means, Earth is effectively reduced to a manageable size. True astronomy is rarely taught, and the instinctive ability to look up at the heavens, outward, away from Self has been replaced by the conditioned command to look inward, toward this Earth and toward Self. If we are unafraid to think of ourselves as part of the whole, we gain a sense of oneness with this Earth and with the universe, and of one part functioning as it should, in unison with every other part, and the significance of the smallest action and reaction is raised beyond measure.

In an unbroken tradition spanning more than 5,000 years, *astrologers believe that everything has meaning* and perceive that meaning according to the premise 'as it is in the macrocosm (the universe), so it is in the microcosm (man as the universe in miniature)'. This concept is further translated into an utterly flexible cosmic language which can describe any factor of life upon this planet in relation to the microcosm — mankind on the collective or individual level. It is a living language composed of *principles that are richly symbolic,* encompassing all the knowledge that man has so far acquired concerning himself and his life upon this planet together with the knowledge that he has yet to awaken to. Astrology is this cosmic language.

In order to translate the cosmic language into human terms the astrologer requires the essential tool of the birth chart which is a map of the heavens that, like the still photograph taken from a moving reel of film, is a representation of the positioning of the planets at a particular time, date and place. Each birth chart is unique, for no two people are alike in every respect from our fingertips to our personalities. It is extremely rare for two people to be born at precisely the same time and place. A Belgian astrologer made a study of such time twins or 'cosmic twins' as they are also called. Born at the same time but 35 miles apart, he found that they not only bore an uncanny physical resemblance to each other, but also shared many experiences in common that had occurred at virtually the same times.

Even though the moment when conception actually takes place is so difficult to establish, since conception can occur at any time during a three day period, some astrologers prefer to study conception charts and the pre-natal epoch in the belief that conception marks the creation of a new life. By common consent, the moment of birth is respected as that moment of totally independent life. C. G. Jung echoed these sentiments when he said, 'Whatever is born or done at this moment of time, has the qualities of this moment of time.' The first cry and the severing of the umbilical cord usually occur within seconds. However, the first cry is deemed the most significant since it is that moment when the infant draws upon life-giving oxygen thereby making the statement, 'I partake of the substance and life of this planet' and formulating the commitment to be all that he or she is capable of becoming. The birth chart is the record of that commitment written in cosmic language.

Establishing a precise time of birth is invariably the astrologer's greatest problem. A birth chart cannot be accurately set up without it. Although the birth time is recorded in Scotland and most European countries, this does not necessarily apply to the rest of Great Britain and many other countries. It is helpful if parents can carefully record birth times of children to the minute. Hospitals are prone to record birth times to the nearest quarter hour. Without a correct birth time, an astrologer must resort to a process of *rectification* which can involve hours and, sometimes, days of calculations and comparisons with important events in the life. There is, however, no guarantee of a successful outcome of such work. In these cases it is possible to erect a *solar chart* based upon the day of birth. Such a chart would provide only generalized information pertinent to anyone born on that day. For a truly individual assessment of the personality an accurate record of time and place, as well as date of birth, are essential.

The circular chart preferred by today's astrologers is thought to have been introduced by Tycho Brahe (1546-1601) who, with the boldness characteristic of his approach to all his work, replaced the accepted rectangular chart of his day. In retrospect, this deceptively simple act provides a correlation with the significant contribution that he made in affecting a profound alteration in man's awareness of the universe, for it was Brahe's remarkably accurate observations that provided the foundation for the later work of Kepler, Newton and Einstein. Gone from the astrologer's work is the rectangular chart and the square favoured by Kepler. Both could be said to symbolize the lateral boundaries of the earthly plane to which man's thinking had been confined. The Earth is not flat but a swiftly moving sphere that is part of the rest of the universe.

No one need be deterred by the astronomical references of the birth chart or their calculation (Chapter 5) for they are all straightforward. The astronomy is best understood if you do not try to imagine the references but to locate them physically. By doing so you will easily understand the reason for the adoption of the circle of the ecliptic as the fundamental circle of the birth chart and its intersections by the horizon which form the four angles.

The word 'horoscope' means 'the view of the hour' and the birth chart (or horoscope) is the view of the heavens as they *appear to be* to us on Earth. We know that the Earth orbits the Sun, but it seems that it is the Sun that moves across the heavens rising and setting each day and it is this apparent movement that creates the circle of the birth chart. The zodiac lies alongside the Sun's pathway and they are synonymous one with the other (see Chapter 3 — The Zodiac). Over the course of a few days you can mark the points in the heavens where the Sun rises and sets. If you were to stand with arms outstretched facing the pathway of the Sun, your left hand would mark the point where the Sun rises, and your right hand, its setting. If you can then imagine a horizontal line drawn across from rising to setting, it would form the **Ascendant** and **Descendant** of the birth chart. In this position you would actually be *facing due South* towards the equator.

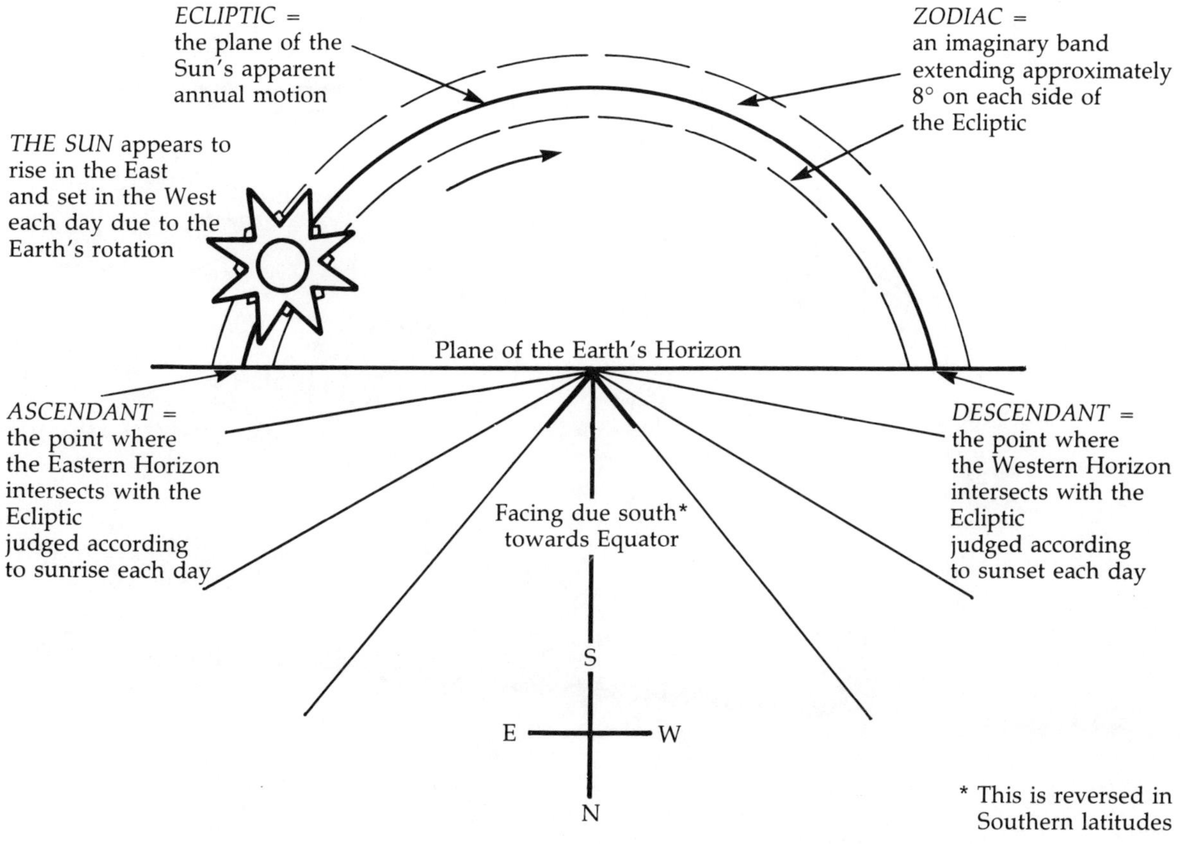

Figure 2 The Ascendant and Descendant

Remaining in this position, imagine a circle that begins from where you are standing climbing up until it cuts through the Sun's pathway (this intersection is called the **Midheaven**). The circle continues on until, on the other side of the Earth, it crosses the unseen half of the Sun's path. (This is the opposite point to the **Midheaven** called the **Imum Coeli** or **IC**). A connecting vertical line between the **Midheaven** and the **Imum Coeli** completes the cross. In this manner you physically create the essential features of the birth chart *and* the prime relationship. The ecliptical path contained within the zodiacal band symbolizes the universe; the axis of the **Ascendant** and **Descendant** crossed by the axis of the **Midheaven** and **Imum Coeli** forms the Cross of Matter symbolizing Earth. Thus the time and place of birth

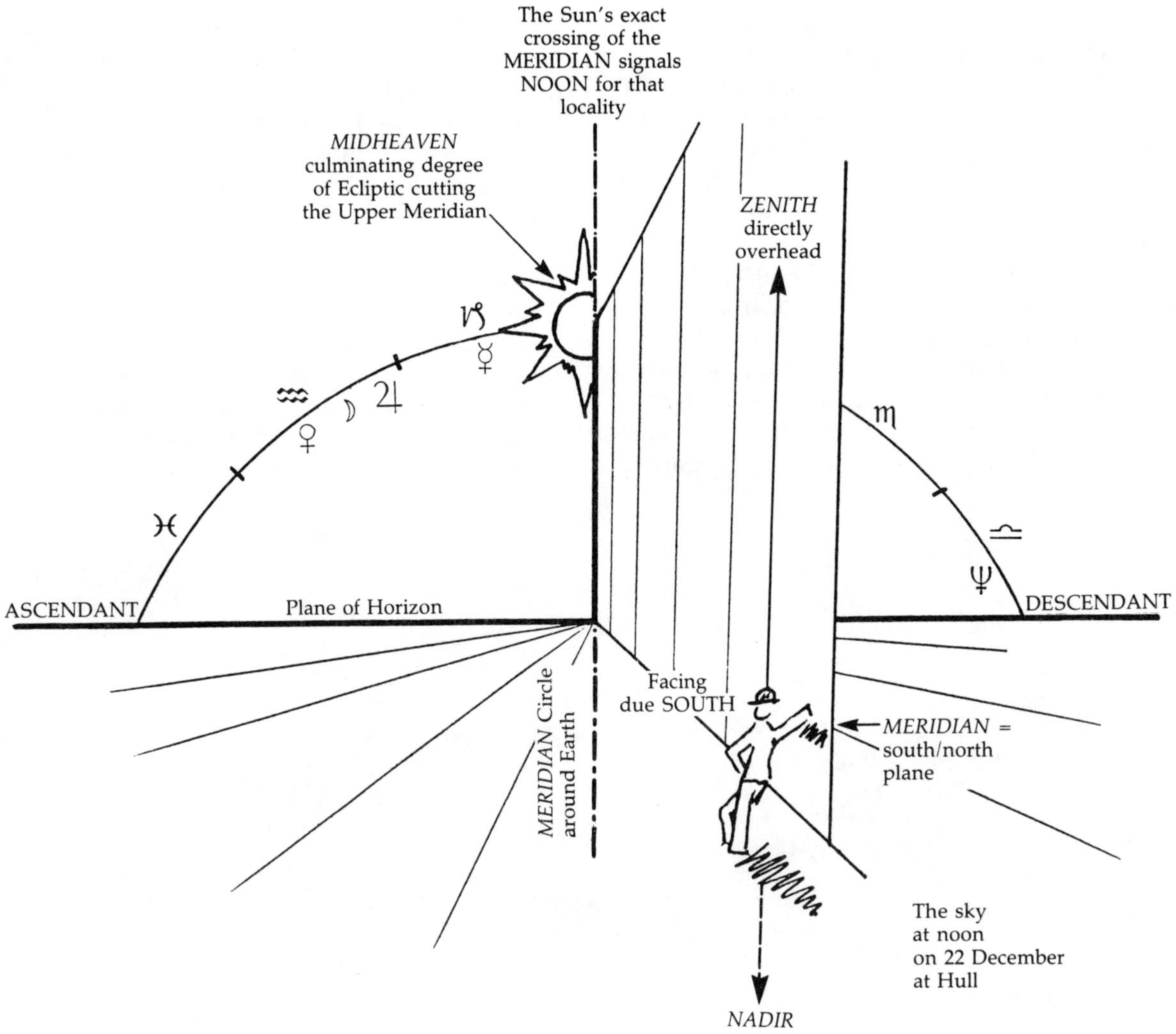

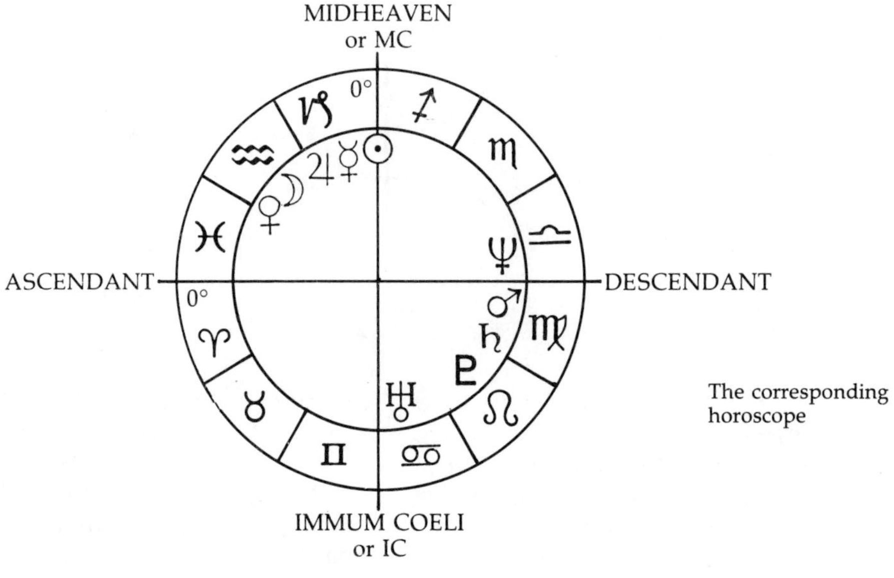

Figure 3 The Midheaven

signify the union between God and man.

Of all Earth's creatures, we have the most highly developed sense of social awareness, having an innate need to interact with our fellow human beings. Each relationship, no matter how fleeting, is of vital significance for it is through them that we learn who we are and how to behave in differing circumstances. If life is a series of relationships, each inter-related and part of a whole that is in essence, the prime relationship, it follows that, if the birth chart is to be truly representative of the individual, each of its features should have meaning according to the facets of that human being, and interrelate with every other feature. The structure of the birth chart itself contains a wealth of meaning.

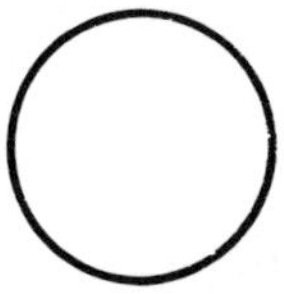

The circle of the birth chart is the symbol expressing timeless eternity, for it has no beginning and no end. Thought by the ancients to be the most perfect of shapes, it exemplifies God and the perpetual yearning of man to attain a state of oneness.

Dividing the Circle of Infinity in two halves is the axis or line of the horizon depicted by the glyph,

representing Earth and all that is contained upon it. It is the conscious state of the here and now; the actuality of life. It is symbolic too, of matter, and of feminine (or negative) energy. This then is the axis of the Ascendant/Descendant established by the **time of birth.**

The **Ascendant** astrologically signifies the manner in which the total personality shown by the whole birth chart is expressed. Whatever zodiacal sign is on the Ascendant of the chart reflects the overall personality traits, for it will show the way in which we approach life. It is the outward expression of our individual life force.

The **Descendant** shows the manner in which we make contact with others, for it is through others that we become fully aware of life. Through the interaction with other people, we are able to grow as individuals. In this manner we draw the world towards us and relate wholly to the life of this planet.

The vertical stroke represents the oneness of God. It symbolizes power descending upon mankind from above. By taking the line from the bottom, the yearning of mankind is shown reaching towards higher matters and to God. It is also symbolic of masculine (or positive) energy. This is the axis of the Midheaven and the Imum Coeli established by the **place of birth**.

The **Midheaven (MC)** signifies the image we have of ourselves and the direction in which we have to strive in order to most fully realize our potential. Because man is created in the image of God, he is meant to perfect himself. This is generally translated into the worldly terms of the aims and ambitions of life. The **Imum Coeli (IC)** indicates how we draw upon the resources of self, our origins and Mother Earth. Armed with the knowledge of who and where we are, we can be confident that our actions will be constructive. In exchange, this planet and its people must be nurtured for we are members of the human race and belong to the Earth.

The horizontal and vertical lines combine to form a cross which is known to be the earliest of man's symbols and found in every culture throughout the world.

As the the symbol of Manifestation and the Four Corners of the World, it expresses our encounter with actual experience and ability to take command of life's conflicts so that they may be brought to a balanced harmony.

The Circle of Infinity enclosing the Cross of Matter symbolizes our capacity to encompass both the spiritual and the material realms. In the union of these symbols, the birth chart signifies our capacity to attain harmony. This means that neither we, nor our lives can be expected to be constantly harmonious. At times, we are afforded privileged glimpses of what harmony means for us. We all long to find some sense of order in the midst of today's apparent chaos. The first lesson is to find peace within ourselves. Reminiscent of the cross-wires focus first used by Kepler to measure the heavens more easily and accurately, we can use this symbol to focus our total beings to interpret its meaning for the individual, or the collective or, indeed, anything whatsoever on the earthly plane.

It is the role of astrology to illustrate or to *illuminate the path* towards attaining a greater sense of inner harmony. It is Ariadne's thread enabling us to find our way through the labyrinth having vanquished the beastly, dark side of our natures represented by the Minotaur. The Seven Youths and Seven Maidens of this myth refer to the Number Seven of the Life Force represented by the Seven Naked Eye Planets according to the polarity of masculine and feminine. Knowledge of astrology can open many doors to understanding the myths and legends of antiquity as well as the allegorical tales of the Bible. In turn, they provide insight into astrological understanding, which aims to give a balanced view of life.

The goal of mankind is to attain a sense of balance between spirituality and materialism, so every feature of the birth chart polarizes with another. Positive and negative are the two poles of the one life force. Positive (masculine) energy signifies cosmic force full of inspiration and ideas busily rushing hither and thither about the universe scattering energy in all directions but unable to be productive until combined with its opposite pole, negative (feminine) energy being Mother Earth, which utilizes form, discipline and logic to contain and harness cosmic force that *together* they might be creatively productive. Each birth chart expresses this concept according to the distribution of planets through the zodiac (see Chapter 3). It does not refer directly to gender or sexuality but to the individual expression of energy. It is possible that this polarity is akin to the essential quality of electricity with its correlating positive and negative poles. Interestingly, the combination of electrical positive and negative poles produce *light*, but when 'earthed' by actual contact with this Earth, *power* is the result.

As the living symbol of the Prime Relationship, the birth chart is in no sense a static entity for it represents the power and potential of the individual life force. Each feature of the birth chart enables us to grow closer to comprehending the uniqueness of every human being. In the same way that the Four Angles (Ascendant, Descendant, Midheaven and Imum Coeli) express the Four Corners of the World, there are four sets of principles, the zodiac, the houses, the planets and the aspects. In keeping with the fundamental tenets of the Prime Relationship, each of these sets of principles inter-relates with the others, forming an extraordinarily simple system that nonetheless enables us to understand the endless intricacies of the human personality.

1. The Twelve Signs of the Zodiac.
2. The Twelve Houses.
3. The Ten Planets (for convenience' sake, including the Sun and the Moon).
4. The Aspects between the planetary bodies.

Together they represent a unique method of comprehending human behaviour by providing a visual image of the complexity of our nature and lives in symbolic terms. Individually they represent:

1. The various expressions of personality.
2. The variety of human experience on the earthly plane.
3. The motivating force of our actions.
4. The differing capabilities to attune to a sense of harmony.

These features not only interact with one another but are seen as extensions of one another. While it is possible to form deductions concerning behaviour by observing only the zodiacal signs or only the planets, no conclusions can be drawn without observance of the whole chart comprising all its details.

An invaluable method of acquiring the information symbolized by the First Principles, is to draw each of the appropriate symbols onto a separate card (index or postcard size) until a whole set of cards is gradually built up — one for each of the twelve **signs** of the zodiac; twelve cards

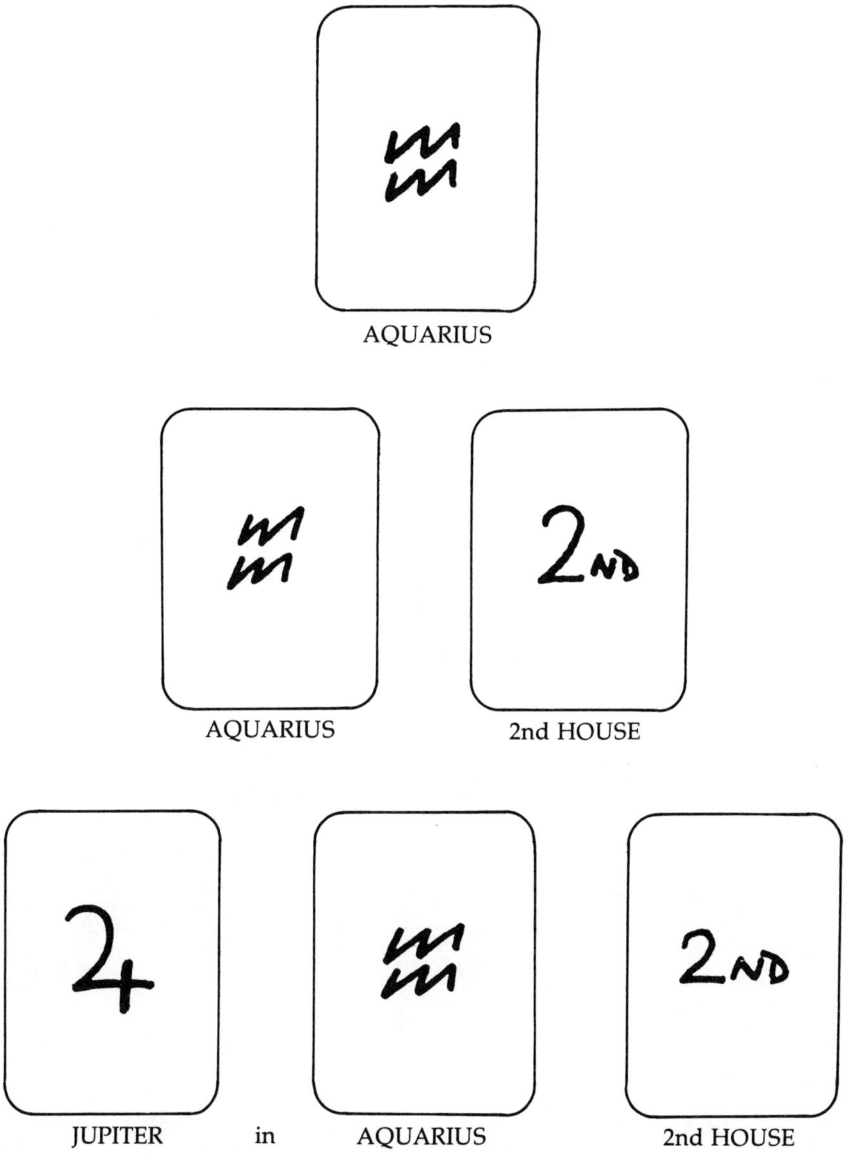

Figure 4 The card system of learning

numbered from one to twelve for each of the **houses** and one for each of the ten **planets**, making a total of thirty-four cards. Later on in your studies, you will be able to add the symbols used for the different **aspects**. Whenever you read anything concerning the signs, houses or planets, place the appropriate card, or cards, in front of you, just within your sightline. In this way you will be unconsciously associating what you are reading with the symbol or symbols in question. It is a known fact that we unconsciously assimilate far more information than we can ever consciously appreciate. When you come to view the symbols in their correct setting, the birth chart, you will find that the wealth of knowledge contained in these principles, can come more readily to the fore. Experience has shown that this method of learning facilitates eventual analysis and interpretation of the birth chart.

Certain keywords were assigned to these principles in the 1950s. They were created to provide ready clues to the knowledge contained by the principles. However, unless they are used as they were intended, they can actually limit your potential to interpret the meaning of the zodiac, houses, planets and aspects according to an individual birth chart. Naturally, you must study in the manner best suited to your needs and you may find the keywords useful to begin with.

Chapter 3
The Zodiac

Extending approximately 8° on each side along the whole length of the ecliptic (the apparent path of the Sun) is the imaginary band known as the zodiac. Within this narrow band that is depicted as encircling the Earth, the remaining planets of our solar system are seen to move. Commencing each year at the Vernal Equinox (around 21 March) and referred to as 0° Aries, the zodiacal band is said to be divided into twelve signs of the zodiac according to the constellations scattered along its length. It truly would require a good deal of imagination to perceive the creatures of the zodiac in those groups of stars. During Ptolemy's time in A.D. 210, the constellations were named to mark more specifically the divisions of the zodiac. Due to the phenomenon of the **precession of the equinoxes**, the zodiac no longer coincides with those constellations. If the Earth were a perfect sphere, it would perform a uniform orbit about the Sun. From space, the Earth is shown to be very slightly pear-shaped, bulging approximately 13 miles (22 kilometres) more around its circumference at the equator (3963 miles or 6378 kilometres) than through its circumference passing through the north and south poles (3950 miles or 6356 kilometres). The gravitational pull exerted by the Sun and Moon endeavours to pull the Earth into an upright position away from its axis which is tilted to the perpendicular. In a similar gyrating manner to that of a slowed-down spinning top, the Earth wobbles slightly 'off course' from a would-be perfect orbit so that the axial points of the north and south equatorial poles of the celestial sphere describe smaller circles around the north and south ecliptical poles.

It takes 25,868 years, or one **Great Year**, for the Earth's poles to accomplish a full cycle around the celestial poles. Because of this swinging movement, the vernal equinox (0° Aries) precesses backwards against the background of the constellations scattered along the length of the ecliptic. The Great Year is divided into **ages** according to the twelve zodiacal constellations, each lasting approximately 2,000 years.

There is a disparity of opinion among astrologers concerning the date of the ending of the current Age of Pisces and the beginning of the Age of Aquarius given as occurring at different points between A.D.1950 and 2740. Hindu astrologers and a minority of those in the West prefer the **sidereal zodiac** which accords with the zodiacal constellations, while the majority of Western astrologers prefer the timeless, symbolic division of the **tropical zodiac** measured annually from the vernal equinox. With further study it is for you to decide which zodiac is more pertinent to your needs, but regardless which zodiac is employed, it is important to appreciate that both trace the Sun's apparent pathway through the heavens, for the ecliptic is fundamental to the astrologer's work. For the purposes of this book, the references to the zodiac allude to the **tropical zodiac**.

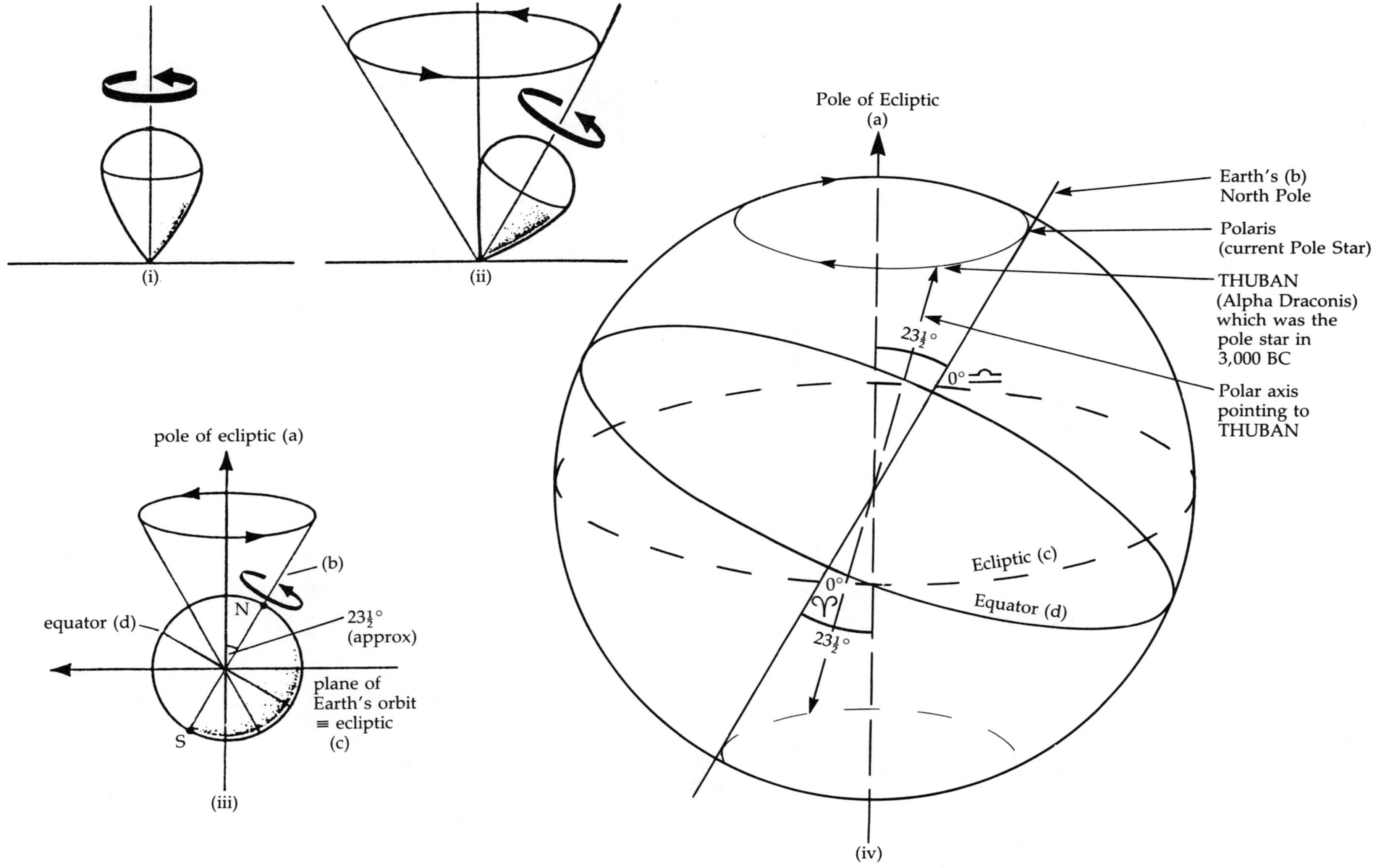

Figure 5 Precession of the Equinoxes

The Mexicans and the Incas are known to have used a zodiac of twenty divisions, while the Babylonians employed eighteen. The Greeks introduced the now familiar twelve-fold division linking the signs of the zodiac more closely with the monthly lunations, being the period between one New Moon and the next and the basis of the annual calender. They retained, as we do still, the Babylonian system of counting in sixties to express angular units (in degrees, minutes and seconds) based upon the perfection of the 360° circle, and for time (in hours, minutes and seconds). The division of the zodiac is arbitrary since it is intellectual in form and purely symbolic in concept. The zodiac is representative of the Prime Relationship between God and man for it is our acknowledgement that our planet, Earth, is a member of a solar system that is a part of the rest of the universe. The starting point of the zodiac, the vernal equinox (0° Aries) and its opposite, the autumn equinox (0° Libra) are those points in the Earth's orbit where the plane of the Earth's equator intersects with the plane of the ecliptic, day and night are of equal length, the Sun rises at virtually 6 a.m. and sets at 6 p.m. all the world over. At these times, deemed sacred by our ancestors, *the Earth is in perfect unison with the cosmos.* Visualized as the unifying, integrated principle that underlies the whole edifice of astrological thought, this theme is given rightful prominence as the foundation of the birth chart. It is the principle of 'At-one-ment' and tells of the need for each of us to work towards understanding our unique individuality in order to fully utilize our energy resources to create a better life for all. It is the ideal that is at the heart of all religious and spiritual teachings, and astrology only differs in that it does not purport to dictate *how* this should be attained. The birth chart is the representation of the principle that it is within the capacity of each of us to make greater use of our individual life force and is, therefore, evocative of our potential to be all that we are capable of becoming. The theme of potential oneness recurs in other features of the birth chart, apart from those expressing

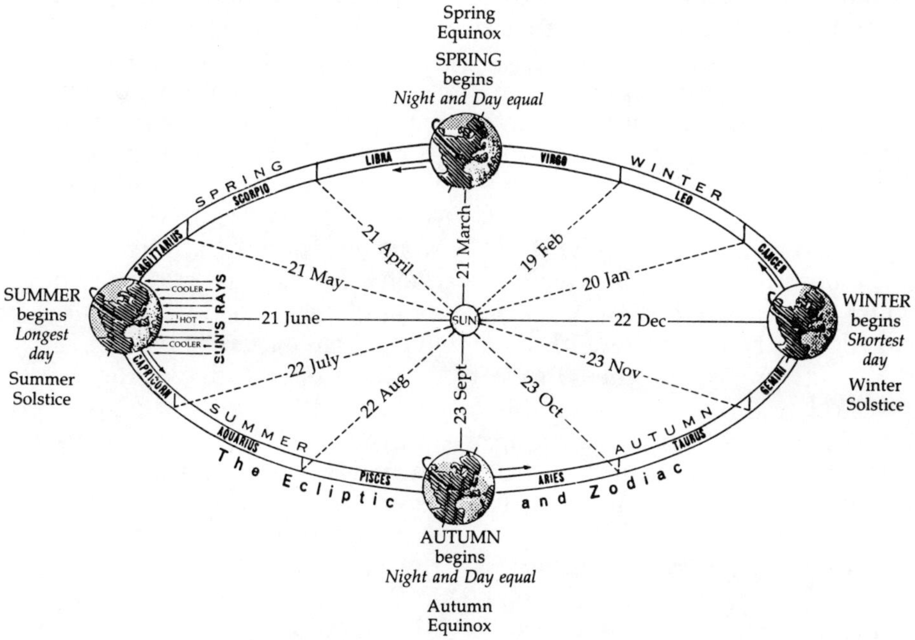

Figure 6 The Earth's Orbital Path
(Showing the Zodiac and the seasons in the Northern Hemisphere)

The Earth is pictured through the Signs of the Zodiac as it orbits the Sun. Because it is the sun that appears to move, it is seen in the Sign opposite to that of the Earth. The Earth is furthest from the Sun at the Summer Solstice when the Sun appears to be in the sign of Cancer.

Extracted from the *Daily Telegraph*'s map, 'The Night Sky'

the circle of eternity; it is seen in the symbols used for the Earth, for the Sun, and in the meaning of the aspect of conjunction, seen as a fusing of the energies symbolized by two planets that are within 8° orb of one another. It is also incorporated in the numerological principle expressed by the number One and concurs with the modern understanding that the birth chart is the first harmonic.

We can also gain some insight into the origin and meanings attributed to the zodiacal circle of the twelve signs. At the vernal equinox on the first day of spring (Aries) an initiatory force of purest energy revitalizes the Earth and opens the way to the acknowledgement of the Law of Polarity (Libra) and the ultimate harmony of the wise use of energy for the greater good of all freely given (Pisces, the twelfth sign).

The twelve signs of the zodiac represent both collective and individual expressions of energy for they are as the Windows of the Soul through which the life force symbolized by the planets is diffused and refracted to express every conceivable behavioural characteristic associated with man. In this way they represent the manner in which we utilize and express our energy. Each birth chart contains every one of the twelve signs of the zodiac and while emphasis has been given to the Sun sign due to the popularized image of astrology in the horoscope columns and the media in general, the position of the Sun on the day of birth represents but one of the twelve signs, and just as a description of the personality would not be complete without reference to the integration of the whole chart and all twelve signs, so it can be appreciated that observation of one sign, albeit a significant one, out of context of the whole, would present only certain rather generalized characteristics.

From the Prime Relationship, which contains the essential meaning of the first harmonic, stems the division which each in its own way depicts further understanding of our potential to integrate and harmonize our energies.

The Polarity of Positive and Negative

The first division of the zodiacal band refers immediately to *free will* and our Divine Right to choose how we should deploy our energy and live out our lives upon this planet. By the division of the zodiac by two into six *positive* signs and six *negative* signs, we are introduced to the manner in which we can either constructively use or misuse our energy. The Law of Polarity explains that a full appraisal of the meaning of life comes only through encountering its extremes. Through comprehension of the difference between ignorance and enlightenment and knowledge of the intrinsic meanings of spirituality and materialism we can take control of ourselves to attain a true sense of wholeness with Self and the universe relating immediately to the Prime Relationship.

In astrology, positive and negative have two meanings: as *expressions* of the type of energy available to mankind (see Chapter 2, page 24); — and in terms of *attitude* that is, the *choice* of whether to opt for a positive or negative course of action when exposed to a particular human experience.

From the simple act of totalling the number of planets in either positive or negative signs, it is possible to derive an immediate understanding of the overall manner in which the personality is expressed. Although it is unusual to find all ten planets in either positive or negative signs, it can and does occur. However, it is more usual to find the energy described as a combination, for example: seven positive, three negative. A predominance of positive signs indicates that the expression of the energy tends to be generally out-going with a readiness to initiate and partake of immediate experiences. A predominance of negative signs does not mean that the individual tends to be a shy, retiring violet but rather that there is generally more emphasis on the feeling nature with the need to examine and value life's experiences in relation to self. In all areas of the birth chart we witness the need of the individual to learn to cope with and understand the manner in which the energy is expressed through our personalities and behavioural characteristics, so the simple assessment of the overall attitudes and expression of energy shown by this distribution will reflect the same idea. Where there is, for example, an even distribution of five positive and five negative, the energies expressed do not automatically cancel one another out but reflect the individual's need to learn to cope with marked fluctuations in behaviour. Invariably, this tendency will improve with growing maturity and self-understanding when the total energy can be controlled and used constructively.

It is interesting to note that C.G. Jung's assessment of personality expression, *extraversion and introversion*, closely resembles the astrological understanding of positive and negative. However, it should be noted that Jung's terms have acquired a popularized image that belies his original intention.

Although only the sun signs were used in the statistical analysis conducted by astrologer, Jeff Mayo, and psychologist, Professor Eysenck, the results showed the same distribution of extraverted and introverted types as the traditional positive and negative signs.

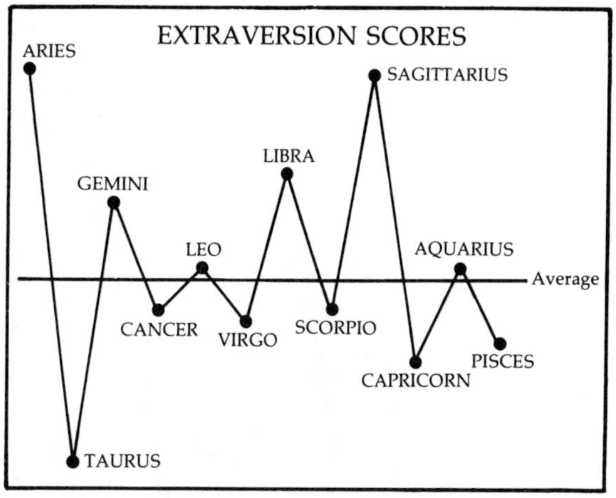

This concurs with similar analysis by John Addey of 'Seven Thousand Doctors' in which he found that the distinctive wave form reflecting the alternating positive and negative signs around the 360° circle is that of the sixth harmonic (6 x 2 = 12 signs).

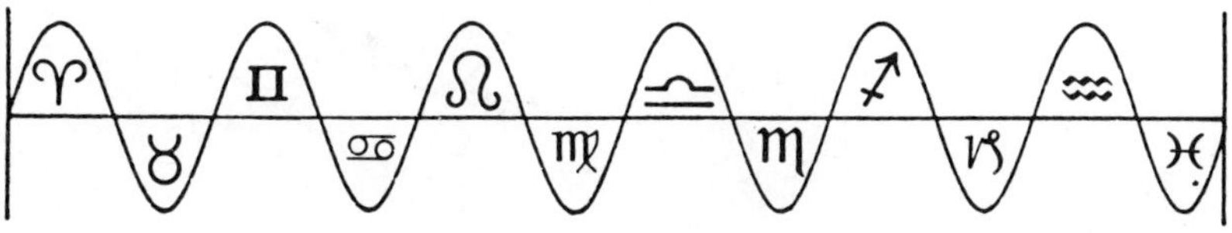

The Principle of Polarity is reflected in other features of the birth chart. Each of the signs of the zodiac has its polar opposite so that the meaning of one is enhanced by knowledge of the other. It is, therefore, wise to study the meaning of the zodiacal signs in tandem. Thus Aries is coupled with Libra, Taurus with Scorpio, Gemini with Sagittarius, Cancer with Capricorn, Leo with Aquarius and Virgo with Pisces. Polarity is also expressed by the division of the 360° circle by two as in the instances of the meanings accorded to the aspect of opposition being the 180° distance between two planetary bodies and the second harmonic.

The Triplicities (The Elements)

The next main division of the zodiac is the grouping of three signs according to the four fundamental natures, Fire, Earth, Air and Water, more usually called the Elements or the Triplicities; Tri - referring to the number Three signifying unity, for where there may be conflict in duality as in the instance of number Two, number Three symbolizes the unifying factor and the capacity for ultimate creativity once the extremes of materialism (positive) and spirituality (negative) have been mastered. Energy is in constant motion, for the ultimate goal is creativity.

By assessing the distribution of the ten planets in the zodiacal signs and the Ascendant and Midheaven according to their Triplicity, it is possible to gain rapid insight into *the manner in which we perceive life*. Distribution varies from one individual to another, for example: Fire 2 + Asc; Earth 6 + MC; Air 2; Water 0. Such an individual would be described as predominently Earth and would, in general, approach life in a manner associated with the nature of Earth.

Three Signs are grouped together sharing in common certain characteristics.

The Fire Triplicity (Aries, Leo, Sagittarius) Full of enthusiasm, the strongly Fire type demands immediate action and involvement. Capable of feeling the heartbeat of this planet, they are governed by the desire to live life to the full. Their lesson in life is to inspire others so that mankind might continually progress.
Key Phrase: 'Now I am here, let's get on with it!'

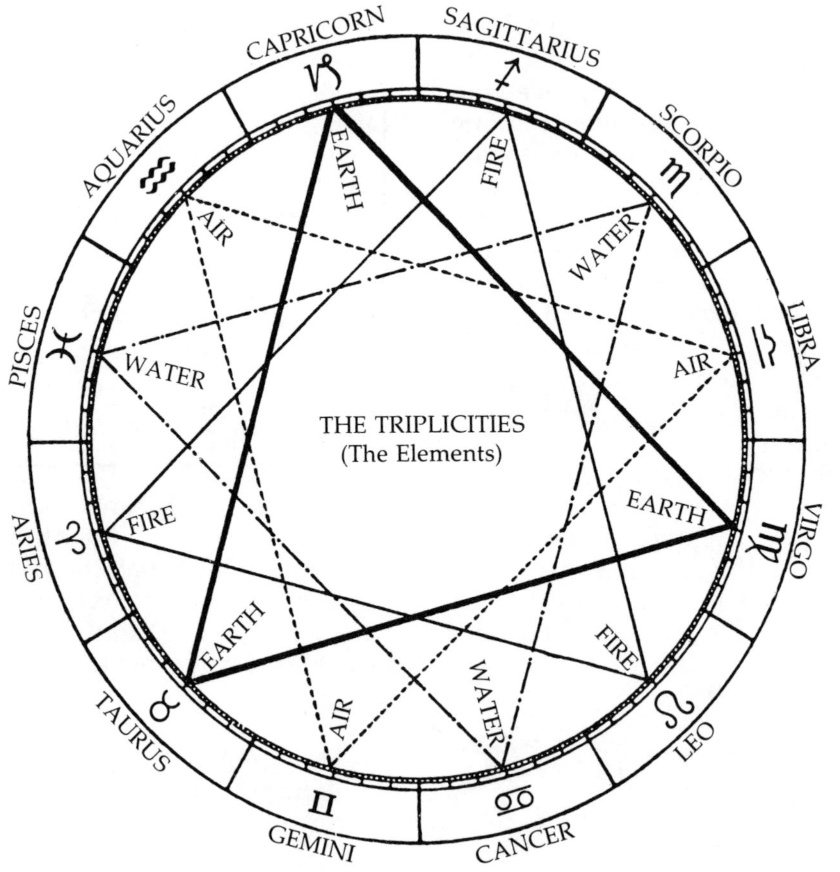

Figure 7 The triplicities (the elements)

The Earth Triplicity (Taurus, Virgo, Capricorn)
Invariably practical and thrifty, strongly Earth types tend to be cautious until they fully understand. Appreciative that this Earth provides for her inhabitants, they feel honour-bound to be productive. Their lesson in life is to value and preserve the physical being — this planet and the Body of Man.
Key Phrase: 'I shall wait until I know what it is all about!'

The Air Triplicity (Gemini, Libra, Aquarius)
Insatiably inquisitive, the strongly Air types are easily able to communicate thoughts and ideas. Curiosity leads them to open new gateways to further knowledge. Through the interchange of trading cultures, man recognizes he is one with all men. Their lesson in life is to teach that the Breath of Life is the joy of all.
Key Phrase: 'I have to know what is going on and why!'

The Water Triplicity (Cancer, Scorpio, Pisces)
Capable of intense sensitivity and compassion, the strongly Water types can comprehend that which is not necessarily seen but felt on both the collective and personal levels. Their lesson in life is to bring to awareness the Beauty of the Human Soul.
Key Phrase: 'I shall wait and see if my first impression is correct!'

The 'lack' of a Triplicity refers to the lack of tenancy by planets, Ascendant or Midheaven and, therefore, emphasis of that Element. Each chart contains all four Triplicities, for every human being is capable of using their energy creatively. Very often the 'lack' can indicate the need to over-compensate. For example, the lack of Fire can reflect the need to drive oneself constantly to take the initiative; the lack of Earth can indicate the strong need for tangible proofs of security; the lack of Air does not mean lessened intelligence but often the great need to prove the intellectual ability; the lack of Water often reiterates and verbalizes feelings as if this shall lend form to their existence.

The association of the Triplicities with Jung's Functions, 'intuition' (Fire); 'sensation' (Earth); 'thinking' (Air) and 'feeling' (Water) has been attempted by a number of able astrologers with varying degrees of validity. Your own knowledge and experience of the concepts involved in astrology and in Jungian analytical psychology should be explored thoroughly so that you can formulate your own conclusion.

The Triplicities are expressed in other areas of the birth chart through the division of the 360° circle by Three, as in the meaning given to the third harmonic and the 'trine' aspect, being the angular distance of 120° between two planetary bodies, and the 'Grand Trine', which is a *triangular configuration* formed by three planets within trine aspects of one another. It can occur that the energies involved can be taken for granted; the natural inspiration of the Grand Trine in Fire can emerge as reckless audacity and a love of thrills; the constructiveness and power of practical application of the Grand Trine in Earth can emerge as blatant laziness or overt materialism; the mental and manual dexterity and ability to formulate concepts of the Grand Trine in Air can lead the person to live on his wits or disregard disciplined study altogether; the remarkable capacity for compassion of the Grand Trine in Water can manifest as weak dependence on others or being prey to feelings and fancies. In this manner it is possible to create problems for oneself where, with relatively little effort, much that is good and of positive value could occur.

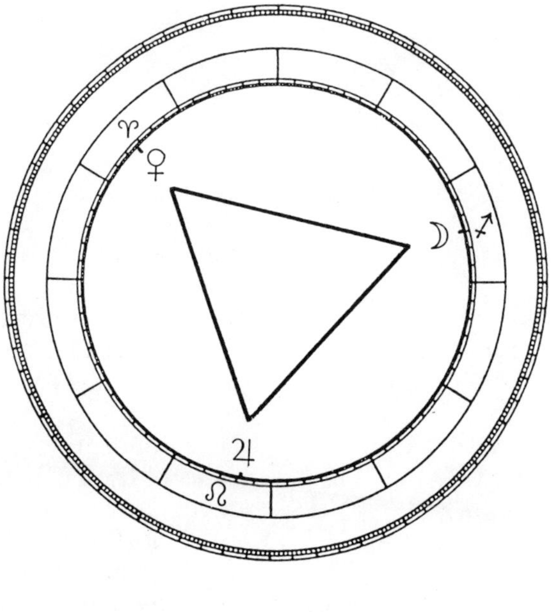

Figure 8 Grand Trine in Fire

The Quadruplicities (The Qualities)

The division of the zodiac into three groups of Four signs known as Cardinal, Fixed and Mutable relates naturally with the number Four of Manifestation. The Quadruplicities describe *the quality* of our lives according to our confrontation with reality as it must be on this Earth. Each of the four signs forms a Cross of Matter and is a further dimension of the Prime Relationship.

By assessing the distribution of the ten planets, the Ascendant and Midheaven according to their Quadruplicity, it is possible to gain insight into *the manner in which we encounter life*. Distribution varies according to the individual's life pattern, for example: Cardinal: 5; Fixed: 3 + Asc; Mutable: 2 + MC: Such an individual would be described as being strongly Cardinal.

Four Signs are grouped together sharing in common certain characteristics.

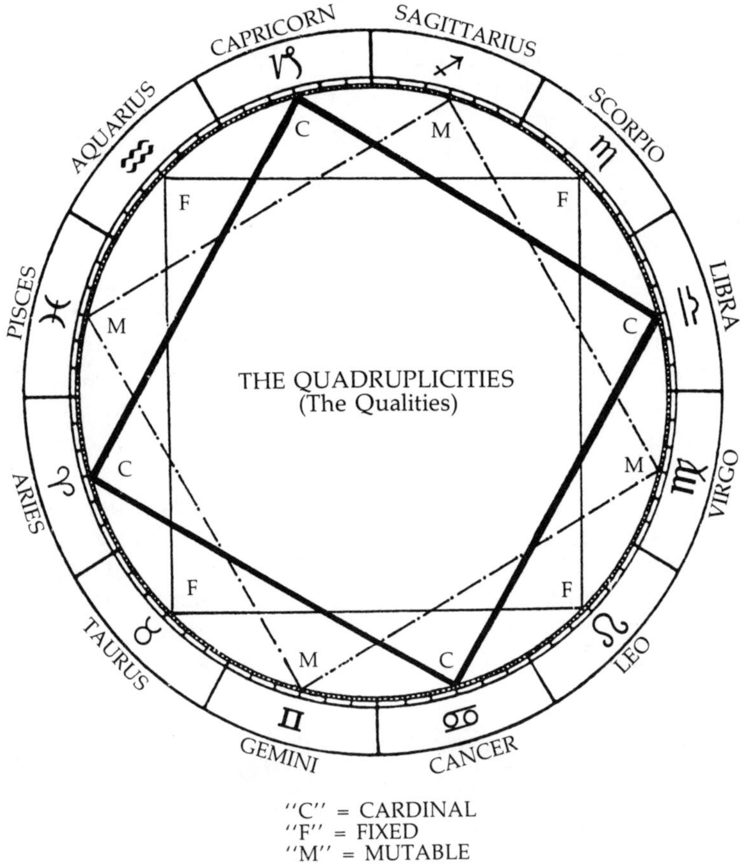

Figure 9 The Quadruplicities (the Qualities)

The Cardinal Quadruplicity (Aries, Cancer, Libra, Capricorn)
Operating from a personalized viewpoint, strongly Cardinal tend to dynamically take the forefront of any activity. Excellent at initiating and organizing others, they may well be disorganized themselves. Their lesson in life is to encourage the living of life to its full potential.
Key Phrase : 'Why is there no peace for me?'

The Fixed Quadruplicity (Taurus, Leo, Scorpio, Aquarius)
Bound by the quality of their emotional response, strongly Fixed need to be secure, unconsciously acquiring habits and traditions that are difficult to alter. Their lesson in life is to provide for and to sustain all mankind.
Key Phrase: 'Don't rock my boat!'

The Mutable Quadruplicity (Gemini, Virgo, Sagittarius, Pisces)
Endlessly searching for the answer to the mystery of Life, strongly Mutable adapts to any contingency. Versatile and egalitarian, they can be too diffuse, wasting time and energy. Their lesson in life is to constantly revitalize thought and belief.
Key Phrase: 'If I only knew why!'

The Quadruplicities are expressed in other areas of the birth chart through the division of the 360° circle by Four as in the meaning given to the fourth harmonic, the 'square' aspect, being the angular distance between two planetary bodies of 90° and the configuration of the Grand Cross and the T/Square, which are often referred to as the Dilemmas. Every chart contains each of the Dilemmas. They represent the human condition and all the issues that a human being can possibly encounter on this planet, for our personalities are shaped by the circumstances of our lives. It is also true to say that character is destiny, since we create and shape our lives according to the calibre of our characters. In the interpretation of an individual Dilemma it is important to note that the conditions and problems in question *operate simultaneously* giving

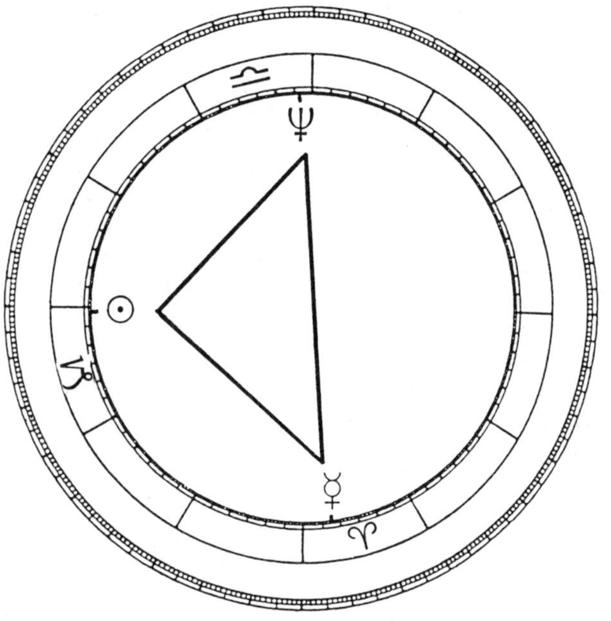

Cardinal T/Square

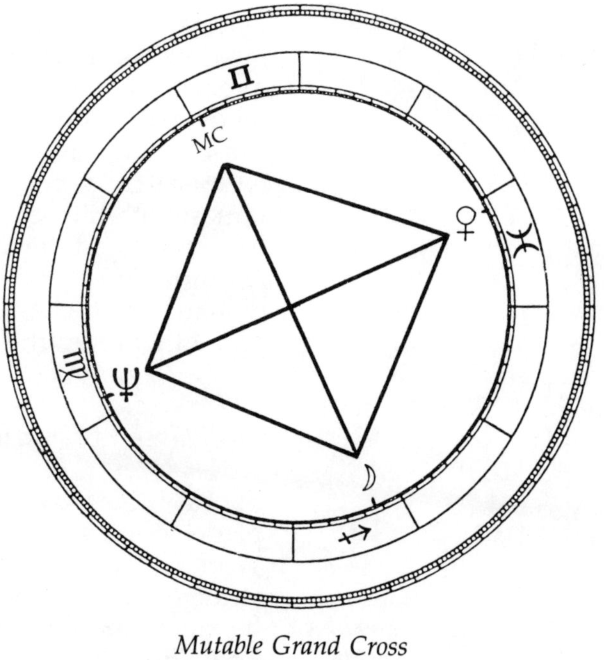

Mutable Grand Cross

Figure 10

pertinent clues concerning the overall life pattern.

The ability to tackle a Dilemma positively and overcome its problems to a large extent tends to be more prevalent where any of the Cardinal signs or houses (see Chapter 4) are involved, for the challenges are usually of a *personal* nature. Aries — the need of space to be oneself; Libra — the partner's needs (whether business or marriage and often both at the same time!). Cancer — childrens' needs and one's duty to parents as their child, the home, which could involve anything under and including the roof! Capricorn — the need to pursue, as well as the demands of a career or position in life.

Those with a Fixed Dilemma tend to be most prone to conditioning, for the problems mainly involve the *emotional* or *traditional*. Taurus — the need for tangible evidence of security; Scorpio — the need to share fully; Leo — the desire to prove oneself and to ensure the perpetuation of self through the offspring; Aquarius — the surrender of self for the needs of society.

The Mutable is the most difficult of the Dilemmas to control due to its elusive nature, for the challenges involved are all *intangible*, giving rise to much discontent: Gemini — too many ideas and plans often lacking control of the mind or tongue; Sagittarius — boundless enthusiasm, hope or optimism and often the genuine quest for a suitable religion or code of behaviour; Virgo — the need for truth as a reality and the realization of perfection; Pisces — the incurable romantic, the wish to believe in someone or something, the martyr.

A simple grid showing the distribution of Triplicities and Quadruplicities can provide an excellent starting point to analysis of the birth chart. In terms of Number, 3 × 4 reminds us of the individual qualities associated with the twelve signs of the zodiac.

	F	E	A	W	
C		2	1+Mc	1	4+Mc
F	1		3		4
M	Asc	2			2+Asc
	1+ Asc	4	4+Mc	1	

The Individual Signs of the Zodiac

Although someone might describe himself as 'a Leo' or 'a Scorpio', it can be appreciated that we all have some Leo, some Scorpio and, indeed, the characteristics associated with all the signs of the zodiac, to a greater or lesser degree, in our personalities. The birth chart utilizes all twelves signs of the zodiac to reflect the differing types of personality and behaviour common to us all for they are *expressions of life*. An individual sign is emphasized, indicating the prominence of those particular characteristics, by the positioning of the ten planets, or by being the sign on the Ascendant or Midheaven. The person concerned would then be described as being strongly of that sign even if the Sun doesn't tenant that particular sign.

Each of the twelve signs contains knowledge concerning the *why* of being. The first six signs relate to *personal* factors. The final six describe the manner in which the individual reaches out beyond self to the world. The following descriptions of the zodiacal signs must serve as a brief introduction only. For the avid student of astrology, further study of their endless correlation with human behaviour should continue *ad infinitum*.

Aries (Positive, Fire, Cardinal); Ruling planet: Mars
Seeking to prove the veracity of his own experience, the strongly Aries type rushes headlong into action fully prepared to meet the challenge of pioneering new avenues of thought and deed. Unless respected, the normally dynamic, free-flowing energy rapidly dissipates. In common with its polar opposite, Libra, the Aries type needs to be motivated, requiring total immersion in a cause that must perpetually fire his enthusiasm. Open, direct and completely honest with himself, such a lack of guile can be interpreted by others as being rather thoughtless and tactless. Extremely demanding, he has to learn tolerance of self and others. In the birth chart generally, Aries, symbolizes the need for *self-understanding*.
Key Phrase: 'I have to know who I am'

Taurus (Negative, Earth, Fixed) Ruling planet: Venus
Work is as essential as oxygen to the strongly Taurean type. By being productive he states the fact of his existence and can know how to give Self freely to a purpose. Often mistakenly accused of being boring or pedantic this sign represents the realization of true material values for the resources and beauty of this planet are our legacy. More secure when grounded in matter, the strongly Taurean type links with his polar opposite, Scorpio, requiring tangible proof of survival and the power of creation.

The need for security may be transferred to possessions which could wrongly be allowed to supersede human values. In the birth chart generally, Taurus symbolizes the

need for *self-worth.*
Key Phrase: 'I need to see what I am'

Gemini (Positive, Air, Mutable); Ruling Planet: Mercury
Mentally alert and alive to endless possibilities, the strongly Geminian type tends to be eternally youthful in outlook and appearance. He is driven by eager curiosity to explore the realms of infinite knowledge, attempting to rationalize even 'the Unknown' with devastating logic. Yet the tantalizing fact of duality is that he is so often out of his depth when confronted with his own often complex personality. Whereas polar opposite Sagittarius draws upon an apparently bottomless reservoir of optimism to maintain self-confidence, bouts of deep depression can catch the Geminian unawares. However, they usually stem from the depletion of nervous energy.

In the birth chart generally, Gemini symbolizes the need for *self-examination.*
Key Phrase: 'I need to know why I am'

Cancer (Negative, Water, Cardinal); Ruling Planet: the Moon
Tender-hearted but often touchy and extremely sensitive, strongly Cancerian types change from day-to-day. Desperate to freely express themselves, they fear the consequences of their vulnerability becoming, rather like their polar opposite, Capricorn, extremely defensive and self-protective. Male and female alike, we all have Cancer in our natal charts and by nurturing the newly-born, the survival of the human race is assured. Tenaciously clinging to that which is fundamental to society, the family of man is perpetuated. No matter how eager to found their home, until convinced that it will last, Cancerians tend to be reluctant to settle down.

Seen in the birth chart generally, Cancer expresses the sense of *belonging.*
Key Phrase: 'I must know my origins'

Leo (Positive, Fire, Fixed); Ruling Planet: the Sun
Pride in Self is both the strength and the weakness of those with Leo emphasized in the natal chart. Warmly generous and gracious with others they demand far more of themselves. Apparently flamboyant and fun-loving, the need for constant approbation and attention betrays the seriousness with which they view themselves. Such over-consciousness of Self can mean enormous pressure to perform well and be in control at all times particularly in terms of Self versus society, as expressed by polar opposite, Aquarius, whereby this type of behaviour opens him up to the physical, mental and emotional problems associated with stress.

In the context of the natal chart, Leo signifies our sense of *self-importance.*
Key Phrase: 'I am capable of becoming more'

Virgo (Negative, Earth, Mutable); Ruling Planet: Mercury
Probably the most under-estimated and least understood is the overtly Virgoan type. With her sheaf of corn symbolizing the fruitful harvest, the Virgin represents the fusion of the physical with the purity of spiritual understanding; the warmth of the Earth is crystallized by the power of the mind so that even the minutest thought and action is relevant and serves a useful purpose particularly should it be in the Human cause. More critical of self than of others, its polar opposite, Pisces, desires an ideal of perfection while Virgo aims to visualize and live by impossibly high standards.

In general, Virgo natally represents the capacity we all have to *discriminate.*
Key Phrase: 'I must always strive for perfection'

Libra (Positive, Air, Cardinal); Ruling Planet: Venus
To encounter the extremes of materialism and spirituality is the lot of the person with Libra well-emphasized in the natal chart. Fluctuating moods, changes in energy are symptoms of the need to acquire balance which is mainly learned through acknowledging that it is the power of thought that rules the physical body. Once equilibrium is attained it is as difficult to maintain. Motivated so often by someone else's needs, this type must learn tolerance of life, for life has a habit of lacking a cohesive pattern. Libra must exemplify harmony but, like Aries, the lesson must first be learned through Self.

Libra's position in the natal chart indicates the necessity to *polarize* energies.
Key Phrase: 'I must justify my existence'

Scorpio (Negative, Water, Fixed); Ruling Planets: Mars and Pluto
Often overwhelmed by the intensity of their feelings, the Scorpionic types tend to be secretive and self-protective until able to truly trust themselves to others, and are reluctant to share of Self rather than risk possible domination. Disturbingly penetrating, the observational power, drawing as it does on conscious and unconscious sources of the fundamental issues of life and death, acts as a catalyst to bring about startling surges in development and access to enlightenment. Shades of Taurus, however, are visible in Scorpio's preference to cling to the known and tangible together with the familiar trait to be sceptical of everything. Scorpio in the natal chart speaks of how we attempt to *survive.*
Key Phrase: 'I am not alone'

Sagittarius (Positive, Fire, Mutable); Ruling Planet: Jupiter
The bow of the Archer and the arrow-like glyph point the way towards the centre of our galaxy reminding us of the confidence of the strongly Sagittarian personality, and his uniqueness for he is one with the universe. Gemini seeks a definition for Life but it is as if Sagittarius were in possession of a 'Divine Passport' to explore every nook and cranny of this planet as well as all the knowledge ever assembled by man. With disarming frankness he will enthuse about yet another new 'answer' and the quest will begin afresh.

Sagittarius expresses our individual capacity to attain a sense of *wholeness.*
Key Phrase: 'I love to live'

Capricorn (Negative, Earth, Cardinal); Ruling Planet: Saturn
Even if the first half of the life seems strewn with obstacles and has a dampening, sobering effect; dogged determination will have its reward, for those who have Capricorn strongly emphasized in their chart tend to be proverbial late developers who successfully establish careers and a fine position in life long after others have ceased to be active. Self-defensive and cautious, in accord with Cancer, a tough exterior often disguises a warm heart and a delightfully cryptic sense of humour. Society reaps the ultimate rewards of this personality who willingly pays responsible attention to duty and honours his commitments.

Natally, Capricorn signifies the capacity for *conscious morality.*
Key Phrase: 'Nil Desperandum'

Aquarius (Positive, Air, Fixed); Ruling Planets: Saturn and Uranus
Energy is in constant motion, and those who are strongly Aquarian serve to remind the world not to stand still, for mankind must progress ever onward. Established convention is there to be overthrown, to pave the way for new thoughts and ideals that will better mankind as a whole. Capable of helping the world to integrate, the Aquarian can be at a loss, often being deliberately disruptive or alienating himself rather than confronting an emotional involvement, unlike Leo who lives to love. Ceaselessly analytical, there is often an unconscious, unwanted desire to test the love and friendship that others have for him. In general Aquarius depicts our *humanitarian instincts.*
Key Phrase: 'I belong to the family of man'

Pisces (Negative, Water, Mutable); Ruling Planets: Jupiter and Neptune
It is within the capacity of the type of personality with Pisces emphasized, to understand the true meaning of Faith in Self, and in the greater, Governing Power of Life. Unfortunately, Pisces tends to learn such lessons the hard way, usually through seeming to lose sight of themselves only to discover that that which they needed never actually deserted them. While it may be possible to accuse them of swimming in opposite directions to themselves, perhaps becoming martyrs to reality or victims of illusion, as the sign of the Healer of Mankind, Pisces is often dominant in charts of those dedicated to caring for others. Seen in the birth chart, Pisces expresses our *expectation* of ourselves and Life.
Key Phrase: 'I wish I could come back some other time!'

Chapter 4
The Houses

Planet Earth is our home and so it is very much taken for granted. We are educated to know certain facts concerning our Earth and its relationship to the Sun at the centre of our solar system. It is, for me, a miracle that the ancients were able to determine this without any of the advantages of our modern technology. We still use references to the Sun which are geocentric, Earth-centred, in orientation. Most beginners of astrology and astronomy have difficulties with associating the references that they have from looking down at a globe of the Earth to the measurements in the heavens. You will find it far easier if you leave study of the globe until you are familiar with picturing the view of the universe as seen from this planet. While astrologers are fully aware that the Sun is at the centre of our solar system, the birth chart relates specifically to the view of the universe as seen from a particular place on the Earth's surface at a particular time. The method of doing this is called a House System.

Why Should There be a House System?

In essence, the houses form a trinity with the planets and the signs. If the planets represent the life force and the signs of the zodiac allow for the visualization of the life force in all its myriad forms of expression, the houses provide the link which indicates *how that vital energy may be experienced in tangible form expressed as human activity here on Earth.*

The houses, therefore, enable the astrologer to examine the potential use of this energy expression on the mental, emotional, physical and spiritual levels of personality. The astrological houses are the marriage of universal spirituality with everyday reality. The more intimate your knowledge of the houses, the more flexible and the more profound will be your understanding of life. According to the House Systems in general use, there are twelve divisions. These twelve houses should be treated as a total whole and, as in the instance of the twelve signs of the zodiac, no chart will lack any of them. In effect this means that every human being is capable of reaching out to every conceivable area of life experience as the natural extension of the Prime Relationship, the concept of the macrocosm and the microcosm incarnate.

The houses relate specifically to the Earth's daily rotation upon its axis. It is not feasible to attempt to depict the houses as moving and to create a diagram, the Earth stands still as the pivot of the birth chart. Just as our view of the heavens shows the apparent motion of the Sun, so the zodiacal band can be made to rotate according to whatever might be the Ascendant.

Which House System to Use?

If a House System is a means of viewing the Prime Relationship between God and Man, it can only be you who decides which system most clearly embodies your feelings

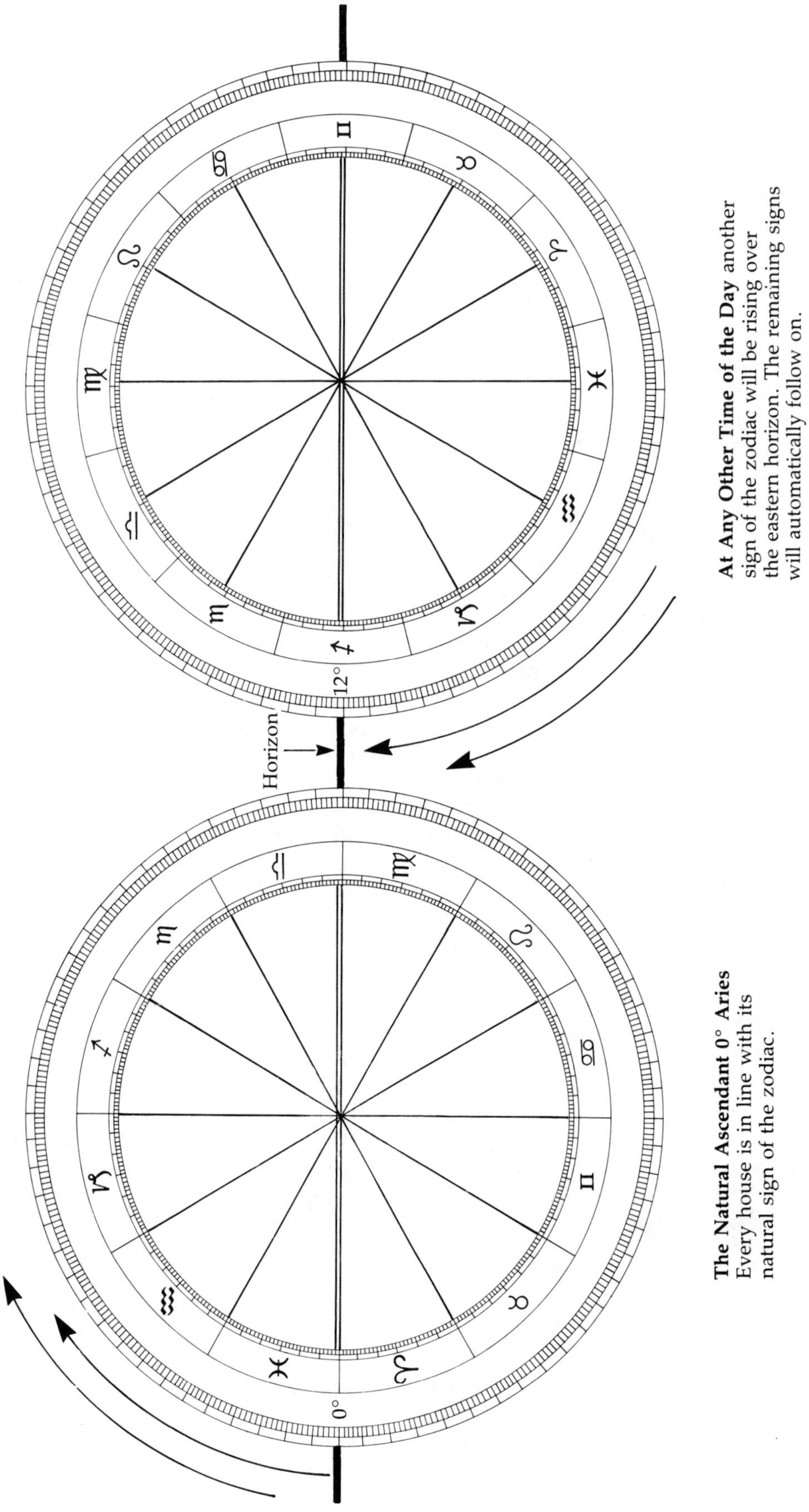

The Natural Ascendant 0° Aries
Every house is in line with its natural sign of the zodiac.
0°
Horizon
12°
At Any Other Time of the Day another sign of the zodiac will be rising over the eastern horizon. The remaining signs will automatically follow on.

Figure 11 The Ascendant

about this most individual matter. It is the most questionable area in astrology and you may, like German and the more scientifically orientated astrologers, prefer to discard the houses altogether. It will be seen, however, that even this will reveal certain fundamental attitudes. This is possibly because the houses refer to the central meaning of Earthliness. To be 'earthed' and grounded in matter is to respect and to be able to freely express the feeling nature. To be scientific in orientation has come to mean the denial or disdain of the feeling nature. Science may be able to analyse the tangible, visible factors of life but has not found the means thus far to measure or analyse the feeling nature of Man. The more mechanistic the attitudes are of the astrologer or society in which he/she finds him/her self, it seems, the more reluctant is the desire to employ any House System.

It is possible to research varying methods of house division and you are urged to acquire a reasonable idea of their bases so that you may make comparisons and choose the system that you feel most closely suits your own outlook on life. There are a number of systems in use at the present time, the most popular being Equal House, Campanus, Placidus, Koch and Topocentric.

All House Systems are methods of dividing the heavens as seen from Earth. The house divisions are based upon the daily, twenty-four hour view that this Earth has of the ecliptic. Each of the subdivisions passes over the horizon in approximately two hours. Although most systems present an apparently rigidly spokelike framework of twelve evenly spaced houses, the area of the ecliptic covered by each of the houses varies according to the place of birth because the different latitudes can alter the viewpoint of the ecliptic.

In keeping with the spherical shape of this Earth, the houses rotate in a circle. Astrologers down the ages have maintained the perfection of the 360° circle. The sexigesimal system of counting created by the Babylonians has not been surpassed. It continues to be used to express *angular units* in degrees, minutes and seconds as well as *time* in hours, minutes and seconds. The number 360° is extremely flexible. It is divisible by all the Pythagorean numbers one to ten with the single exception of the number seven. This is interesting in terms of symbolism for seven is the number meaning the life force which is represented in the birth chart by the planets, initially the Seven Naked Eye Planets (see Chapter 5, page 61).

Descriptions of the many existing House Systems are given competently in Ralph Holden's *The Elements of House Division* and only a brief discourse will be given here of the House Systems mostly used at the current time simply to illustrate something of the spiritual or philosophical nature that underlies the various systems. There is a general tendency to think of the houses from a purely mundane point of view which can limit this fertile area for interpretative purposes.

The Equal House system owes its popularity mainly to G.E.O. Carter, Margaret Hone and the two main British teaching bodies, The Faculty of Astrological Studies and The Mayo School of Astrology. It is known to have been used in India 5,000 years ago and was favoured by Ptolemy (A.D. 100–178) who was undoubtedly the largest single influence on astrological understanding for 1,400 years. It is the simplest of all the systems used today for its basis or primary is the ecliptic itself. The twelve house lunes are formed as symbolic extensions of the twelve zodiacal signs creating a visible link between the universe and the Earth. It is thought of as a pure system by those astrologers seeking to examine the essential spirit or soul of the individual. Commencing from the Ascendant, the 360° circle of the ecliptic is divided into twelve equal portions of 30° each. It is the House System which has been used for the analysis in the final chapter of this book.

Critics of the system complain that since the house lunes, and cusps, the actual division lines, are based solely upon time, the place of birth can be an arbitrary matter thus rendering the chart unscientific and applicable to anyone whose time of birth might coincide. However, the fact that the MC/IC axis rarely coincides with the cusps of the tenth and fourth houses can be seen as an advantage in interpretation whereby they allow for a more subtle indication of self identity (MC) and the root consciousness (IC) of the individual. It is not unusual

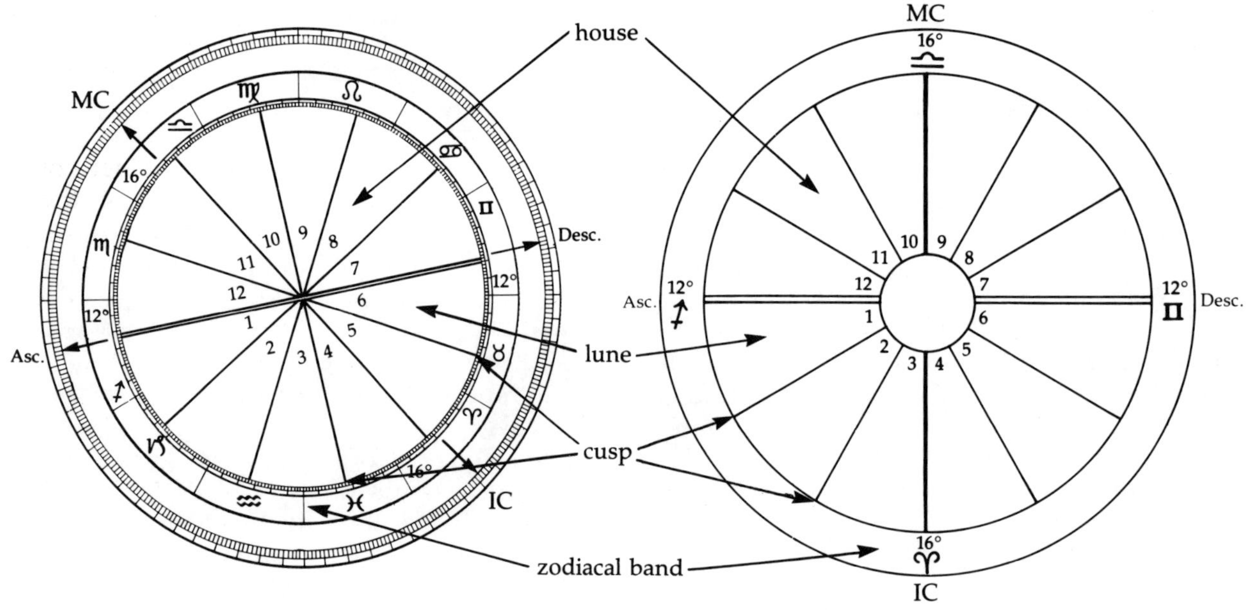

Equal House System

House cusps are determined by the Ascendant. In the example above, each cusp is 12° of every following sign of the zodiac, e.g. The 10th House cusp is 12° Virgo.

Quadrant System

House cusps are determined according to which Quadrant system is used.

Note: These charts are taken from the No.1 and No.2 chart forms published by the Faculty of Astrological Studies. They are on sale at astrological bookshops.

Figure 12 The House Systems

to find astrologers making use of this system in conjunction with one of the following Quadrant systems since the Equal House system aligns more closely with the soul or personality than with the more external circumstances of life. The latter is more prominantly shown via the Quadrant systems.

The Cross of Matter formed by the Four Angles, Ascendant, Descendant, MC, IC, is the fundamental basis of the *Quadrant* systems. It was the contention of Porphyry (A.D. 232–304) that the Four Angles should correspond to the cusps of the first, seventh, tenth and fourth houses respectively. The implication here is that the individual is confronted with a total commitment to being on this planet.

The resulting four Quadrants were divided in two by the Greeks to create eight house lunes but the twelvefold division with the trisection of each of the Quadrants proved more natural and acceptable. Simply from the point of view of number, the division by two would create a system singularly dedicated to a profoundly mathematical and materialistic outlook whereas the trisection involves the number three, denoting Man's capacity to be creative within the framework of his earthly existence.

The flaw with Porphyry's system is that if the primary of the ecliptic is retained, the house lunes automatically become unequal. It then becomes necessary to create alternative methods of measuring the heavens. In the thirteenth century Campanus evolved the first major departure from Porphyry's method. Because the Four Angles are based upon the daily rotation of the Earth upon its axis, Campanus contended that the intervening house cusps should concur with the Earth's diurnal motion and the corresponding celestial sphere not upon the ecliptical path. He proposed that the Prime Vertical which passes through the east and west points of the horizon, zenith and nadir of the observer's points is applicable only to the earthly references of the horizon and the celestial sphere. The resulting Quadrants of the Prime Vertical are then trisected to form the house lunes, passing through the north and south points of the horizon. This creates a chart based upon both time and place of birth. The rigid conservatism of the Middle Ages held sway influencing the mind of Man to think only along fixed lines. It is interesting to note that the shape of charts were then either square or rectangular which may possibly have given rise to the supposition that the Earth was flat.

It is rather surprising that the American astrologer Dane Rudhyar who has proved to be so innovative favours the Campanus system but he maintains that it is extremely revealing in his strongly psychologically orientated work.

In the intervening centuries, numerous systems were proposed that drew upon terrestrial measurements and references such as the equator and the Earth's axial rotation. Three systems that divided time rather than space or the ecliptic, were devised, most notably Placidus and the modern Birth Place or Koch. The Placidus House System created by Placidus de Tito (1603 - 1688) became generally used because of the ease with which it could be printed in table form. Since its publication by Raphael in 1821, it has been consistently included in early ephemerides which have been distributed throughout the world. The time taken for the degrees of the ecliptic to move from the Ascendant to the Midheaven is noted and trisected to become the cusps of the eleventh and twelfth houses. This is repeated for the arc from the Imum Coeli to Ascendant to derive the cusps of second and third houses. It has come under a great deal of criticism for it cannot cope with latitudes greater than 60°. The Sun's positioning in the birth chart using Placidus always mirrors the time of birth as if a cosmic clock-face. It is during this period in our history that Man has become increasingly more preoccupied with time and the need for precision; indeed, the whole pace of life revolves around the clock.

The modern systems of Koch and Topocentric have been thought far superior to those that have gone before, especially the oft ridiculed Placidus. However, the basis of Koch is similar to that of Placidus except that the Quadrants are trisected equally whereas Placidus calculates the house cusps independently. This system was devised by Walter Koch (born 1895) and since its first publication in 1921 has gained much popularity particularly in Germany, its country of origin, and the rest of the continent.

First published in 1961 by Wendel Polick and A.P. Nelson Page of Buenos Aires, the Topocentric House System relates directly to the latitude of the birthplace rather than to divisions of time. It has been promoted in Great Britain as the most precise House System mainly by Chester Kemp and Geoffrey Cornelius. However, the house cusps tend to be virtually the same as those derived by using the Placidus House System. Its distinct advantage is that there are tables available for lattitudes from 0° to 90°.

The continental method of entering Placidus, Koch and Topocentric house cusps on an Equal house chart form which shows very clearly the unequal size of the

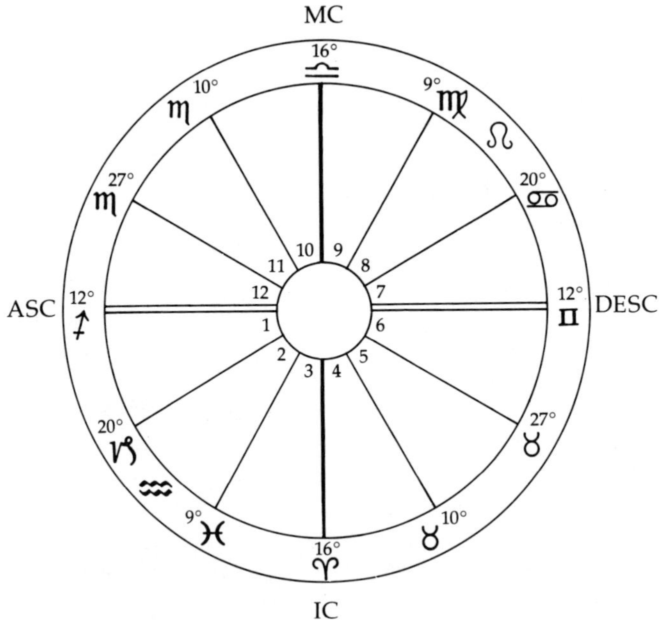

Usual quadrant method

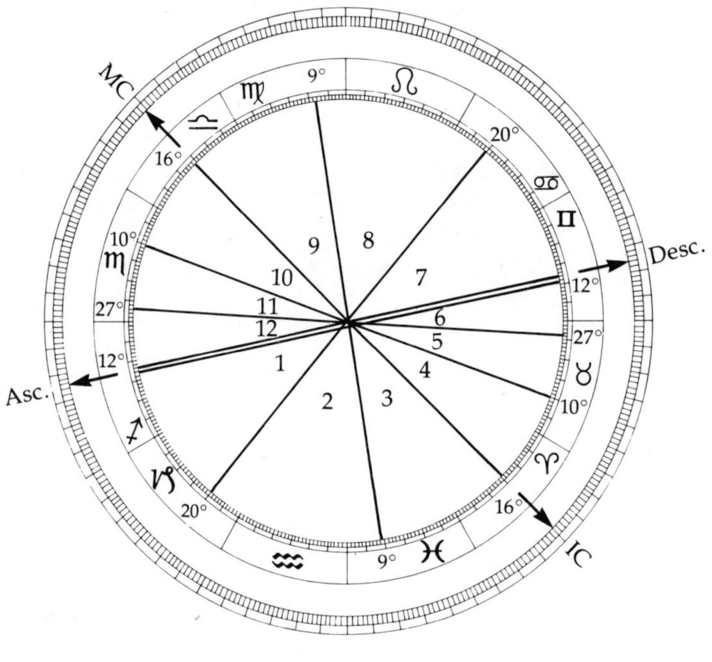

Continental version showing unequal houses

Figure 13 House cusps accordings to Placidus

houses by these systems, is becoming adopted by some of Britain's top astrologers. This could be a reflection of the awareness of the need to blend science and the feeling nature; however, it could also be said that it is neither one thing nor another and, therefore, a reflection of the confusion that is prevalent in so many societies during these changeful times.

Tables of houses are available for these more popular methods. It is advisable to purchase copies of Raphael's *Tables of Houses for Northern Latitudes* and *Tables of Houses for Great Britain* which are not expensive. The house cusps in these tables have been determined by the Placidus House System. Refer to the reproduction of *The Tables of Houses for Hull* at latitude 53° 45′ North. These tables are also suitable for the Equal House System since the

TABLES OF HOUSES FOR HULL, Latitude 53° 45′ N.

Sidereal Time.	10 ♎	11	12	Ascen ♐	2	3
H. M. S.	°	°	°	° ′	°	°
12 51 32	14	8	26	10 52	18	7
12 55 14	15	9	26	11 34	19	8
12 58 57	16	10	27	12 16	20	9
13 2 40	17	11	28	12 58	21	10
13 6 24	18	11	28	13 41	22	12

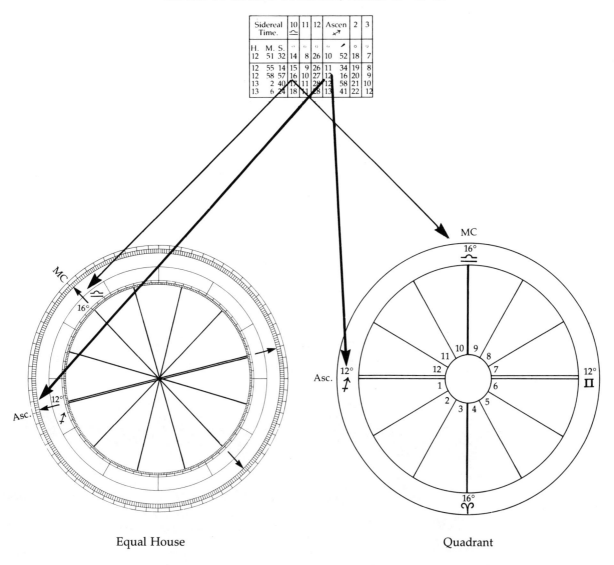

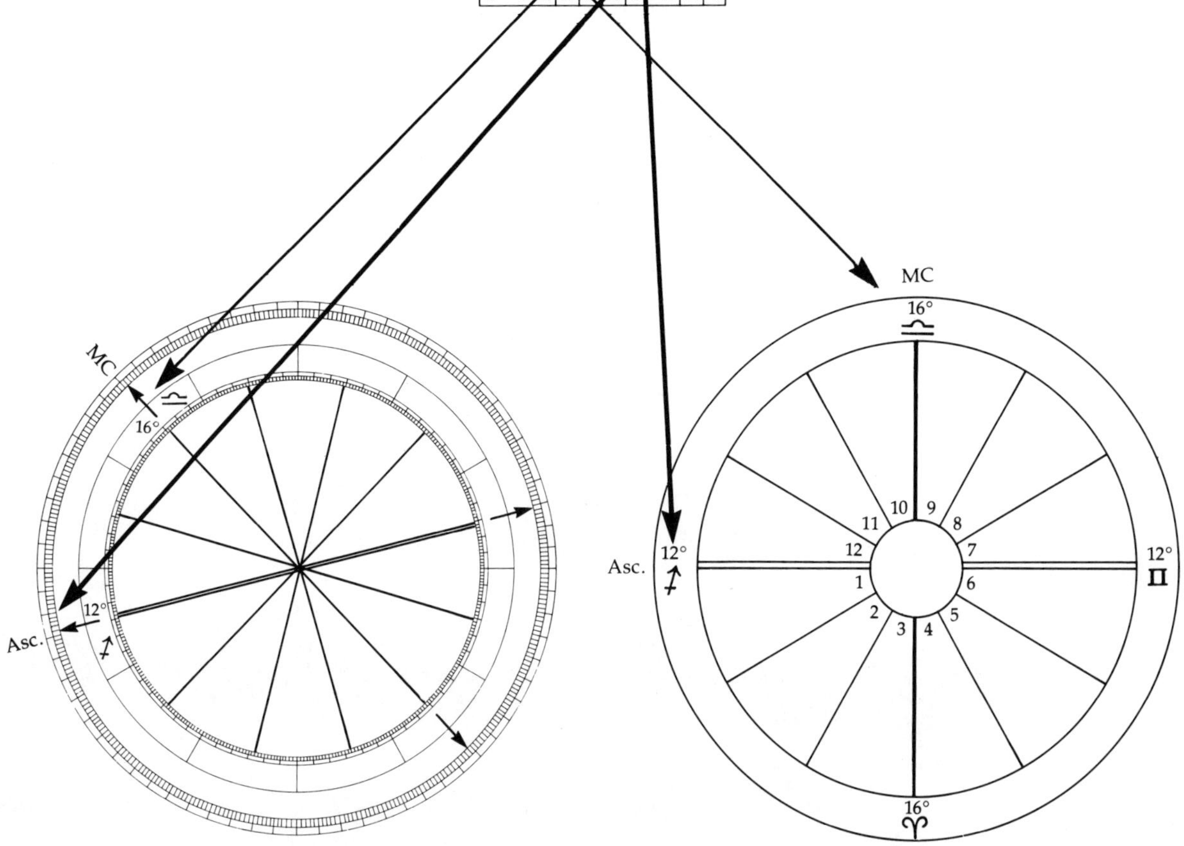

Equal House

Quadrant

Figure 14 The Ascendant and Midheaven in the tables of houses

Ascendant and M.C. only need to be extracted. They may also be used for the Koch system but while the formula for doing so is not especially complicated, the beginner is advised to initially adopt either the Equal House or Placidus system. Once experience of their workings has been gained, there will be plenty of time to experiment with the other House Systems until you determine the one that proves most suitable for your purposes.

The Interpretation of the Houses

The houses flow from the Ascendant in an anti-clockwise direction numbered one to twelve completing a full sequence in much the same way as the signs of the zodiac complete the full circle of the ecliptic. Be wary of a tendency to limit the interpretation of the birth chart by only examining those houses which are *tenanted* by one or more planets. By a system known as *dispositorship* no house is omitted from the total scheme. Each of the houses will have one of the signs of the zodiac on its cusp. Referring to the preceding example Equal House chart (Figure 12), Virgo is on the tenth house cusp. The whole quality surrounding this house will be amended by the quality of its ruling planet, Mercury (see Chapter 5 — The Planets). Although this may seem rather complicated at first, it quickly becomes an automatic process.

Sidereal Time			10 ♎	11 ♎	12 ♏	Ascen ♐		2 ♑	3 ♒
H.	M.	S.	°	°	°	°	′		°
12	0	0	0	27	16	1	31	5	20
12	3	30	1	28	16	2	10	6	21
12	7	20	2	28	17	2	49	7	22
12	11	1	3	29	18	3	28	8	24
12	14	41	4		19	4	8	8	25
12	18	21	5	1	19	4	47	9	26
12	22	2	6	2	20	5	27	10	27
12	25	42	7	2	21	6	7	11	28
12	29	23	8	3	21	6	47	12	29
12	33	4	9	4	22	7	27	13	
12	36	45	10	5	23	8	7	14	2
12	40	27	11	6	23	8	48	15	3
12	44	8	12	7	24	9	29	16	4
12	47	50	13	7	25	10	11	17	5
12	51	32	14	8	26	10	52	18	7
12	55	14	15	9	26	11	34	19	8
12	58	57	16	10	27	12	16	20	9

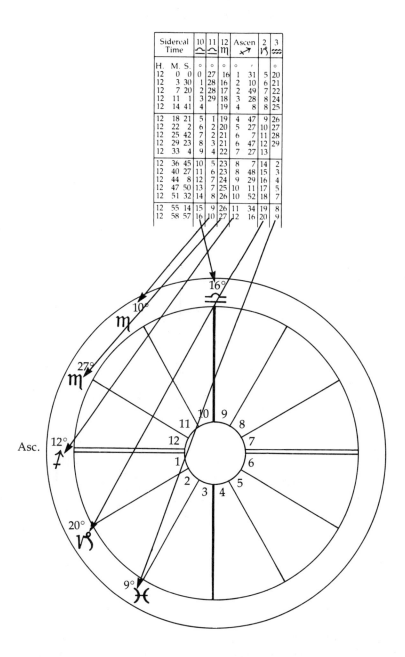

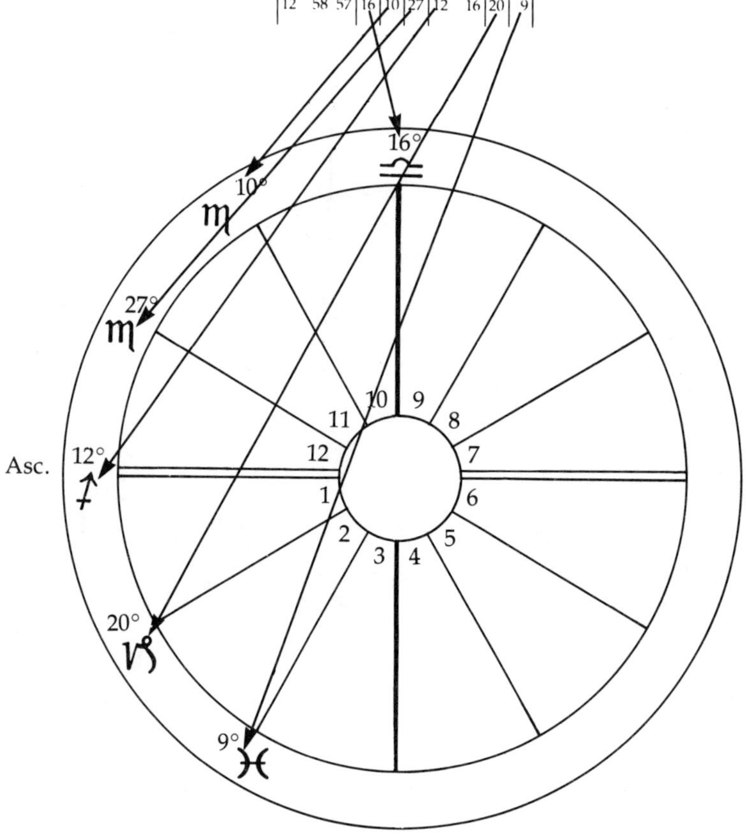

Figure 15 The Placidus House System

Hemisphere Emphasis

The overall emphasis of energy shown by the distribution of the ten planets throughout the birth chart can aid understanding of the houses as well as enabling ready insight into the total personality. The chart can be seen as four semi-circles, the first created by the Ascendant/Descendant axis which cuts the chart into two halves, the top half being south, facing the equator, and the bottom half, north. The second division is created by the MC/IC axis which also divides the chart into two halves, the left being the eastern hemisphere and the right, the western hemisphere.

A strong distribution of planets in the *southern* hemisphere indicates a tendency for an individual to feel at ease in worldly situations. With a lack of emphasis in the lower half of the chart where a certain lack in understanding oneself can prevail, there is often a conscious desire to seek greater self-understanding. Being confronted constantly with the enigma of one's own

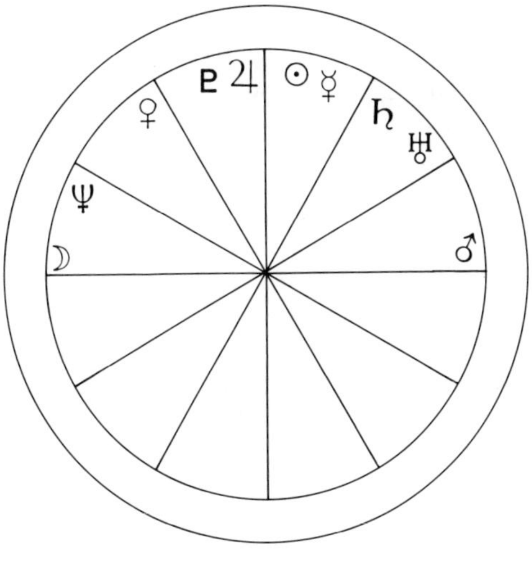

Southern Hemisphere Emphasis

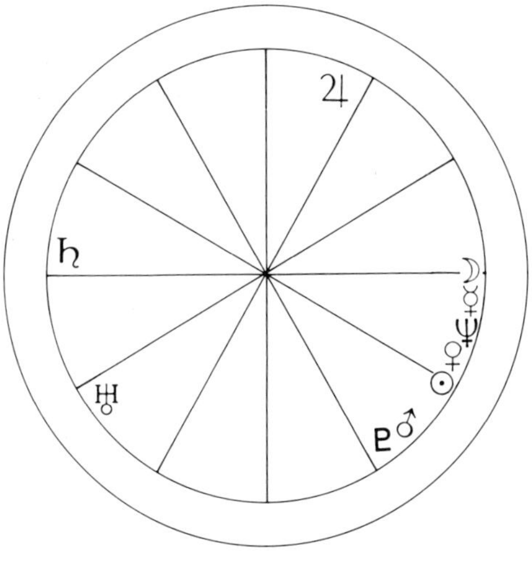

Northern Hemisphere Emphasis

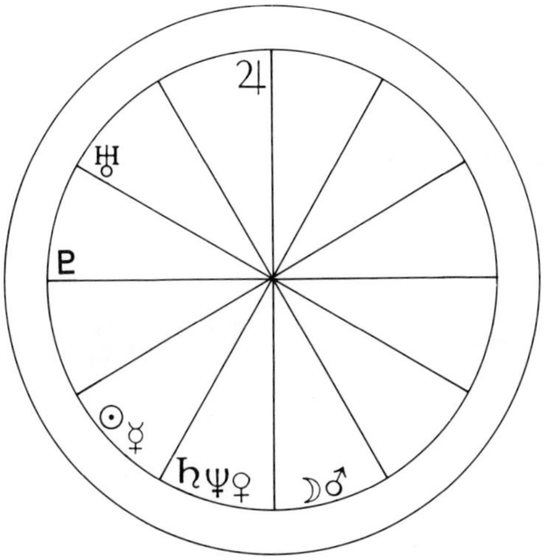

Eastern Hemisphere Emphasis

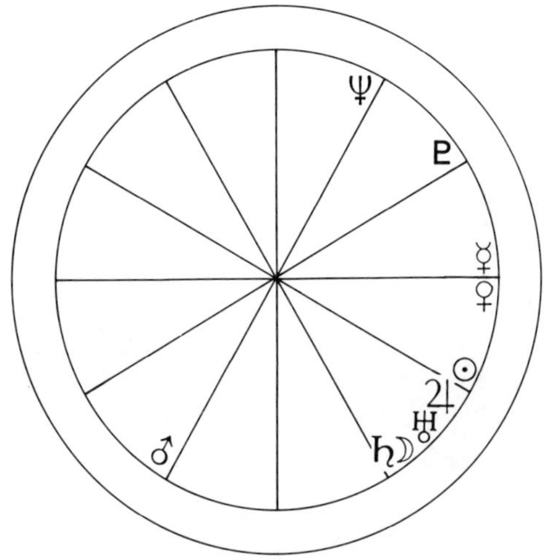

Western Hemisphere Emphasis

Figure 16 Hemisphere Emphases

personality can be extremely frustrating.

With a greater emphasis on the *northern* hemisphere, when there is a larger number of planets in the bottom half than in the top, there can be an associated sense of knowing who one is but of not knowing how to cope especially well in society.

With an *eastern* hemisphere emphasis, it is easier to be in command of one's own destiny, being able to be decisive and forthright about life. This may well be accompanied by a desire for someone or something else to assume the responsibility for self. The onus being so constantly with oneself can seem most burdensome at times.

A *western* hemisphere emphasis invariably suggests a personality who is often the victim of external circumstances. The individual is forever confronted with life and it is often found that this type longs to be free to make his own decisions.

The houses share a common theme, that of the need for the individual to acquire certain life experiences, some of which may be actually desired, whereas others are necessary in the shaping of the personality.

The starting point of each house is referred to as the *cusp*. The cusp of the first house is the Ascendant, with the houses following on, numbered one to twelve, in an anti-clockwise direction. While some astrologers infer that the 'influence' of one zodiacal sign overlaps into another and we hear of people being born 'on the cusp' of a Sun sign, this overlapping, or orb allowance, applies to houses rather than to signs. The majority view is that there is a demarkation from one sign to another which commences at 0° and ends at 29° 59′.

However, the houses are linked closely with the signs of the zodiac following their natural sequence, thus the first house has an association with Aries, the second with Taurus, the third with Gemini and so on. In precisely the same way that the twelve signs of the zodiac are divided by two, three and four, so divisions of the twelve houses by the same numbers provide further information concerning their meanings.

The first six houses, in common with the first six signs, are more expressive of personal matters. The last six houses, in common with the last six signs, are more expressive of worldly matters where self is in contact with others in a truly worldly sense. Each house rules a different sphere of activity.

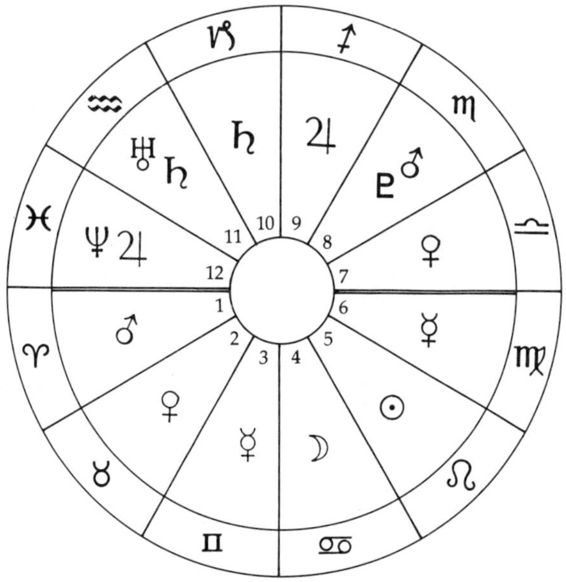

Figure 17 The natural rulerships

The Meaning and Rulerships of the Houses

The First House (ruled by Mars and associated with Aries)
As the Ascendant is the cusp of the first house, they are taken as being synonymous with one another. The first house is the most prominent of the houses since it involves the overall manner of self-expression and the general manner in which behaviour is expressed and attitudes and outlook on life are formed. New people, places and interests will have bearing on the shaping of the personality. Health comes under the jurisdiction of this house for the temperament and behaviour are so affected by the state of health and vice versa. The sign on the Ascendant will show the most likely problem areas in this respect.

The Second House (ruled by Venus and associated with Taurus)
Inner resources as well as financial prospects are expressed by this house and it is clear that these matters in turn affect the way in which the personality is used and expressed, for everything revolves around the degree of self-worth, being the value that is placed upon oneself. It is the physical house governing the body for that is our most tangible asset.

The Third House (ruled by Mercury and associated with Gemini)
Known as the House of Communication, it governs the written and spoken word and all forms and means of making communication with others. Not surprisingly, those involved in agencies and in selling, have a prominent third house. Ruling brethren, neighbours and indicative

of the capacity to study, it can give insight concerning the direction of thoughts and the capacity for learning.

The Fourth House (ruled by the Moon and associated with Cancer)
This house rules the unconscious desire to set down roots and create a home. It governs the feeling of the hearth as well as its bricks and mortar; the family into which one is born, as well as the family one will eventually create. It rules the parents, in many instances the mother, but invariably the parent who is the greater influence during the caring years.

The Fifth House (ruled by the Sun and associated with Leo)
The inner child and sense of creativity gives rise to that feeling and desire for pleasure and pleasure-seeking. It may well be that a romantic liaison, or even the birth of a child, causes a reappraisal of the world in which we live so that life is coloured according to the emotions. Anything that spells fun, including theatre, show business, entertainment, even gambling or speculation come under the jurisdiction of this house. It can also describe the likely children, the image of the father and how one is likely to behave towards one's children.

The Sixth House (ruled by Mercury and associated with Virgo)
Described often as the House of Work and Health. The sign on its cusp will describe the manner in which work is tackled, colleagues, associates and the capacity for work in general. Clearly the physical health and mental well-being have a direct bearing on the capacity to work. It rules service to others, which also involves the military. Traditionally, small animals are governed by this house.

The Seventh House (ruled by Venus and associated with Libra)
This house rules personal relationships of all kinds, as well as partnerships, which can be both business or marriage. It rules the manner of dealing with other people, hence its traditional name, the House of Open Enemies.

The Eighth House (ruled by Mars and Pluto and associated with Scorpio)
Associated with this area are the fundamental issues of birth, life and death together with those stronger feelings which may be hidden, even from oneself. The ancients must have been familiar with the easy translation of emotions and sexuality with money and possessions for this sharing house governs both the deeper emotional feelings, the sexual act and earned income, for this is the value society places on one's worth. It rules the handling of other peoples' money, taxes, insurance, legacy and inheritance.

The Ninth House (ruled by Jupiter and associated with Sagittarius)
Ruling the mind's processes, this house is naturally associated with higher learning, philosophy, colleges and universities. It is a guide to discovering moral codes and general behaviour. Since the mind is allowed free reign so the physical body is able to cover long distances. Thus this house is associated with long-distance travel and, in terms of the mind, the spiritual realms.

The Tenth House (ruled by Saturn and associated with Capricorn)
Just as the Midheaven describes the direction of the ego so this house governs career, ambitions and achievement. It shows the respect and esteem afforded by others and has bearing on the position in life to which we not only aspire but can attain. It is often thought to describe the father since it is frequently his position which determines the later public standing of his offspring. Even in our more enlightened society, the tenth house in a female chart very often describes her husband since it is his position which directly affects hers.

The Eleventh House (ruled by Saturn and Uranus and associated with Aquarius)
Often called the House of Personal Hopes and Wishes, it describes one's aspirations as well as the areas that are of most importance in a deeply personal sense. It involves issues of a deeply personal nature, expressing feelings concerning society and humanity as a whole as well as friends, and acquaintances. Contact with society begins through one's friends, hence the linked association of clubs and societies under the jurisdiction of this house.

The Twelfth House (ruled by Jupiter and Neptune and associated with Pisces)
Sometimes referred to as the House of Seclusion, it infers that private place within us that only we know exists. Those private feelings that are never voiced to anyone. It is from this innermost area that is gained one's self-identity, for it determines the degree of belief that we have in ourselves. It is a most vulnerable area for it is there that we are capable of deceiving ourselves. Not for nothing did the Ancients regard it as the House of Hidden Enemies for we are, fundamentally, our own worst enemies. It deals with the health of self and others, and so rules hospitals, institutions, welfare and prisons. We are all capable of making prisoners of our own selves in one form or another.

Polarity

When analysing the birth chart, it is wise to examine the houses according to their polarity for each has a relationship with its opposing house. Each of the polarities forms an axis across the chart.

The Axis of the First and Seventh Houses
Indicative of the impact of being, for it is concerned primarily with relating and the reaching out into life to exchange ideas, feeling and understanding with others. The interchange of self with others creates mutual influences that amend attitudes. It is the force of personality that affects the mood and behaviour of those with whom we come into contact and vice versa.

The Axis of the Second and Eighth Houses
Being part of this Earth, none of us escapes the basic rhythms of existence. The fundamental pattern traced from birth to death encompassing the sexual rhythms concerns the fact of being and thus has direct bearing on the formation, power and usage of personality.

The Axis of the Third and Ninth Houses
The Mind of Man supersedes all his attributes. This axis involves movement and the covering of distances, mentally, physically and spiritually. The intellect demands more knowledge and education for the sense of enquiry should have no limitations.

The Axis of the Fourth and Tenth Houses
The challenges of career and the establishment of a particular position in life are invariably linked to the type of general life-style and quality of living. The stability of a happy home environment can provide tremendous incentive establishing a sense of purpose that reaches out to the rest of the community.

The Axis of the Fifth and Eleventh Houses
Life itself is a gamble, for the changing, disruptive character of society can never be fully predicted. No-one is exempt from the responsibility of self to other human beings. The desire for a rich, full life, being of value to society, initiates from the creative source of self.

The Axis of the Sixth and Twelfth Houses
To be of use provides a sense of purpose, to be idle encourages apathy. Involving our expectations, the harm that can be done through self-criticism, self-deceit and the harbouring of thoughts and fears that cannot seem to be shared can assume guilt and anxiety about the whole process of living and being oneself. The translation of energy into service can benefit all Mankind including oneself. Perhaps we need the confrontation with ill-health of self or a loved one in order to understand priorities.

The Division of the Houses by the Numbers Three and Four

The triplicities (elements) and quadruplicities (qualities) can be applied to both the signs of the zodiac and the houses. Every birth chart contains all twelve houses to indicate that every human being has access to any and all knowledge that is available on this earthly plane. It is not essential to personally experience every facet of human life in order to comprehend its meaning. However, through modern technology the pain and the pleasure of all the peoples throughout the world can be witnessed in our living rooms. Unquestionably modern man is able to make contact with a broader spectrum of human experience than at any other time in recorded history. Divisions of the houses by three and four enable the astrologer to relate worldly experience in connection with individual man.

Division by Three

The division of the twelve houses by the number three creates a means of understanding how we relate to life, for life is seen in terms of our relationships to others (see Figure 18). The first four houses, first, second, third and fourth, all refer to the relationship One to One. These houses relate specifically to the gathering of self-knowledge and self-awareness, for the prime duty that every human being has is to 'Know Thyself'.

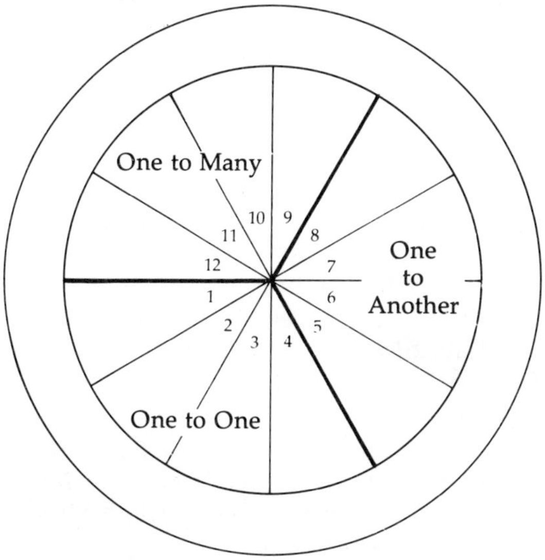

Figure 18 Division by three — relationships

In the second sequence of four houses, fifth, sixth, seventh and eighth, the object is to learn to cope with personal relationships, One to Another. To share all that one is and has with another human being means to give freely of Self.

The third sequence of four houses, ninth, tenth, eleventh and twelfth, acknowledges the need of the relationship one to many and the need to learn to share the same air space with the teeming multitudes of people on this planet.

Division by Four

Any division of the houses by the number four into sequences of three houses each draws upon the concept of the Cross of Matter (see Figure 19). The individual is confronted with the reality and responsibility for him/her self and life as it is. The first three houses indicate the intimate knowledge of ourselves that must be gained through the experience of life in order to know who we are.

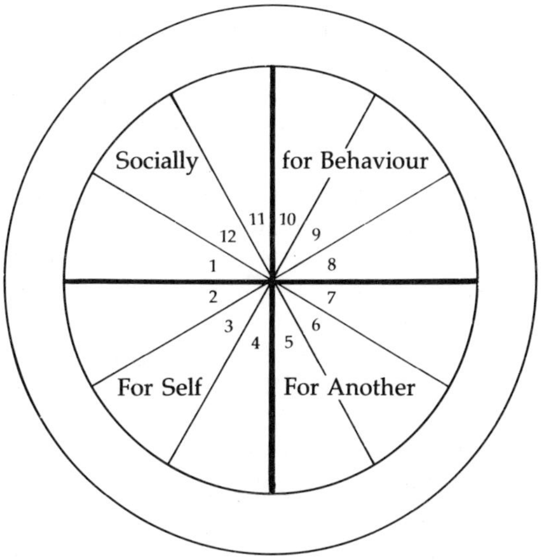

Figure 19 Division by four — responsibility

The second sequence, fourth, fifth and sixth houses, shows the capacity to procreate, to give of ourselves, caring for those with whom we are closely connected.

The third sequence, seventh, eighth and ninth houses, expresses the responsible adult, for our behaviour directly affects others.

The fourth sequence concerns our responsibility to society as individuals and on a collective level, for if there is any suffering in this world then we are all responsible because we allow it to happen.

Angular, Succedent and Cadent Houses

The more familiar method of dividing the houses by a sequence of four is similar in essence to that of the quadruplicities (see

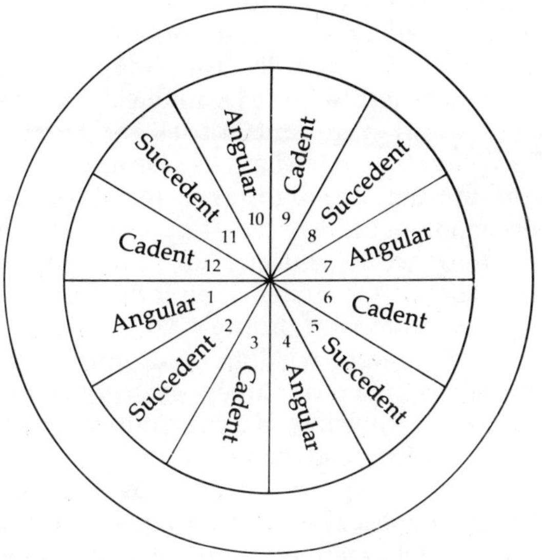

Figure 20 The angular, succedent and cadent houses

Figure 20 and refer to pages 33–36). The angular houses represent those areas of life where human experience is met head-on for we attract those experiences that we need in order to become who we are.

These houses reflect immediate connection with life through the individual's unique prescription for living. The home life (fourth), involvement with other people (seventh), and sense of honour (tenth) are shaped and coloured according to our personalities (first). (Refer also to the Four Angles, pages 23–24).

Linked with the four fixed signs of the zodiac, the succedent houses are those areas of life which are most grounded in matter. They refer to the familiar, the known, the values according to which life is lived. What we are (second) is invariably translated into what we have. Who we are (fifth) is bound up with self-respect. If we value ourselves, we can function in a creative manner, bringing up children to have pride in themselves. The eighth concerns what we are prepared to do for money in terms of earned income and especially for other people, hence the translation again between the feeling nature and money. It is easier to argue about the cost of an item than to struggle with the emotions or sexual nature. That which the individual stands for (eleventh) has wider, social implications. Anarchy would prevail without social values. The responsibility of the succedent houses is to give back to the Earth what is used, that is, giving back the Gift of Life. How often is it said, 'we get out of life what we put into it.'

In common with the four mutable signs of the zodiac (see page 36), the cadent houses are concerned with the intellect. In the angular and succedent houses can be seen the potential of Man to dominate his environment through the force of his personality and feelings. The cadent houses are those which reflect Man's true superiority above the animal kingdom, for he is able to dominate through the power of mind, learning, wisdom and spirit. The houses numbered three, six, nine and twelve are divisible by the number three telling of the knowledge afforded by the power of creativity. United as the four cadent houses, they show Man's ability to express that creativity on the earthly plane.

Finding the Local Sidereal Time

Newcomers to astrology are often deterred by the seemingly complex calculations required to set up a birth chart. The truth of the matter is that the calculations are not difficult at all. The only reason that they seem so bewildering at first is that they are new. Like everything else, it is simple when one knows how. Probably the most tricky part of all the calculations is counting in multiples of sixty rather than in the familiar multiples of ten. The fact that both angular units and time are expressed in the Babylonian sexagesimal system makes life actually much easier for the astrologer, for the two are interchangeable. A car moving at sixty miles per hour travels one mile in one minute. A planet moving 2° (120 angular minutes) in one day, travels 15 minutes in three hours.

We take the matter of telling the time completely for granted. It is a simple matter of looking at a watch or a clock or taking a time check from the broadcasted chimes of Big Ben. The story of the development of clocks and man-made time is a fascinating one but for our purposes it is important to know that navigators, sailing the high seas, were responsible for creating Standard Clock Time from the positioning of the stars. Astrologers must work backwards, converting clock time to 'time reckoned by the stars', otherwise known as *Sidereal Time*.

The Ascendant, Midheaven and house cusps of a birth chart are calculated from the *Local Sidereal Time* of the birth place. A relatively simple formula that is based upon certain logical steps, is required to convert the given clock-time of a birth to the local sidereal time. (See page 57).

Astrologers and astronomers prefer to work in sidereal time because it is the more accurate means of measuring time. Explanations of the how and why of time are not strictly essential in the erection of a birth chart, but understanding the how and why of what you are doing can help to eliminate the possibility of making errors during computation. Knowing the reasons for the various steps that are taken clarifies the process and will also prove an advantage if you wish to make use of an electronic calculator or computer.

In order to set up a birth chart, there are three co-ordinates which are normally taken for granted that should be understood: clocktime; GMT; longitude and lattitude.

What is Clock Time? (See p.57, step 3)

We are all familiar with clock time since it is a matter of merely looking at a clock or watch. Most clocks perform two complete revolutions in a twenty-four hour period and these are noted in hours and minutes, either a.m. or p.m.; in European countries the twenty-four hour clock is mostly employed. Clock time is based on the standard GMT (Greenwich Mean Time) that is used throughout the world.

What is GMT? (See p.55 and 57, step 4)

GMT refers to the mean solar time on the Greenwich Meridian. What does that mean? Because the Earth is tilted in its elliptical orbit, the length of each day varies throughout the year, apart from the spring and autumn equinoxes, when the Sun rises at 6 a.m. and sets at 6 p.m. all the world over. True solar time is recorded by sundials, all of which are sometimes fast and sometimes slow, depending on the time of year. The mean is the average of successive transits of the Sun from a fixed point of observation and the sight chosen for this was Greenwich. But why Greenwich?

Greenwich Observatory was clearly visible to shipping and naval companies along the River Thames. It was established in 1676 in order to determine longitude and latitude so that navigation might be made safe for the British Navy and shipping in general. Although French navigators preferred a Paris based ephemeris, by 1788, of all the world's shipping, 72 per cent used charts based upon the Greenwich Meridian.

What is the Greenwich Meridian?

It is sometimes thought that the meridian is a special circle which applies only to Greenwich but this is not so. Every locality has its own meridian. A meridian great circle is merely a reference for anywhere on the Earth's surface according to the place of observation, facing towards the equator. This great circle passes through the north and south points of the horizon, the corresponding north and south poles of the celestial sphere and the zenith and nadir of the observer. That moment when the Sun is exactly on the meridian of a given place, was declared to be noon. This intersection

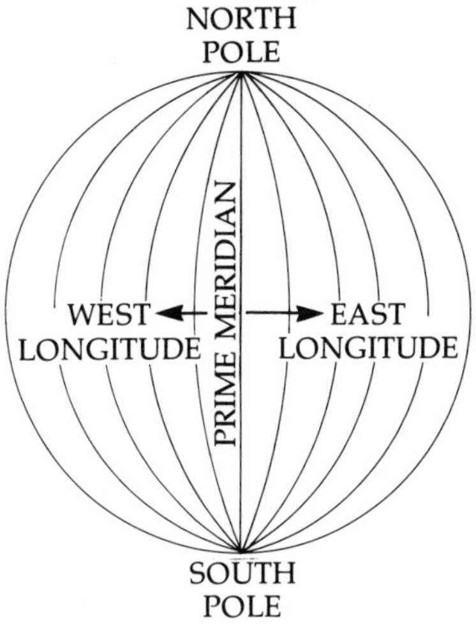

Figure 21 The meridians

of the Sun's apparent path with the meridian of a given place is the Midheaven in the birth chart (see page 22). The meridian at Greenwich was designated the Prime Meridian by an international conference in 1884, fixing a common zero for longitude and time reckoning throughout the world. The Prime Meridian could have been set anywhere else in the world; indeed it had been argued that the Great Pyramid in Egypt, Jerusalem, or Ptolemy's choice, the Canary Islands, would be far better suited to this purpose.

World Standard Time Zones (See p.54 and 57, step 5)

Commencing at the Prime Meridian at Greenwich, the globe of the Earth is marked off into twenty-four zones 15° apart, making a total of 360°, extending 180° east and 180° west of Greenwich and meeting at the International Date Line. Zones *east* of Greenwich are termed *minus* zones, with local times ahead or faster than Greenwich, and those *west* of Greenwich are termed *plus* zones, which are behind or slower than Greenwich. All clock time within a zone conforms to the standard of its designated meridian. Some areas in the world give time zones in half hours. There are still some countries which do not conform to the time zone system. It is vital to be sure of the zone's standard time; otherwise serious errors in the conversion of clock time to GMT can arise, negating the birth chart. Time zone charts or maps are easily obtainable from stationers or observatories. Most atlases provide the same information.

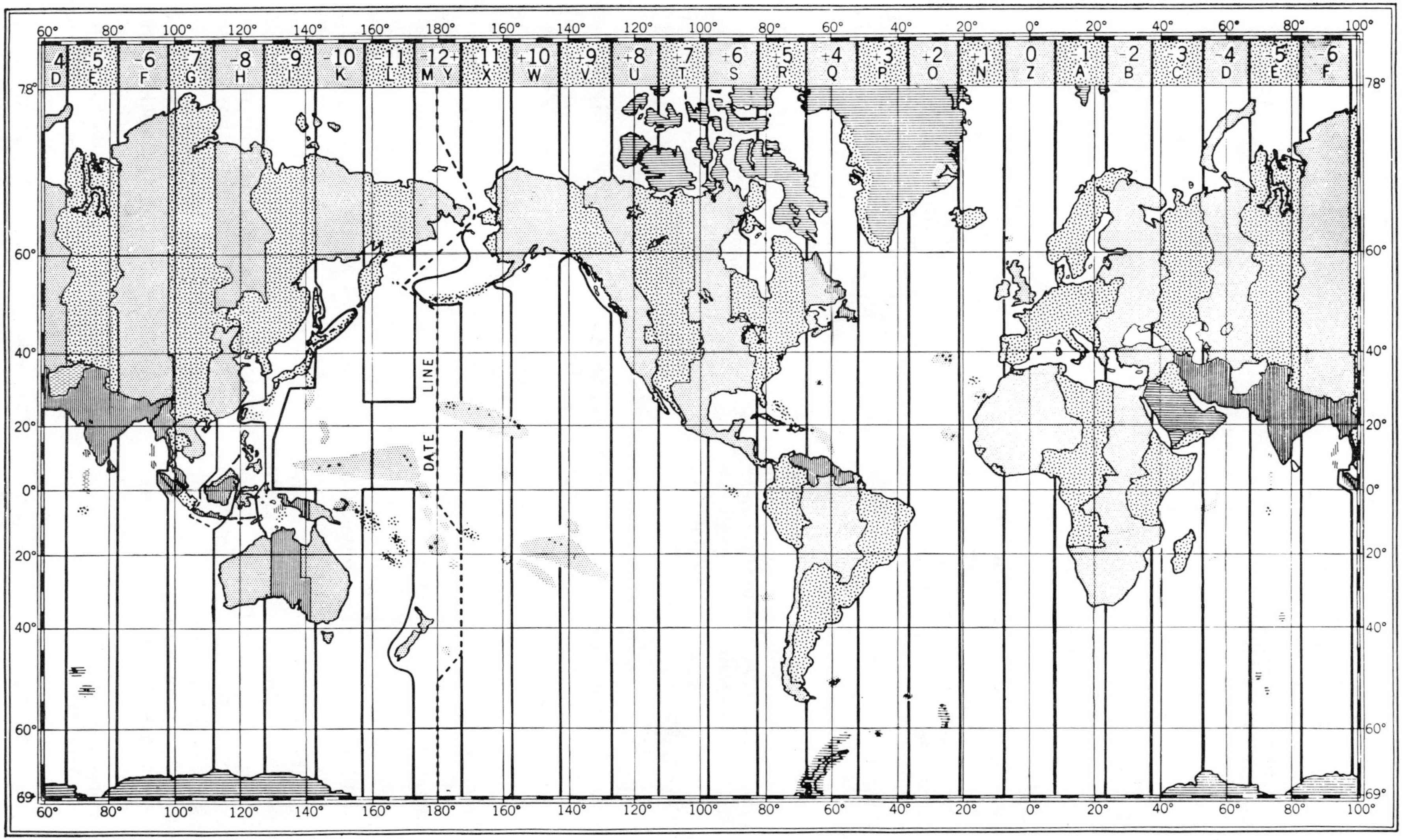

Figure 22 World Time Zones

Longitude Equivalent (See p.57, step 2)
In the endeavour to convert clock time to local sidereal time we need to find out what is the actual time according to the locality of the birth. For any locality differing from that precisely on the Prime Meridian at Greenwich, a difference in terms of longitude must occur. Because the Earth rotates 360° in each twenty-four hours, it must rotate 1° in four minutes. Degrees and minutes of longitude, calculated in sixties, can easily be converted to hours and minutes of time. To obtain the longitude equivalent, according to time, simply multiply degrees and minutes of longitude by four (minutes). For example, Hull, with a longitude of 0° 20′ west of Greenwich, has a local mean time variation from GMT of 1 minute 20 seconds (0° W 20′ x 4 = 80 seconds = 1 minute 20 seconds). Because it is west of Greenwich it is *plus* GMT meaning that in Hull noon actually occurs at 12.01.20.

The American Federation of Astrologers has produced very helpful *Longitudes and Latitudes throughout the World* and *Longitudes and Latitudes in the U.S.* A good atlas with a gazeteer will also give the longitudes and latitudes for most localities. (See p.57, step 1.)

Daylight Saving Time (See p.57, step 6)
In 1916 the British Government introduced Daylight Saving Time, adding one hour to GMT during the summer months — a measure quickly adopted by other countries at war. Reintroduced from 1941 to 1945 and used again for the sake of economy in 1947, British Summer Time lasted throughout the year with a further hour being added during the summer months, called Double Summer Time (DBST). In order to conform with the rest of the countries in the E.E.C., Britain experimented during 1968 to 1971, keeping British Standard Time (BST), which meant adding an extra hour to GMT throughout the whole year. Because of Britain's northerly latitudes, where winter days are so short, it was regarded as a failure and the experiment was abandoned. Since 1972 Britain returned to its own standard of keeping GMT in the winter time and British summer time (BST) in the summer. This means that clocks 'Spring forward and Fall back'. There is no consistency or standard laid down for the time of year when Daylight Saving Time is employed by various countries. It is necessary to check this out very carefully and while it is possible to check with the appropriate embassy, the following books are most useful: *Time Changes in the World, Time Changes in the U.S.A.* and *Time Changes in Canada and Mexico,* all by Doris Chase Doane. *Natal Charting* by John Filbey provides the dates of all the time changes for Great Britain from 1916.

Why is it Necessary to Convert to GMT? (See p.53 and 57, step 4 and 11)
Most ephemerides used by astrologers give the planets' positions according to the sidereal time either at noon or at midnight GMT. A birth chart may be constructed from any given clock time for virtually anywhere in the world, converting it first to GMT from any zone standard. GMT is often referred to in other countries as Universal Time (UT).

What is the Difference Between Mean Time and Sidereal Time?
Mean time is derived from the average of successive solar days, creating a day which is exactly 24 hours long. The sidereal day is 23 hours 56 minutes 3.455 seconds long and is the true daily rotational period of the Earth upon its axis. This means that there is a difference in time between the sidereal day and the mean solar day of 3 minutes 56 seconds. Originally measured according to the successive transits of stars over the observer's meridian, sidereal clocks in observatories are set at 0 hours 0 minutes 0 seconds when 0° Aries is on the meridian of a given place. Since sidereal time is reckoned according to longitudinal meridians, it will not vary, regardless of latitude, as can be seen in any tables of houses. During the course of the year there is a daily increment of 3 minutes 56 seconds in the sidereal time. This increment can be traced in any ephemeris whether for noon or midnight, in the column headed Sidereal Time.

Does any Correction Have to be Made from Clocktime to Sidereal Time? (See p.57, step 8)
Since sidereal time is shorter than mean time by a total of 24 hours in a year, which is

approximately 4 minutes (3m 56s) in a day, or approximately 10 seconds (9.86s) each hour, it is necessary to make a correction from clock time called the *acceleration on the interval*. Thus for a birth time given as 7.15 a.m., the acceleration on the interval would be: 7h 15m x 10s = 72 seconds = 1 minute 12 seconds, which must be subtracted if using a noon ephemeris or added if using a midnight ephemeris.

What is the Sidereal Time for the Place of Birth? (See p.57, step 12)

Just as there is a difference between standard time and local mean time so there is a difference between sidereal time and the local sidereal time at a particular place. To determine the precise local sidereal time, the longitude equivalent must be added or subtracted, according to whether it is east or west of Greenwich, to or from the sidereal time reckoned at GMT.

Ephemeris Time

Some ephemerides, including the annual *Raphael's Ephemeris* during the years 1960-1982, have been calculated in Ephemeris Time (ET). GMT is measured according to the axial rotation of the Earth but this rotation is not strictly regular. Introduced in 1952 and independent of terrestrial longitude, Ephemeris Time is based upon the orbital motion of the Earth measured over many years. The correction from GMT to UT amounts only to seconds and need not be used for astrological purposes, for birth times are usually noted to the minute only.

Why do the House Cusps Vary at Different Latitudes?

The Earth's axis is always directed to the same point in the heavens, the north celestial pole, and is inclined to the plane of the Sun's apparent path at an angle of approximately 23½°. The angle thus formed between the plane of the Earth's equator and the plane of the ecliptic is called the 'Obliquity of the Ecliptic'. Because the signs of the zodiac rise parallel with the equator, they only rise uniformly at two-hourly intervals actually along the equator itself. At any location north or south of the equator there has to be a distortion. The further the distance towards the poles, the greater is the disparity, with some signs ascending faster than others. In the northern hemisphere, the signs from Capricorn to Gemini are known as the signs of Short Ascension, rising more rapidly than the signs Cancer to Sagittarius, which are known as the signs of Long Ascension. The reverse is the case in the southern hemisphere. In the most northerly and southerly latitudes, some signs of the zodiac never rise or set at all, which creates problems with House Systems such as Placidus (see page 41ff). However, it might also be said that the life-style of those who live in the neighbourhood of the Arctic Circle is rather different from those in more populous areas of the world, due to six months perpetual light followed by six months perpetual dark. It is possible to trace the movement from the equator to northerly latitudes via the Tables of Houses, some attaining to 66° north, by tracing the Ascendant and corresponding house cusps at different latitudes but always at the same sidereal time. For example, at the sidereal time 0h 0m 0s for latitude 11° North, the Ascendant is 4° 50′ Cancer; at 12° North it is 4° 50′ Cancer; at 22° North it is 9° 08′ Cancer and so forth.

Births in Southern Latitudes (See p.57, step 14)

A chart for a birth south of the equator can be constructed using the *Tables of Houses for Northern Latitudes* by simply adding twelve hours to the local sidereal time and reversing the signs of the zodiac for all the house cusps, e.g., for a birth in Melbourne, Australia at latitude 37° 50′ South with a local sidereal time of 15 hours 35 minutes 23 seconds, refer to the Tables of Houses for Athens, latitude 37° 58′ North, where the appropriate given Ascendant is 6° Aquarius and Midheaven 26° Scorpio. Reverse signs and the Ascendant will be 6° Leo, Midheaven 26° Taurus, 2nd House 21° Virgo, 3rd 29° Libra, 11th 18° Gemini, 12th 10° Cancer. Astrologers in countries of southern latitudes question the validity of reversing the signs of the zodiac in this manner, feeling that the signs should commence with Aries at the autumn equinox. There has been little work done on this particular area, which appears to be ripe for research.

Follow the numbered 'steps', referring to appropriate sections on given page numbers for full explanations.
(A) = 'Enter information as requested'; (B) = 'Delete as required'; (C) = Examples given on following page:

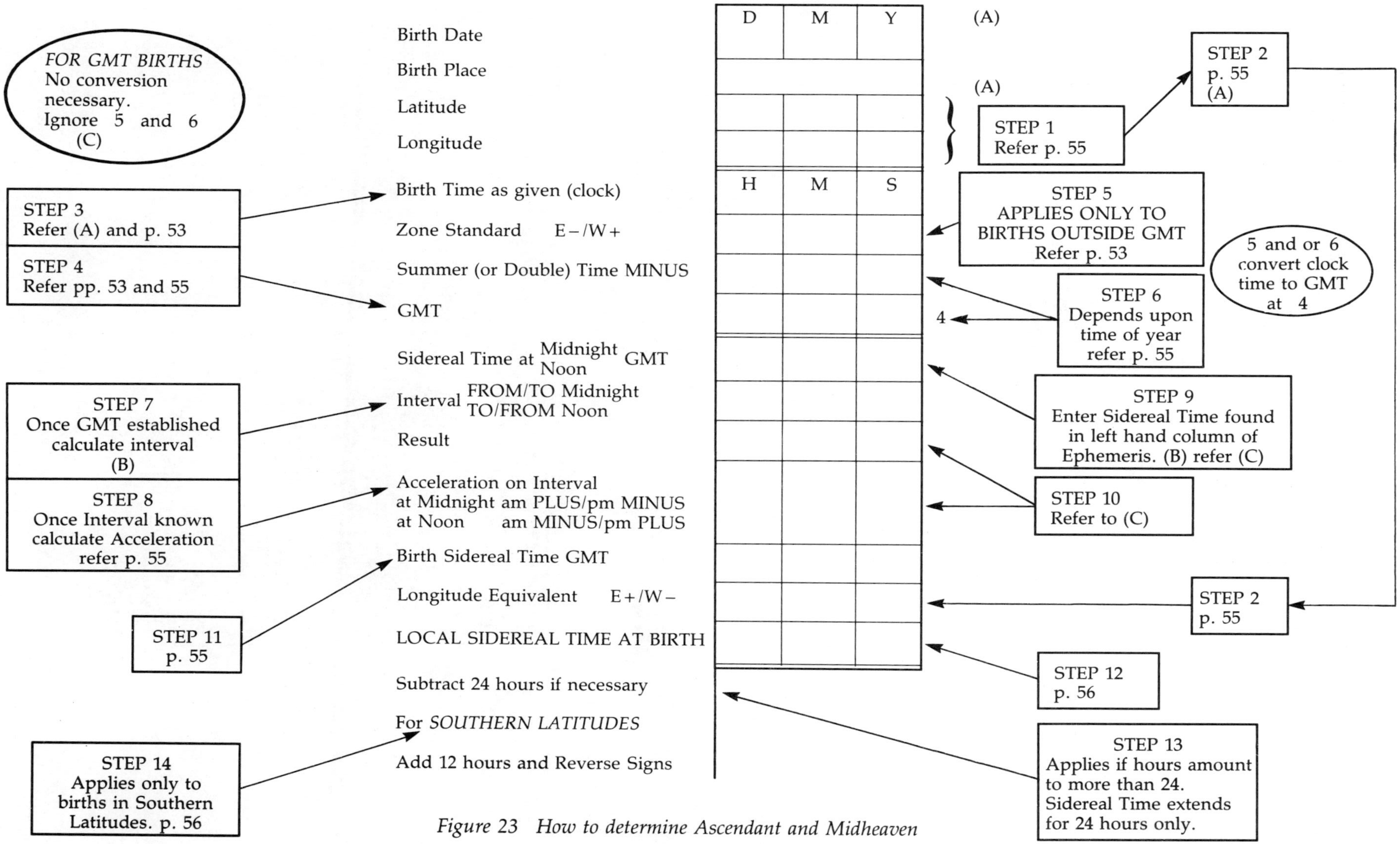

Figure 23 How to determine Ascendant and Midheaven

Using a midnight ephemeris

	D 22	M 12	Y 1949
Birth Date	22	12	1949
Birth Place	HULL: YORKS		
Latitude	53	45	N
Longitude	0	20	W
	H	M	S
Birth Time as given (clock)	6	58	—
Zone Standard E – /W +	—	(G.B)	—
Summer (or Double) Time	—		
GMT	6	58	—
Sidereal Time at Midnight GMT	6	00	52
Interval FROM Midnight (am PLUS)	6	58	00
Result	12	58	52
Acceleration on Interval at Midnight am PLUS		1	10
Birth Sidereal Time GMT	13	00	02
Longitude Equivalent (West MINUS)		1	20
LOCAL SIDEREAL TIME AT BIRTH	12	58	42

Subtract 24 hours if necessary
For SOUTHERN LATITUDES
Add 12 hours and Reverse Signs

(Delete as Required)

Using a *noon* ephemeris

	D 22	M 12	Y 1949
Birth Date	22	12	1949
Birth Place	HULL: YORKS		
Latitude	53	45	N
Longitude	0	20	W
	H	M	S
Birth Time as given (clock)	6	58	—
Zone Standard E – /W +	—	(G.B)	—
Summer (or Double) Time	—		
GMT	6	58	—
Sidereal Time at Noon GMT	18	02	51
Interval TO Noon (am MINUS)	5	02	00
Result	13	00	51
Acceleration on Interval at Noon am MINUS			50
Birth Sidereal Time GMT	13	00	01
Longitude Equivalent (West MINUS)		1	20
LOCAL SIDEREAL TIME AT BIRTH	12	58	41

Subtract 24 hours if necessary
For SOUTHERN LATITUDES
Add 12 hours and Reverse Signs

(Delete as Required)

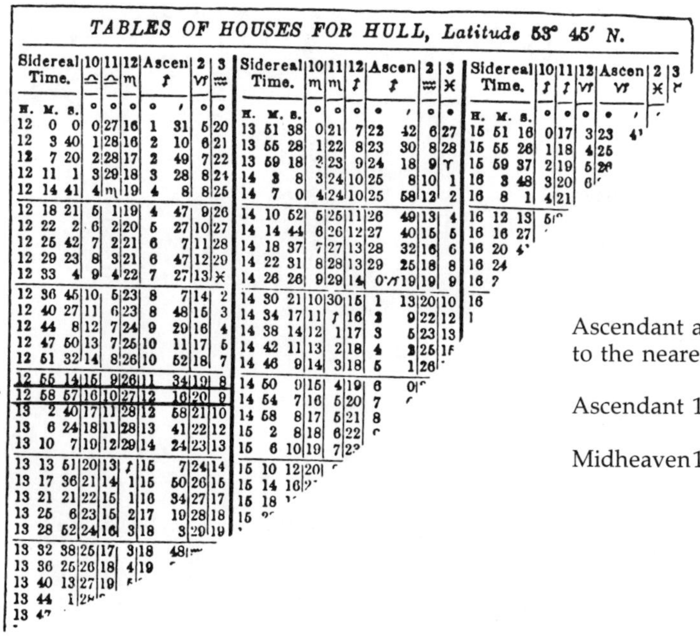

TABLES OF HOUSES FOR HULL, Latitude 53° 45′ N.

Sidereal Time H.	M.	S.	10 ♎ °	11 ♎ °	12 ♏ °	Ascen ♐ °	′	2 ♑ °	3 ♒ °
12	0	0	0	27	16	1	31	5	20
12	3	40	1	28	16	2	10	6	21
12	7	20	2	28	17	2	49	7	22
12	11	1	3	29	18	3	28	8	24
12	14	41	4	♏	19	4	8	8	25
12	18	21	5	1	19	4	47	9	26
12	22	2	6	2	20	5	27	10	27
12	25	42	7	2	21	6	7	11	28
12	29	23	8	3	21	6	47	12	29
12	33	4	9	4	22	7	27	13	♓
12	36	45	10	5	23	8	7	14	2
12	40	27	11	6	23	8	48	15	3
12	44	8	12	7	24	9	29	16	4
12	47	50	13	7	25	10	11	17	5
12	51	32	14	8	26	10	52	18	7
12	55	14	15	9	26	11	34	19	8
12	58	57	16	10	27	12	16	20	9
13	2	40	17	11	28	12	58	21	10
13	6	24	18	11	28	13	41	22	12
13	10	7	19	12	29	14	24	23	13
13	13	51	20	13	♐	15	7	24	14
13	17	36	21	14	1	15	50	26	15
13	21	21	22	15	1	16	34	27	17
13	25	6	23	15	2	17	19	28	18
13	28	52	24	16	3	18	3	29	19
13	32	38	25	17	3	18	48	[illegible]	
13	36	25	26	18	4	19			
13	40	13	27	19	[illegible]				
13	44	1	2[illegible]						
13	4[illegible]								

Sidereal Time H.	M.	S.	10 ♏ °	11 ♏ °	12 ♐ °	Ascen ♐ °	′	2 ♒ °	3 ♓ °
13	51	38	0	21	7	22	42	6	27
13	55	28	1	22	8	23	30	8	28
13	59	18	2	23	9	24	18	9	♈
14	3	8	3	24	10	25	8	10	1
14	7	0	4	24	10	25	58	12	2
14	10	52	5	25	11	26	49	13	4
14	14	44	6	26	12	27	40	15	5
14	18	37	7	27	13	28	32	16	6
14	22	31	8	28	13	29	25	18	8
14	26	26	9	29	14	0 ♑	19	19	9
14	30	21	10	30	15	1	13	20	10
14	34	17	11	♐	16	2	9	22	12
14	38	14	12	1	17	3	5	23	13
14	42	11	13	2	18	4	2	25	1[illegible]
14	46	9	14	3	18	5	1	26	
14	50	9	15	4	19	6	0		
14	54	7	16	5	20	7			
14	58	8	17	5	21	8			
15	2	8	18	6	22				
15	6	10	19	7	2[illegible]				
15	10	12	20						
15	14	16	2[illegible]						
15	18	[illegible]							
15	[illegible]								

Sidereal Time H.	M.	S.	10 ♐ °	11 ♐ °	12 ♑ °	Ascen ♑ °	′	2 ♓	3 ♈
15	51	16	0	17	3	23	4		
15	55	26	1	18	4	25			
15	59	37	2	19	5	2[illegible]			
16	3	48	3	20	6				
16	8	1	4	21					
16	12	13	5[illegible]						
16	16	27							
16	20	4[illegible]							
16	24								
16	[illegible]								
16									
1									

Nearest
SIDEREAL TIME

Ascendant and Midheaven to the nearest degrees

Ascendant 12° Sagittarius

Midheaven16° Libra

Figure 24 Determining Ascendant and Midheaven: a worked example

The Accuracy of the Given Birth Time

If a birth time is not known with accuracy — that is, to the minute, it is wiser to use the Ascendant and Midheaven to the nearest degree. If minutes amount to more than thirty, then round up to the nearest next degree; if minutes amount to less than thirty, then leave the degree as it is. For the beginner to astrology, calculations to the nearest degree will suffice. For more advanced work, using progressions and transits, accuracy of the angles to the minute is most important.

The Computerized Chart

There are different companies available who will calculate birth charts by computer solely from a given clocktime and place of birth. It is also possible to purchase software and floppy discs that have been programmed specifically for home computers but it is most important to make sure that suitable software is available for the type of computer you may wish to purchase. It is recommended that you become familiar with what is required before making such purchases. Beginners are recommended to practise chart calculations manually and perhaps make use of computer companies to verify chart accuracy. (See also Chapter 5, page 112).

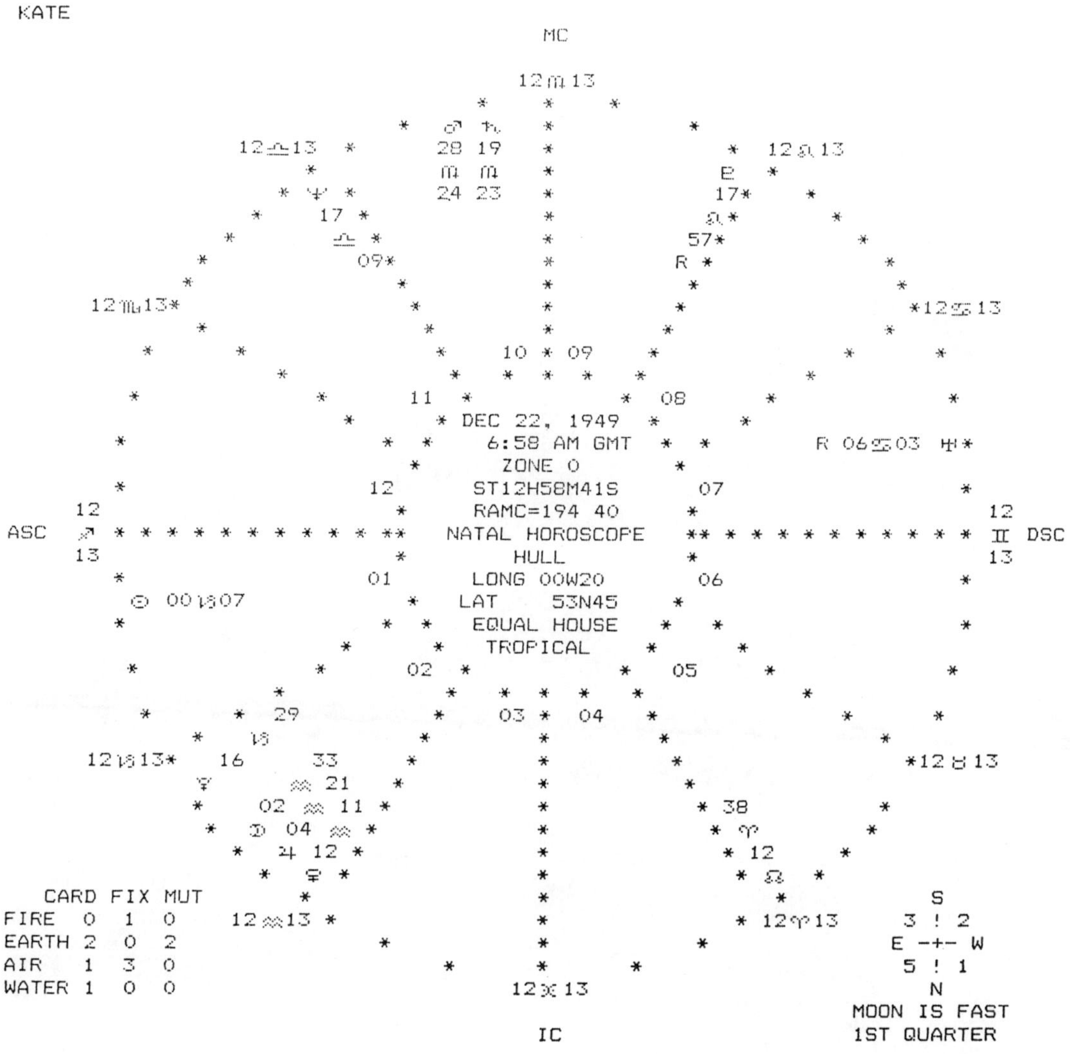

Chapter 5
The Planets

Throughout history astrologers have monitored the movements of the planets in our solar system and found that their rhythmic cycles have coincided with the life lived out by mankind on Earth. While this correlation has been accepted mainly from metaphysical or religious viewpoints in modern times, verification of it is being attempted from a rational viewpoint, upon the erroneous grounds that astrologers maintain that we are directly influenced by the planets. This misunderstanding is the usual basis for the controversy surrounding astrology. (Refer also to Chapter 1.)

Astronomers have suggested that the Sun, the Moon and the planets were originally one body that split apart creating the planets in the order that they are now and the asteroid belt that lies between the orbits of Mars and Jupiter. It is a theory that concurs with that of the 'Big Bang' of the origin of the universe and is equally as speculative. From the astrological view, however, the principles of the individual planets are held to be subdivisions of the one fundamental principle or energy source that lies behind everything.

Astrologers believe that everything in the universe obeys the same natural laws and that the correlating patterning of the planets of our solar system with life on Earth is symbolic of the life force of this universe. All theological works, including the Bible, contain references to the number seven, 'The mystery of the seven stars which thou sawest in my right hand, and the seven golden candlesticks. The seven stars are the angels of the seven churches; and the seven candlesticks are the seven churches.' (Revelation I.20). Such references allude to the Seven Naked Eye Planets: the Sun and the Moon, which have been counted as planets for the sake of convenience, together with Mercury, Venus, Mars, Jupiter and Saturn, all of which are visible in the night sky without the aid of a telescope.

The seven planets and the number seven are synonymous with the life force. Seen within the context of the birth chart

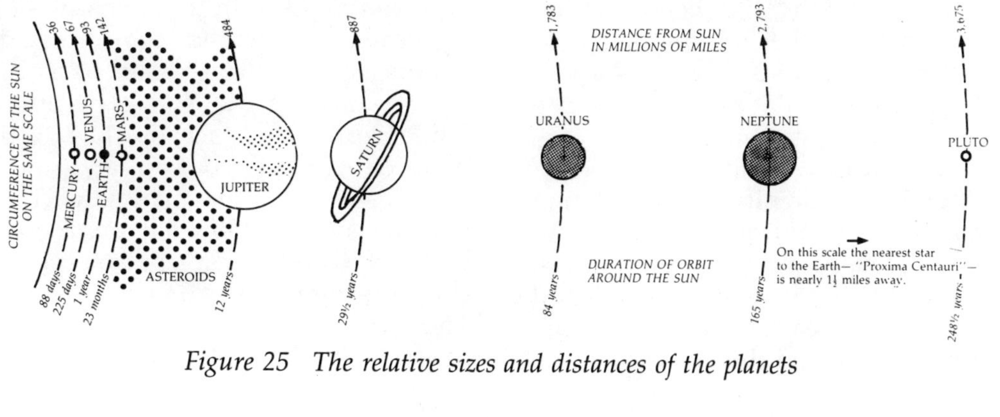

Figure 25 The relative sizes and distances of the planets

comprising the intellectually pure zodiac and the rigid framework of the houses, the continuously moving planets symbolize the the dynamism that propels everything. Their perpetually shifting patterns are representative of the unending changefulness of Creation for change is movement and movement is life. Thus the act of plotting the planets onto the birth chart immediately galvanizes that static entity into life.

The union of the planets with the signs of the zodiac and the houses creates a Trinity that, in itself, is evocative of the creative principle. Three multiplied by four gives the creative number twelve, but it is also important to recognize that three plus four equals the number seven. Physically comprised of the meeting of the vertical line with the horizontal line, seven numerologically tells of the union of the higher, spiritual self with the lower, animal self in the search for the perfection of unfoldment. It is the number of completion yet renewal according to the fullness of spiritual values.

Up to the time when the telescope revealed the infinity of the universe, astrologers depended solely upon these seven planets. With the discovery of Uranus in 1781 and Neptune in 1846 the scheme was amended so that the Sun and the Moon were given special prominence from the seven planets, now Mercury to Neptune. While the emphasis of the number seven was apparently retained, it is interesting to note that increasingly further significance was being given to man's individuality and his behaviour. Since Pluto's discovery in 1930, the symbolism surrounding the magical, mystical seven planets has passed into the realms of history and the scheme has been recognized to have ten planets. In keeping with its mirror image, 'as above, so below', it is since that discovery that mankind has been moving towards a different level of consciousness and attainment. Significant of this more complex stage in man's evolution is the number ten, meaning Oneness with the Greater Whole. It is deemed the number of ultimate perfection, signifying completion or the attainment of purpose, and to that end mankind is being stretched on the rack of the extremes of materialism and spirituality. It is recognized esoterically that the more highly evolved the individual, the more prone that individual will be to encounter difficult life problems and emotional intensity in the understanding that we never get more in life than we can actually cope with. Depth of feeling is not deemed a sign of weakness but evidence of strength of character. On this premise, the collective goal to raise the level of consciousness, albeit for most an unconscious act, shows that mankind has the strength to withstand the pressures of modern life that were completely beyond the knowledge of our predecessors. Everything is of significance in the shaping of the people that we are capable of becoming, and in the shaping of a world that it is capable of being. Astrology reflects this potential, for it is a system of understanding that enables us to gain a finer vision of our lives collectively or individually.

While it is possible to use astrological principles to study collective man, mundane or political astrology is a specialized area with many hidden traps for the inexperienced or untutored. Astrological symbolism is generally applied to individual matters in which the planets serve to represent basic human life principles which reflect the power of creation and the life force and are understood as psychological urges or unconscious driving forces. Each of the planets represents differing facets of personality that are peculiar only to human beings, facets that differentiate us from the animal kingdom.

The Individual Planets

The Sun ☉

The moment of conception has now been captured on film. In that instance of time, it is possible to see that the fertilized ovum begins to rotate bearing a startling resemblance to the shape of our galaxy. Evidence of the fact of the relationship between the macrocosm and the microcosm? Views differ markedly concerning that moment when the soul enters the body; it could be at conception, at some stage during the pregnancy or even at birth. The whole matter is questionable. Not questionable is the fact that when two cells unite, one male and one female, a single cell is conceived. This single cell is pure creativity. It is life. The glyph for the Sun, ☉ is wholly evocative of this crucial event and so serves to represent immediate creativity and the initiating power of the life force. It stands for the capacity to be aware of our central being, for it is ours by the simple fact of being alive. Thus the Sun takes an immensely prominent position in the birth chart.

No two birth charts are identical because the time, date and place of birth create a uniquely individual Sun by virtue of the degree of the sign of the zodiac, the house position and the relationship by aspects with the other nine planets (see Chapter 6, 'The Visual Energies') that tells of the *quality* of creative energy that we usually describe as self-expression. Thus the Sun indicates the individual self and the capacity to be.

We are One by reason of our creation and nothing should divide us from that sense of Oneness. Our worldly condition causes us to feel fragmented, compelling the need to spend our lives endeavouring to return to that prime knowledge of At-One-Ment. Each of us is a seed able to prove its existence by the power of being. Here we can see the reasoning for the rulership of Leo with its pride in the pure sense of being. The desire to rejoice in being alive viewed through the medium of the fifth house becomes clear, as does the polarity with the opposite Aquarius and the eleventh house, for it shows that caring for others comes from extending our energy away from the centre of self outward to others acknowledging ourselves as part of the Oneness of Mankind.

It can occur that the whole of our lives can be spent seeking some reason for being, perhaps qualifying or criticizing every action and demanding something other than being the person we have been born to be.

Much has been written on the positioning of the Sun according to its sign of the zodiac; the familiar Sun signs are easy to research. You may also find it useful to refer to those descriptions of the signs found on pages 36 to 38. The house position of the Sun invariably describes those attributes that we need to learn about ourselves in order to allow free rein to our natural self-expression.

Guide to the Interpretation of the Sun Through the Houses

Sun in the First House

The need is to discover a sense of independence and responsibility for self and one's own actions. It may seem that the prime cause is self, but self for what purpose? A lesson to be learned is not to take oneself too seriously and to be the first to use humour to help restore equilibrium.

Sun in the Second House

The lesson is simply to learn to be. Understanding of the constant drive to be secure comes from getting in touch with one's own resources of self, for therein lies ultimate security. Preoccupation with the physical being and the accoutrements of life does not make up for a lack of sureness.

Sun in the Third House

The feeling of not truly being capable of pursuing life on one's own terms, as if afraid to make a commitment that must stem purely from a sense of self, can give rise to nervous depression. There can be a tendency to live in the shade of another's existence, perhaps a brother or sister.

Sun in the Fourth House

Being overly self-protective can remove the commitment to be part of the world. Cloistering oneself in the guise of nurturing the family and others in the immediate environment can negate the need to nurture the life force within.

Sun in the Fifth House

The potential to attain pure, unfettered self-expression is often obscured by an all-pervading consciousness of self. Often too busy experiencing what life has to offer with little respect or regard for self and the life force.

Sun in the Sixth House

The tendency is to be hyper-self-critical with enormous expectations of what one should be capable of doing. So often aims are daunted by a sense of seemingly everlasting inadequacy. Prone to subordinate own needs too readily.

Sun in the Seventh House

The lesson has to be learned of allowing

oneself to be motivated by others without resentment rather than regarding their presence as an intrusion on one's own space and time. To live in accord with others means learning to live in accord with oneself.

Sun in the Eighth House
There is no divine prescription that life should be easy or simple. Questioning why life must be so intense or fearing that others may claim too much of self merely squanders precious energy. Translating emotions into material terms is a preoccupation unworthy of the life force.

Sun in the Ninth House
Too great an awareness of own behaviour may well give rise to the determination to seek a reason for existence, mainly through the thoughts and ideas of others, until the lesson is understood that it must be gained on one's own terms. Searching along false avenues of hope and being anti-establishment without sufficient reason can be a waste of invaluable energy.

Sun in the Tenth House
The career and a particular position in life can dominate to the extent of superseding the importance of self as an individual. Take away the career and what is left? Society is meant to benefit from such energy but does not require total dedication to the denial of all else.

Sun in the Eleventh House
The desire to alter the social order does not necessarily extend to recognizing that there may be areas of self that could undergo changes too. It is part of the nature of progress that the world must be subjected to disruptions and upheavals so one must be prepared to acknowledge the pressures of a changeable personal life.

Sun in the Twelfth House
The spotlight is turned so successfully on self that there is nowhere else left to hide. Martyrdom can engulf one's being. The answer lies in the surrendering of self to the needs of the Greater Whole. Of course, to achieve this end means the shifting of the emphasis away from self towards others.

The Moon ☽

When we are born into the world we are immediately bombarded by a mass of stimuli and surrounded by all kinds of conditioning influences. The Moon governs the period of life known as 'the Formative Years' for it is during these vital years that we receive the kind of conditioning from our parents (especially the mother) and our immediate environment that will colour our behavioural response to all things for the remainder of our lives.

Subject to early influences in so many subtle ways, it may not be easy to relate the quality of our emotional expression in adulthood to the manner in which we were treated or handled as infants. When *progressions* are used to examine the life-span, the day following birth is said to symbolically represent the first year in the life. Thus a life-span of between seventy and a hundred years will equal approximately three months following the birth. Although this symbolic guide is used only by astrologers, the significance of the first months following birth is gaining greater acceptance both medically and biologically. It has mostly been the prerogative of the parents to observe the remarkable development during this period.

It is often assumed that on its arrival into this world, a baby will automatically be welcomed, loved and cosseted by its doting parents. Sadly, in too many instances this is not so. We can only respond in a subjective way to anything for we can only work from our own framework of reference and are bound to respond to a newly-born infant accordingly. This response must differ in every instance for the world is peopled by individuals. Thus the influences and circumstances surrounding a birth and the vital period that follows will always be different. This difference will be shown by the positioning of the Moon according to its zodiacal sign and house and its relationship with other planets in the birth chart. This dictum applies to each of the planets for, by analysing that individual quality, we can judge how that principle symbolized by the planet in question will manifest itself in the life and personality of each unique human being. The eagerness of those attempting to understand the workings of astrology or to measure human behaviour *per se* by statistics is invariably dampened because of the dilemma of the variety of human expression. If church bell-ringers know that the combination of notes rung by twelve bells can exceed 500,000,000, think of the combinations involved by using twelve signs, twelve houses that rotate in a twenty-four hour period as well as ten constantly moving planets.

Guide to the Interpretation of the Moon Through the Zodiac

Moon in Aries
Highly emotional, volatile and unafraid to take responsibility for own actions. Everything is assessed according to an intensely subjective viewpoint. It can also describe the mother who may well need to pursue her own life independently. Mostly humorous and openly demonstrative, she could be rushing out the door just when her child may need her most.

Moon in Taurus
In the sign of the Moon's exaltation, where it is said to function at its best, for the very simple reason that when instinct is allied with form it is at its most profoundly creative. Evocative of the Earth Mother, fertile and eternally devoted to the betterment of her offspring. Perhaps such care can lead to laziness in adulthood.

Moon in Gemini
Often erratic and disconcerted by sameness or anyone who attempts to tie him down, this type needs the freedom to think or to say anything and everything. The talkative mother who can sometimes provide the child with too much stimulation. Endless chatter may disallow the opportunity to discuss anything truly meaningful. The inheritance is a perpetual state of enquiry.

Moon in Cancer
In its natural sign, the mother tends to be as she should be — as the instinctive nurturer who does not seek credit for an attribute that is perfectly natural. Since the child is allowed to be itself with no hindrance there may well be an inclination to dramatize and to allow the emotions to spill over in adulthood. The response to life ebbs and flows so that moods constantly fluctuate.

Moon in Leo
It is possible that the mother who cannot accept the role assigned to her, to be a mother, may inspire a magnified sense of self-importance in her offspring. In adulthood this can become an arrogant awareness of being on display and yet is capable of being an example for others to follow. The behaviour may well be akin to that of the father.

Moon in Virgo
An aura of perfection surrounds the hardworking mother who always, somehow, manages to be 'there' to administer to the whims of her infant in spite of awkward schedules and, often, poor health. This can produce a source of dissatisfaction in the adult, for nothing and no-one ever quite lives up to expectations thereafter.

Moon in Libra
The well groomed mother may well be motivated more consistently by the needs of her husband than her infant, which can incline the baby to adopt a willingness to please both parents. This can result in an affable, considerate, yet often indecisive nature in the adult.

Moon in Scorpio
Tradition gives this as the most difficult position for the Moon; its *fall* being the opposite sign to that of *exaltation*. The mother who demands and imposes stringent standards upon her child. She is able to share her life with her husband and family but jealously guards them against the rest of the world. Thus the adult can be extremely self-protective, feel easily threatened and yet is capable of single-mindedly concentrating his/her own resources to the completion of any goal.

Moon in Sagittarius
The quality of inspiration surrounding the nature of the adult lends the belief that the Divine Right of Choice is a personal attribute. Usually marked independence and outspokenness has been encouraged by an intelligent, philosophical mother who understands full well the value of good education and a freely enquiring mind and spirit.

Moon in Capricorn
A planet is traditionally considered poorly placed when in the sign opposite that of its natural rulership (*detriment*). It is possible that the Mother's life was hard. The child often grows up before its time, knowing from too early an age the necessity of having to shoulder responsibility. The adult can have an overly serious, inhibited manner, being governed by the external or actual rather than the instinctual.

Moon in Aquarius
An unusual life-style can cause the mother to have too little time or patience. The baby only knows a sense of isolation. The habit of difficult or rebellious behaviour to attract more attention to itself tends to produce an adult who shuns emotional commitments in favour of less demanding platonic friendships. Mother and child often eventually become understanding friends.

Moon in Pisces
Life can be painful but out of suffering can come the faith and knowledge that it can be beautiful. At any age, the emotions are highly tuned and sensitive to the most subtle alterations in atmosphere. The mother may be weak in some way. Perhaps the health is poor, necessitating hospitalization, or she is unable to cope with life, seeking solace in various forms of escapism. The adult only feels happy when there is something to worry about.

Guide to the Interpretation of the Moon Through the Houses

Moon in the First House
With such a finely tuned response to life, there is immediate contact with the environment so that moods and reactions ebb and flow according to the local atmosphere. Clearly a good position for anyone needing to be in touch with the pulse of general trends, for example a journalist, market researcher or historian. Tendency to contract infection is likely.

Moon in the Second House
Can be intensely needful of security, requiring evidence that all is well. It is possible to lose that sense of reality unless 'earthed' by possessions, money, the physical body or the Earth itself, hence the peace that descends when gardening. The bodily functions may be affected by fluctuating degrees of self-worth so that weight may be gained or lost depending on inner sense of well-being.

Moon in the Third House
The nervous system may be very highly strung giving rise to a restless searching for a motive for being. May possibly 'mother' a brother or sister regardless of any disparity in ages whilst being prey to responding to their moods and whims. A love of gadgetry and anything that can provide more free time for thinking and learning is welcomed.

Moon in the Fourth House
Ruler of Cancer, the Moon is comfortable in its own house with instinctual awareness of the importance of the family circle. The same yardstick applies with the male chart and there may be a ready response to the call of 'Queen and Country' viewing the home as the bastion of society.

Moon in the Fifth House
Aware of the impact of self and the need for self-expression, like a dancer stepping in tune with the rhythm of Oneness, the inclination is to place oneself in the limelight. Not surprisingly, this is a good position for those involved in the performing arts.

Moon in the Sixth House
This is the workaholic who responds keenly to matters involving work, colleagues or anyone who needs help. Endlessly fussing over details that usually escape the notice of others, this type has a tendency to be willing to give of self for the good of others and is, therefore, more likely to be an employee rather than an employer.

Moon in the Seventh House
While capable of being the reflection of the spouse, the influence of the mother would be strongly apparent in personal relationships. For example, the man who needs to marry the facsimile of his mother or the woman who seemingly cannot escape seeing history repeat itself. The signs are obviously important — in Aquarius, for instance, there could well be a completely instinctive search to find someone diametrically different to the mother or who would shock her totally.

Moon in the Eighth House
Often confronted by very stark issues, there is a tendency to have an intense response to life. At times, the fear of being engulfed by the pain of life may be as great as the torment of death. Extremely emotional and vulnerable, the inclination is to be self-protective. A defensive air may well camouflage the need to be with another human being.

Moon in the Ninth House
Restlessly searching, yet a feeling of being part of the Greater Whole inspires an almost arrogant self-confidence. This type is meant to set standards for others by his own example and so may well be unafraid to adopt the position and policy of the 'loner'. Fortunately, he is able to be at home with anyone anywhere in the world. Interestingly, Michel Gauquelin's statistical work has revealed the high incidence of the Moon in the ninth or twelfth houses in the charts of writers.

Moon in the Tenth House
Opposite in position to the Moon's natural house, there can be a sense of isolation, of not being completely at ease out in the big, bad world. The way to survive is to do the expected and carve out a career yet retain a very private corner for oneself. The mother, and women in general, are often significant in aiding and sustaining a career.

Moon in the Eleventh House
Awkward, gauche and cantankerous, this type tends to find life a constant challenge. So charged with electricity that actual sparks can fly when touching other people both literally and metaphorically. There is that feeling of not really belonging to the world and yet being entrusted to be one of its keepers. Personal life is extremely important and should not be thrust aside for the sake of larger issues.

Moon in the Twelfth House
Fully capable of enjoying own company and motivating self to function freely, this type is able to nurture the psyche so that it will respond to life and glow in the dark like a glow-worm. Well able to draw upon unnameable forces for inspiration, for there is an instinctive awareness that there is more to life than can be seen or touched.

Mercury ☿

As the baby begins to acknowledge his surroundings, working from his centre of being (the Sun) with instinctual demands made upon his parents or guardians (the Moon), he reaches out to those beyond that immediate circle, recognizing brothers, sisters, cousins and those with whom he daily comes into contact, neighbours and family friends. It is this next stage that is governed by Mercury. He uses tactile awareness to become more familiar with that widening environment. Much to parents' dismay, objects are tested with the tongue and the lips. Although not able to understand it as such, the infant is being conditioned by the feelings and attitudes of his brethren. Is he welcomed by the elder brother or sister as an ally, or resented as an interloper? Perhaps as a first or only child he is allowed to perpetuate his central position of attention. The *lack* of siblings in a family can be as great an influence as the likelihood of the sibling rivalry that has its roots in the initial contact.

The quality of Mercury according to its individual character shown by its sign, house and aspects with the other planetary bodies, will describe the quality of the relationships between brothers and sisters or feelings concerning them but it will mainly be used to represent the nature and expression of the mentality and the capacity to be consciously aware. It also signifies manual dexterity and the ability to use implements or tools. Of course, animals communicate with one another but their capacity to do so bears little relation to the complexities of human speech that vary so extensively that no voice pattern is precisely like another.

Mercury is used to signify our sense of enquiry, our curiosity that reaches out with a never-ending thirst for more knowledge. It follows that the type of schooling and education will have a profound effect on the individual. Some of us are slow to learn or have little interest, whereas others find it a source of never-ending joy. Some find that learning comes most easily in the earlier part of the life whereas others only truly begin to study once they leave formal education behind them. There are also those individual teachers who have such a marked influence, colouring the whole, attitude, for good or ill, to any kind of task, that 'there is no such word as can't!' Refer also to the sections on the third and ninth houses, which are associated with the learning process and influence of educational standards.

There is, in general, a readiness in young people to open themselves up to experience and to share their thoughts and feelings by communicating verbally, as well as through the written word, and it is far from unusual to find young people talking through the night, an activity seldom shared by those beyond their early twenties.

It may be said that life is consciousness but perhaps it is more valid to say that it is consciousness that makes us truly aware of the meaning of life. Consciousness of life automatically lends form and substance to any action. Without consciousness there is no necessity for anything to exist, yet it is not necessary to be able to see or to touch something to be aware of its existence. It is consciousness that lends purpose, meaning and dignity to everything.

The distribution of the planets, signs and houses is in no sense accidental. There is no chance factor concerning the assignation of the rulership of Mercury to the signs of Gemini and Virgo and the corresponding third and sixth houses. In Gemini the mind is stimulated to question and to rationalize, and is then allowed practical and creative outlet in earthy Virgo so that ideas may be refined and made useful. It is no coincidence that the ruling planet of the two opposing signs and houses is Jupiter. Traditionally, Jupiter rules both Sagittarius and Pisces, the ninth and twelfth houses. The relationship formed between Mercury and Jupiter is that of knowledge and wisdom.

Mercury, the messenger of the gods, is the 'light-bringer' causing the dark of ignorance to be lit by enlightenment. According to Greek legend Mercury, who was known as Prometheus (See Appendix, page 167), stole fire (inspiration) from the heavens to benefit mankind, and also taught useful arts to raise the condition of mankind above that of the animal kingdom. For his actions, the gods Jupiter and Mars ordered that he be chained to the 'Rock of Earthly Existence' and then to be tormented for ever by the 'Vulture of Remorse' which tore out his ever-renewed liver (which is that part of the body ruled by the planet Jupiter). In his attempt to redeem mankind, Prometheus had been tainted by its evil and propensity to pain. How often is it that enlightenment and wisdom come through the medium of pain and suffering?

In each twenty-four hour period, as night follows day, the Earth is said to inhale and exhale which is symptomatic of expansion and contraction. We expand our lungs to inhale the life-giving oxygen of this planet and on the breath that is exhaled is born the Word. It is knowledge that expands our consciousness of life, making it possible to fly to the outer reaches of the universe on the wings of the mind, and it is enlightenment that leads us to return to the centre of all things. Through the Mercury principle we can extend ourselves by widening the mind, for it is this that places us in direct communication with the Greater Whole.

The individual quality of Mercury will be shown in the birth chart by its position according to its sign, house and aspect with other planetary bodies.

Guide to the Intepretation of Mercury Through the Zodiac

Mercury in Aries

Capable of utter honesty and completely defeated by anything remotely subtle or devious. An original thinker who often wastes valuable time and energy in proving he had the idea first. He has to learn that it is the idea that is more important.

Mercury in Taurus

Mind can be stubbornly entrenched along particular lines. Thinking springs from the fountain of self-worth and most matters are judged according to the way that values have been moulded since early childhood.

Mercuy in Gemini

Loquacious and prone to ceaseless chatter, the nervous system is invariably highly strung. Perhaps because the mind is so fine and capable of comprehending anything and everything there can be a virtual denial of its power, perhaps as a mental form of self-protection.

Mercury in Cancer

An absorbent, impressionable mind, often

with an outstanding memory. The tendency to draw upon the past can create a love of history. The needs of the home and loved ones are often uppermost in the thoughts. The home environment can be used as an excellent study area once carefully organized.

Mercury in Leo
Often geared solely for the purpose of its own world, the mind can actually be extremely powerful when fully controlled to aim at a particular purpose. Being self-opinionated or complacent where own knowledge is concerned can cause the well of wonders to dry up.

Mercury in Virgo
This finely tuned mind so capable of utter precision and detail can be extremely productive. A tendency to be overly concerned with chasing elusive perfection can lead to self-defeating humility, inducing a state of constantly working below levels of competence.

Mercury in Libra
Often highly intelligent and fair-minded but prone to justify thoughts and actions needlessly. Requires motivation in order to utilize intellect sufficiently and can relinquish goals, or fail to commit self to a particular line of thought or study, through indecisiveness.

Mercury in Scorpio
A mind that can be uncannily probing and perceptive, yet much mental anguish can be caused through giving way to dark thoughts and the nurturing of grudges. Without careful and constructive channelling into suitable areas such harbouring of frustrations or vindictive thoughts can discolour the whole personality.

Mercury in Sagittarius
Marvellously enthusiastic and highly principled, there is a tendency to be lazy when it comes to acquiring essential information and qualifications. Brave and bold in so many instances in piercing through sham to get at truth, there is often little or no follow-through to make use of such knowledge.

Mercury in Capricorn
Can have a very serious view of life, often assessing its darker side before being prepared to acknowledge there might be anything else. Very practical but unhappy where there might be any risks involved. Often takes up studies late in life with eventual successful conclusions.

Mercury in Aquarius
A highly intelligent and bold thinker who can become entrenched in pursuing certain areas of thought in a surprisingly dogmatic and autocratic fashion. Often inventive with a leaning towards scientific enquiry.

Mercury in Pisces
The mind works in may ways and on many levels. Depending upon the mood, thinking can be extremely artistic and creative and then suddenly muddled and almost stupid. The latter is often part of the process in which bouts of depression act as periods of gestation for creative efforts. Facts, both useful and useless are absorbed without any apparent effort.

Guide to the Interpretation of Mercury Through the Houses

Mercury in the First House
With a ready openness to the immediate, comprehension is sought concerning what is actually taking place. The mind is much orientated to the present and the personal.

Mercury in the Second House
Makes connections readily with that which can be seen, felt and truly recognized. There is usually a need to either write down or make thoughts visual in order to gain greater comprehension and acceptance.

Mercury in the Third House
Honour-bound to be curious and to seek out all knowledge. However, the scope of the area involved varies from one individual to another. It might be small so that thoughts and the capacity to be voluble may centre around local gossip.

Mercury in the Fourth House
Inner restlessness can be eased by recognizing that the mind is bound to the Roots of Being, having been nurtured by a

caring and intelligent mother to think of others and their needs. Often delights in history and the study of origins.

Mercury in the Fifth House
Often voluble and temperamental because of the need to work through the highs and lows of the creative process. Able to visualize and retain childhood memories and to think simplistically, paring away the extraneous.

Mercury in the Sixth House
Being so concerned with chasing elusive perfection, a tendency to be overly modest can cause serious underestimation of capabilities. In this way limitations can be self-imposed. Usually highly intelligent with an inclination to adopt studies and interests for their usefulness.

Mercury in the Seventh House
Usually seeks an intelligent, witty, talkative partner. Great importance is placed on intelligence so that a distinction and bias is made of people according to their thinking ability or educational standard. A born negotiator and never happier than when mediating on behalf of others.

Mercury in the Eighth House
The quality of individual Mercury is very important in this especially subtle area of the chart. The thinking may simply revolve around the most basic necessities of life or it could be capable of examining the recesses of the ultimate mystery of life or, indeed, any of the shades in between.

Mercury in the Ninth House
Although inclined towards profound thought, the mind can become lost *en route* in a myriad of thoughts. There is a tendency to search endlessly for an answer. A mind prone to exaggerate and to diffuse energy by scattering it over a wide field, if channelled, it can tune in to the infinite.

Mercury in the Tenth House
Thoughts aspire to promote a healthy outlet for energies. Often given to mundane interests and thoughts but the social conscience usually encourages the desire to voice the ills that hinder the founding of a good social order.

Mercury in the Eleventh House
An electric mind that envisages the demands of larger social issues. Often refuses to accept another's opinion simply out of the habit of being and seeing self as 'different' from the rest of the world. The stimulating company of kindred spirits is like food and drink.

Mercury in the Twelfth House
There is a search for the confirmation of existence and comprehension of the Unknown. It is not enough to instinctively understand the plight of the less fortunate even though such efforts eventually lend purpose to the whole life.

Venus ♀

Armed with instinctive awareness and educated to employ mental resources to think about his actions, the young person passes out of the awkward stage of adolescence. He is now ready to reach outwards beyond himself to make all forms of associations

Mercury and Venus are known astronomically as the *inferior planets* for their orbits lie between the Earth and the Sun. According to astrological understanding Mercury and Venus share a close relationship. In common with Mercury, Venus rules both an Earth and an Air sign, in this instance Taurus and Libra, telling of the natural ability to link, to correlate, and to relate not only to our fellow human beings but also to things and to concepts. The principle of Venus expresses the very human need to comprehend, that is, to seek an answer that results from the Mercurian impulse to question. It is the intelligent recognition that something lacks symmetry or order, that a picture requires straightening, the appreciation of beauty as created by nature or man.

Venus governs those years when the young person feels compelled to move into the outer world beyond the confines of the known areas of home and school to begin to experience relationships with others — not solely those of an essentially romantic or emotional nature but all associations with other people. It is through the sparking of ideas (Air) and the sharing of experiences with others that we can grow closer to that ultimate union of Self with the Greater

Whole. A casual remark by a fleeting acquaintance can, in some instances, trigger off greater understanding of oneself or one's circumstances. Remarks exchanged by complete strangers can significantly alter one's mood or attitude in a way that could have far-reaching consequences.

Human beings are gregarious creatures. We need one another and we have to learn to live peaceably with one another on this very crowded planet. It is fascinating that out of those millions, two people will find each other and, in the main, live out their lives in a manner that is in accord with the tradition of polarity, as part of a growth process that ensures the survival of homo sapiens.

In the birth chart Venus is used to signify the capacity for a particular individual to form links in close association with others. In any relationship there will be an interchange with a fellow human being. It is through the individual quality of Venus shown by the sign, house, aspects with the other planetary bodies and the assessment of the seventh house and Libra that the type of response to another human being will be shown. By taking the sign on the cusp of the second house together with the positioning around the chart of Taurus, the ability to respond to form can be gauged. Colour, pattern and shape, whether it is sight or sound, is pleasing. Rhythm and harmony differ according to the tastes of the individual for they all have bearing on the emotional nature. The most typical reasons cited for any marriage break-up are lack of communication (Mercury), financial and sexual problems (Venus and Mars). There is often a translation of emotional and sexual problems into financial matters, mainly because money seems to be so much easier to relate to, especially in a society which places so much emphasis on material values.

Guide to the Interpretation of Venus Through the Zodiac

Venus in Aries

Strong sensuality makes for attraction to and for the opposite sex, but ensuing relationships are not always well handled, mainly because of very personalized attitudes that can mean being touchily explosive. Usually sincere and honest about self, and despising any form of deviousness or insincerity in anyone else.

Venus in Taurus

In its own sign, Venus links readily with the fundamental rhythms of life and physical harmony so that musicality and an excellent speaking or singing voice may well be likely. However, with an inclination to be lazy and indolent much effort must be made to make a successful career from such attributes.

Venus in Gemini

A fascinating and stimulating companion, there is a tendency to seem fickle or inconstant since mood fluctuations make it hard to create stability. May well form more than one serious attachment during the lifetime.

Venus in Cancer

Empathetic and caring, there can be a vulnerability that few suspect. Sentimental and easily moved by the plight of others. Can cling, sometimes too strongly, living through the partner in preference to pursuing own interests.

Venus in Leo

Capable of easy self-expression, often with a high degree of artistic ability. Demonstrative and full of largess but so aware that everything stems from self. Needs approbation and to be loved rather than risk being hurt. May have a glamorous image of what love should be.

Venus in Virgo

Discriminatory faculties are exceptionally finely tuned. Extremely 'choosy', seeking the perfect life partner, but why not? The desire is to have an enduring relationship with a compatible mate, but it is possible to create difficulties by maintaining impossible expectations.

Venus in Libra

When in its own sign, Venus denotes the ability to create co-operation with and among others, linking people together for the common good. Tendencies to be overly concerned with justifying behaviour and actions can lead to being more of the pacifier, giving way to the partner's needs for the sake of harmony.

Venus in Scorpio
Opposite its natural sign Venus is said to be in its *detriment*. Life tends to be seen through high-focussed lenses so that all energies are devoted to a single issue or person. When in love everything else is superseded. A degree of objectivity is required to balance thinking, otherwise jealousy or severe heartache can ensue should the relationship break down.

Venus in Sagittarius
This is the position of the freedom-lover who longs to dictate how others should live. Easy-going and generous of spirit but not of self. There is often an attraction to those from other lands or who have interests that are new and stimulating to offer. There can be a tendency to shy away from any long-term commitment.

Venus in Capricorn
This type takes time to develop confidence and trust that he or she will not be betrayed or hurt. Very deeply feeling hidden by a somewhat austere exterior. Desires only honourable commitments and relationships and believes strongly in the sanctity of the marriage vows.

Venus in Aquarius
A friendly mien that prefers to be non-commital, and so is more inclined to flout convention rather than risk being tied down in an emotional relationship. Finds it difficult to relate to subjective attitudes for the mind cannot relate to small-scale matters.

Venus in Pisces
Said to be in its sign of *exaltation*, the feeling nature is especially sensitive. It is important to seek some sort of artistic or creative outlet for there is an easy identification with human weaknesses including one's own! Tendency is to idealize and romanticize the image of the loved one out of proportion to the reality.

Guide to the Interpretation of Venus Through the Houses

Venus in the First House
Naturally pattern-cognitive with excellent co-ordination that creates an easy, relaxed self-expression. Can be given to self-indulgence, mainly due to a heightened awareness of own needs.

Venus in the Second House
A genuine lover of comfort fond of the best that life has to offer. Relates readily to the goodness of Earth and its produce. Preference for gardening, sculpture, etc.

Venus in the Third House
An excellent mind capable of integrating thought and feeling to a finely tuned degree. Such an ability to communicate inevitably encourages writing and public speaking skills.

Venus in the Fourth House
Able to create an environment in which others can be nurtured and encouraged to be creative in their own right. Thus the home can be utilized as a working area to good effect.

Venus in the Fifth House
Good health and physical co-ordination and thus robustly able to encourage forms of self-expression, especially among young people. Delights in play and may sometimes be accused of not taking life seriously enough.

Venus in the Sixth House
There is often a distinct ability to understand the need for detail within the larger framework. Invariably attracts the best of attention from those in the healing professions and co-operation from helpful colleagues. Most associations are made through work, including meeting the marriage partner.

Venus in the Seventh House
Sympathies tend to lie with other people whereby their needs and wishes may supersede those of oneself. There is a tendency to relate all matters to the loved one's needs and this type does not generally come into his own until married.

Venus in the Eighth House
Life is generally seen according to the fundamental issues of sufficient income and emotional well-being. No matter how cushioned the background may be, there may well be a sense of insufficiency. Can be

unhappy unless it is possible to delve deeply into the most intimate recesses of everything; it is always the unknown quantity that is unsettling.

Venus in the Ninth House
At home and at ease anywhere and with anyone. Can take own good fortune for granted, giving way to an interminable longing to be somewhere other than where one is, which in turn creates a restless exposure to new ideas, places and people and an insecurity of itself.

Venus in the Tenth House
There can be much soul-searching in the earlier part of the life to find the appropriate outlet for energies. Often highly creative but also keenly people-conscious so may well pursue an artistic career which may eventually be superseded by one of the helping professions. The career line is usually very healthy and productive, going on long into old age.

Venus in the Eleventh House
Highly intelligent approach to personal issues with a degree of detachment that is enviable. Links readily with social problems and the betterment of society. This is a good indication of the ability to create long-lasting friendships.

Venus in the Twelfth House
Enjoys solitude and the peace of own company which is sufficient motivation to opt for an occupation to work undisturbed. Tends to be private or even secretive about feelings and the way that a relationship might be going, as if making it public might harm or destroy it in some way.

Mars ♂

Now that the young person has acquired a sense of value, he is able to communicate and mingle with other people and has the ability to accumulate possessions recognizing them as symbols of his worth in terms of society. He feels a sense of self-assertion and the wish to be independent. With the determination to be self-reliant and self-sufficient comes the desire to achieve something in life which stems purely from, and can only serve to satisfy, oneself. To leave a nest that may be very comfortable, safe and warmly secure, to create a life wholly for oneself demands courage, audacity and an enterprising spirit for these are now the tools with which to survive in the big, bad world. These are the energy drives that astrologers assign to the red planet, Mars.

The quality of Mars depicted in the individual birth chart shown by sign, house and aspects will signify the quality of courage in the individual personality. Not everyone can boldly pursue their own ends with such daring. Some may lack the courage to step beyond their own front door. There are as many shades and variations as there are people on this planet.

It is often thought that Mars is only associated with selfishness, ruthlessness and a flagrant disregard of another's feelings, but this possibly reveals the lack of knowledge of its full meaning. This planet also serves to represent the human ability to laugh. It is humour and the capacity to laugh that is the antidote to pain and, indeed, any of man's negative emotions or states of mind such as anger, hatred, despair, etc. A close combination of Venus and Mars will reflect in the birth chart of a comedian that magical sense of synchronicity — co-ordination that times the delivery of a line or gesture to gain the biggest laugh. By the same token, such a performer would need a strong Mercury in order to put such a performance across to his audience. Thus each planet is shown to have meaning in the scheme of the chart so that one planet is not isolated from another.

First of the *superior planets* that lie beyond Earth's orbital path (see page 61), Mars is taken astrologically to symbolize that sense of reaching out beyond known frontiers that we recognize in its rulership of pioneering Aries. The Mars principle expresses the survival instinct; that fighting spirit that will do all in its power to keep oneself and one's loved ones alive; that understanding that progress ensures the survival of the species. It is shown in the ability to initiate change for it takes courage to recognize the need and the time to move on. It is the audacity and ability to take the lead that inspires others to follow.

Through Mars is seen the desire to win, to be the first past the post, to want to be the managing director of one's own company; in command of one's own destiny and able to challenge life on one's own terms. It is not surprising, therefore, to find that Mars is a dominant feature in the map of the athlete or the self-made man or woman.

Guide to the Interpretation of Mars Through the Zodiac

Mars in Aries
Powerful in its own sign, energy streams very freely so that emotional nature is very open — what you see is what you get. Prone to irascible states of temper but grudges are rarely borne. Quick to anger but just as quick to forget. Easily able to make decisions and will shrug off errors.

Mars in Taurus
Extremely stubborn and wilful but unable to deny self its animal needs. Excellent physical co-ordination that needs a constructive outlet. An implacable enemy.

Mars in Gemini
Disputive and often volatile, there is a tendency to alternate between flashes of genius and belligerence. Sarcasm and cynicism can mar the capacity to think brilliantly. Can have problems holding self to a purpose.

Mars in Cancer
Moody and unpredictable, can feel threatened very easily. Highly subjective attitude and self-protective should self or loved ones be challenged. Can give way to periods of weakness through rapid depletion of energies. The home can be a very productive area.

Mars in Leo
The large, benefic and generous personality who is actually capable of being extremely selfish. It is usually a matter of pride that, 'I can accomplish all!' Strongly self-motivated and gains tremendous joy and zest from being alive.

Mars in Virgo
Can be overly hard-working to the point of exhaustion. Extreme pettiness or small-mindedness can mean that valuable energy is squandered on incidentals. High efficiency is enviable but states of anxiety or worry deplete energy resources.

Mars in Libra
Extremely creative and capable of galvanizing others to be productive. Most difficulties lie with the decision-making process whereby indecisiveness and looking to others for direction denies real capabilities. Can be hindered by a disputive nature that loses its cool rapidly due to others' behaviour that is thought below par.

Mars in Scorpio
A veritable powerhouse of concentration with a highly tuned sense of enquiry that is totally tenacious when seeking the truth. However, can be prone to brooding intensity and may well dislike communicating feelings and thoughts to anyone. Capable of nurturing grudges and often will endeavour to seek recompense long after the event.

Mars in Sagittarius
Invariably anti-establishment and independent in outlook. Highly energetic and often competitively involved in physical activities well into middle age. Thereafter, energies tend to revolve more consistently around philosophy and comparative religion.

Mars in Capricorn
In its sign of exaltation, high productivity is carefully and assiduously channelled to the greatest effect. Will work constantly for however long it takes to attain success, and usually achieves original goals in notable fashion.

Mars in Aquarius
Often deliberately cantankerous and perverse, tends to defy conventional attitudes. Inventive, original and highly-strung, there is a need to work in a wholly independent fashion even though popular and well-liked.

Mars in Pisces
Prone to be disliked or disbelieved for no rational reason. Very emotional and often mistakenly believes self to be weak or overtly vulnerable. Can be unhappy and malcontented if energies are not wisely used.

Guide to the Interpretation of Mars Through the Houses

Mars in the First House
Combative and competitive, with the need to arrive first at any destination regardless of circumstances. Accident prone. Invariably bold and decisive creativity, governed by inspiration, is subject to dramatic phases.

Mars in the Second House
Strong emphasis on the physical and material. Very protective of self and own possessions with much energy expended on proving the reality of existence. Powerful sensuality that can tend to lack subtlety.

Mars in the Third House
Impulsive behaviour can lead to accidents and difficult situations generally, so that tolerance and tactfulness need to be acquired to fulfil potential. Sibling rivalry can prevent the successful conclusion of studies.

Mars in the Fourth House
Domestic arrangements can be chaotic but it is also possible to use the home for an active work area. Disputes with parents are often short-lived; honesty regarding own shortcomings helps of course!

Mars in the Fifth House
Impatient and argumentative. Children may be something of a threat to peaceful existence. Capable of being rude and overbearing but extremely creative when energy is correctly channelled.

Mars in the Sixth House
Attraction for careers in the Armed Forces or areas where speed or danger are involved. Quite apart from accidents, health can be very trying with possible inflammatory diseases or surgery necessary at some stage in the life.

Mars in the Seventh House
Combative attitude, for there is a tendency to feel threatened and unsure of self which might goad partner into outbursts of temper. Honesty is sought for but not always achieved for trust is difficult.

Mars in the Eighth House
Proud and extreme depth of emotion and capable of profoundly contacting the meaning of life and death states. Excellent position if involved in criminology, research or psychology, for example.

Mars in the Ninth House
The earnest seeker after truth. Determinedly seeks to test the limitations of endurance of both the physical body and the mind. Enthusiasm lasts only as long as interest is sustained.

Mars in the Tenth House
Energetically pursues career aspirations while flouting convention and possibly antagonizing those in authoritative positions. Excellent for the self-made or self-employed person.

Mars in the Eleventh House
Personal issues are of vital importance. Necessary to create a positive outlet for energies; otherwise disputes with others can be extremely likely. The born group organizer who dislikes being organized by others.

Mars in the Twelfth House
Resentful and fearful of the consequences of being confronted with the resources of self. Exceptionally capable of working in seclusion or campaigning for the benefits of others. Needs always to err towards the philanthropic.

Jupiter ♃

Fired with the enthusiasm to leave home and to set up a completely independent lifestyle, the young person may well find himself confronted with the awareness that there must be some sort of social order. Man does not and cannot isolate himself from his fellows. A social system has certain standards and codes of behaviour to which all must adhere in order for that society to function for the greater good of all. For the most part, society rests its tenets upon religion, for religion means 'way of life'. It is via the outward practice of daily life that man indicates his recognition of the Divine Power that commands his obedience and reverence.

The planet Jupiter signifies that drive in all

human beings to adhere to certain principles of behaviour. Just as moral codes differ from one society to another, so too, there are subtle variations from one individual to another. It represents the good opinion that one has of oneself, for self-confidence stems from moral certitude, faith in the rightness of one's actions and optimism in the future.

If movement is life, then it is not meant for mankind to be complacent or self-satisfied, nor to accept that knowledge and understanding is his divine right, for life would then be without challenge (Mars) and there would be no progress. Jupiter rules that period in the life when it is most possible to prosper and to gain a position that is coloured by social attitudes, when one is seen to be what one is. Traditionally, Venus and Jupiter were regarded as the Greater Benefics concerned with good fortune and prosperity. While this compounded a materialistic view of these planets' meanings, it can be appreciated that through the rulership of Taurus, Venus allows us to examine the individual's attitudes to money and possessions. In Jupiter's instance, the trappings of success can buy the freedom to function in society as one wishes and to use that ability to enhance the lives of others, notably through the benefits of education and learning. It also allows for the freedom to move about without let or hindrance in the physical sense and in the mental sense through the freedom to think for oneself and to make knowledge the prerogative of all human beings, hence the association with the publication of the written word.

Because Prometheus stole fire from the heavens, Jupiter ordered Vulcan to create the first woman, who was called Pandora. When she married Epimetheus, she gave him a box from which issued every kind of human ill which spread throughout the world. All that remained at the bottom of the box was Hope, which could bring its influence to bear in easing the troubles of mankind. Hope does spring eternal, for without it there is little purpose to life. In using Jupiter to signify hope and optimism, its quality according to its position by sign, house and aspects will reflect the differences in terms of a hopeful attitude, for some people bounce back readily from difficulties whereas others find it immensely hard to retain any degree of optimism. Coping with the 'ups' and 'downs' of life is usually seen as an overall life pattern as well as swings in temperament. These are usually very clearly discernible through the relationship between Jupiter and Saturn (see page 134. The Aspects involving Jupiter and Saturn).

Sagittarius is ruled by Jupiter for it is that particular sign which links us most readily with the rest of the universe and reminds us of man's capacity to be inherently wise with a fountainhead of knowledge that links individual man directly with the Greater Whole. Small wonder that the mind tends towards more philosophical lines from middle age onwards. Jupiter expresses the desire to know and understand the 'why' of life. 'Knowledge knows from the outside, but wisdom realises from within' (Bessie Leo).

Guide to the Interpretation of Jupiter Through the Zodiac

Jupiter in Aries
The fun-loving, free-roaming spirit who loves to play at life. Tends to maintain a high degree of optimism so long as self is clearly in control.

Jupiter in Taurus
Desirous of a first-class life-style; possessions are often treasured. There is a need to visualize concepts by either writing them down or drawing them.

Jupiter in Gemini
The mind never knows when to cease and can create much out of little or diminish that which could be great. Planning and applied study can mitigate mental laziness.

Jupiter in Cancer
A strong sense of purpose governs actions. Invariably sincere and can be genuinely inspired. Often erring towards the philosophical with maturity and may well hold strong spiritual or religious views.

Jupiter in Leo
Full of *bonhomie* and a genuine desire to please. Can be autocratic but sincerely concerned to give of the best of self and anything owned.

Jupiter in Virgo
A strong sense of morality and awareness of the need for particular standards that can sometimes stifle growth. Can be overly critical and unjust in outlook.

Jupiter in Libra
Genuinely affable and sociable with a strong sense of justice which should be utilized for the good of many and not only for the immediate family circle. Expects others to behave well at all times.

Jupiter in Scorpio
Very cautious until sure of situations or the feelings of others. Prefers to keep a low profile. At times, given to sudden phases of unusual behaviour which can be found rather startling. A need to let off steam should be indulged.

Jupiter in Sagittarius
Generous and good-spirited, this freedom-lover believes that he has *carte blanche* on life. Resources of energy and finances need careful handling, otherwise they can be easily squandered. Easy come, easy go!

Jupiter in Capricorn
There is a reluctance to fully imbibe of life. A sense of caution dampens enthusiasm and the potential to gain more from life. This tendency improves later on in life when the physical energy finds it more difficult to keep pace with ambitions.

Jupiter in Aquarius
Strongly humanitarian with a strong sense of justice for all mankind. Philanthropic by nature and an advocate of civil rights. This type may well be concerned with the ecology of this planet.

Jupiter in Pisces
Devoted to an ideal, especially if it involves anything that would benefit others. Can be lazy and unsure of direction in the first half of the life. Tunes into the pain of mankind but willing and able to be of service.

Guide to the Interpretation of Jupiter Through the Houses

Jupiter in the First House
Benevolent, open-hearted and invariably very 'lucky'. Attracts many of the good things in life almost as if entitled to them. Because there is an expectation of being well treated, that is usually what occurs.

Jupiter in the Second House
Traditionally held that the second and tenth are the ideal positions for the attainment of an excellent position in life. Family background may well assure material success and general well-being but even those of humble origins have an attitude that poverty never touches.

Jupiter in the Third House
Usually excellent relationships with helpful, supportive siblings and has the desire to always think well of them. Enjoys learning but may well take natural aptitude too much for granted.

Jupiter in the Fourth House
Has a general sense of well-being and is at ease in any circumstances. Enjoys a first class life-style in congenial surroundings and is ever the welcoming, gracious host.

Jupiter in the Fifth House
There is a likelihood of intelligent, philosophically inclined children. Relationship with own father is invariably sound, with mutual respect for one another's chosen life-style. Could squander good fortune through taking too many risks.

Jupiter in the Sixth House
Excellent physical health and robust constitution that may possibly be taken for granted. The love of good food and a tendency to indulge self should be monitored and curbed. Supportive and amiable colleagues help to create pleasant working atmospheres.

Jupiter in the Seventh House
The intelligent, affable and potentially wealthy partner who grows increasingly philosophical with the years. The tendency to take the marriage partner for granted could create problems where none need exist.

Jupiter in the Eighth House
Plenty of potential to create good income sources. There may well be an inclination to live on the surface of life rather than worry

about its vicissitudes, which can form a kind of protective screen from any connection with the sordid or scandalous.

Jupiter in the Ninth House
High-minded and philosophically inclined, especially with growing maturity. Outlets are found in academic fields but there may well be a propensity to travel and live a full life before settling into such mental pursuits. The law or politics could prove attractive.

Jupiter in the Tenth House
This is the position for the large thinker who can conceive enormous yet practical plans. The successful outcome of ambitions and the attainment of a fine social position is highly likely.

Jupiter in the Eleventh House
Although able to attract delightful friends who will do all that they can to assist, there can be a tendency to be lazy and indolent. Friends will succour and care, but only for so long! Reformist ideas should be pursued.

Jupiter in the Twelfth House
Goodly belief in self ensures that nothing can really damage sense of self-esteem. This is often the 'Old Soul' who responds to an inner compulsion to help make the world a better place for all.

Saturn ♄

The furthermost of the seven planets that can be seen with the naked eye, in an orbit taking twenty-nine and a half years to complete, Saturn appears dull and ponderous by comparison with luminous Venus and Jupiter. Marking the final boundary of our Solar System, Saturn was traditionally viewed as 'The Greater Malefic', being associated with the boundaries of mankind which were translated according to anything that pronounced a limitation on human activities. Thus, Saturn became known as the harbinger of all doom and gloom. In keeping with the other principles used in astrology, Saturn was seen to have its good points, as the Purifying Angel on the premise that out of total humility and the shame of utter degradation gleams the pure, shining spirit of martyrdom and sacrifice. Not surprisingly, Saturn was found difficult to interpret!

Man's development has ever kept pace with his celestial discoveries. The introduction of the telescope revealed the ringed world of Saturn as the most gloriously awe-inspiring sight befitting the lofty and dignified position this planet has come to hold in modern astrology. Coinciding with the new-found ability to look beyond that which was known, man could begin to comprehend the reality of his place in the universe. It was as if the shutters had been removed from our thinking. Mankind had embarked on the journey to maturity.

In the light of modern thought, Saturn is more appropriately called, 'The Great Teacher'. Today it is commonly accepted that its meaning has a far wider implication. Human beings share the common destiny of having to cope with problems at some stage of their lives. Some people tend to cope with the most arduous difficulties with relative equanimity whereas others tend to go under at the first hint of anything being in any way wrong. Saturn will provide clues concerning the kind of problems that might be encountered in the lifespan as well as the manner in which they may be tackled. Time and time again we are confronted with lessons which must be learned before it is possible to go on to the next stage in our development. It is important to recognize that life's lessons tend mainly to be learned during the difficult and dark periods so that we need to tackle such times not only with a positive spirit, but with the conviction that a great deal can be gained from them that will aid our on-going human development. Although it is a truth that we never actually experience more than we can cope with, there are those inevitable periods when we must discover our own limitations. If we can manage to face those times with fortitude, patience and forbearance, our difficulties should be overcome and we can reap the rewards of lessons well learned, gaining the kind of wisdom that comes from hard-won experience.

Mankind cannot be exempt from the experience of boundaries. Frontiers prevent the freedom of movement between countries. Nationality and social background leave their imprint on our attitudes to life, erecting barriers that limit individual self-expression. Ever since babyhood, barriers have been imperceptibly imposed. In the birth chart, Saturn rules those signs and houses in opposition to those ruled by the Sun and the Moon, signifying the earthly experience that will shape the Soul. In the normal course of development, a baby will constantly test itself, pushing against the limits that the parents set down for safety's sake. The next step and stage of experience is vital to its progress yet, without such limits, the baby could become insecure, fearful or wildly undisciplined. The process does not alter in adulthood. The urge to take that next vital step must be heeded. The boundaries may have widened but they must continue to be challenged. While it is easy to recognize those limitations that society imposes, less obvious is the tendency to inflict them upon ourselves through attempts to live by particular standards of behaviour based upon opinions which may well have their roots in early conditioning. Just as in babyhood, such limits provide a haven, a sense of security representing that which is known and, therefore, understood.

Guide to the Interpretation of Saturn Through the Zodiac

Saturn in Aries
Self-expression is so dampened that the personality tends towards such overcaution that the decision-making process is rendered rather ineffectual. Nevertheless it is possible that the individual will be placed in situations where he is constantly required to make decisions quickly.

Saturn in Taurus
This can be a very productive and positive position involving the creative alliance of Venus as ruler of Taurus. There is a tendency though to be bound by material problems and to remain the victim of past conditioning. Values can be all too easily disrupted by immediate happenings.

Saturn in Gemini
The difficulties that may be encountered involving communication, such as speech defects, poor hearing, shyness, etc., which can have a profound effect upon studies, must be overcome regardless. Difficulties may also be expressed through phases of depression or an inability to cope with fluctuating states of energy. High nervous tension means the need to relax more when dealing with others.

Saturn in Cancer
It is as if the father of the household has been confined to the home against his expressed wish and he resents it mightily. The desire to be worldly can be denied or suppressed just as the warmth of feeling associated with Cancer may be dimmed or withdrawn. The woman may find herself constantly at odds, attempting to pursue a consistently active career while fulfilling her obligation to maintain a stable and happy homelife for her family.

Saturn in Leo
An insidious sense of oppression inflicts itself upon the consciousness as if to deny the personality its right to a true part of the Spirit of Life. This can create a feeling of inadequacy and the taking of self too seriously which can make one appear older than one's years.

Saturn in Virgo
The discriminatory faculties can be so heightened that nothing is ever quite good enough nor meets with one's demands for perfection, creating a sense of dissatisfaction with oneself and life in general. Nervousness and a fear of being touched can complicate life to a marked degree. Expectations should be raised yet can become so narrow that the life evolves as confined or restricted. A prison created by thought and deed.

Saturn in Libra
Being pattern-cognitive and artistic, creative endeavours can be of a very high order. In common with any Venus/Saturn combination the emphasis is on productivity, for it is what is actually done that becomes significant. Any lack of equilibrium can be overcome through self-control. Emotional inhibitions are likely to be resolved given time.

Saturn in Scorpio
It may well be found easier to work and live among those where no emotional involvement is likely. However, the lessons to be learned are emotional for it is

important to learn to share of self freely. To be fearful of being dependent upon another human being can require a good deal of soul-searching to discover its causes.

Saturn in Sagittarius
Difficulties occur in maintaining self-confidence and optimism about the future for there is a tendency to be easily discouraged. Since self-respect is paramount, the blame for anything going awry rests with oneself, having a generally dampening effect. There is usually a preference to associate with those older or wiser. Since there is a constant need to have knowledge, those who appear to have such knowledge are afforded great respect.

Saturn in Capricorn
The proverbial late-developer who will work consistently and assiduously towards ultimate goals, often achieving aspirations in the latter part of the life. Often serious and single-minded, there may be a certain lack of compassion for those not quite so able. However, those who persist in spite of any setbacks earn undying respect.

Saturn in Aquarius
Traditionally, Saturn rules both Capricorn and Aquarius. Respect for institutions lasts only as long as they fulfil their purpose. Scientifically aware, austerity may be tolerated only for a certain length of time for it has to be justified. There is a sense of knowing what is most important or viable. On a personal level, self-denial does not necessarily provide what matters most nor the loved ones most desired.

Saturn in Pisces
While it may seem easier to wear an air of defeat rather than risk the possibility of depression, it is a false illusion. A fear of being demoralized can create such apathy that the beauty within oneself can be totally denied. Everyone is capable of being his own worst enemy but it is not necessary to martyr oneself in the process. It is more important to raise the consciousness and acquire self-confidence through faith in self and the goodness of life.

Guide to the Interpretation of Saturn Through the Houses

Saturn in the First House
A sense of inadequacy and self-denial discolours the personality so that there is a tendency to feel ill at ease and self-conscious. Making contact with new people and new environments can be very painful; however the lesson shown is that one must learn to use one's personality to acquire open attitudes to life and to others and thus to discover oneself.

Saturn in the Second House
While restrictions tend to be placed upon the financial structure, it is nevertheless possible to acquire excellent business acumen from experience. Any obstructions should be interpreted as challenges by which a sense of security can be attained. The lesson to be learned is to comprehend the true meaning of materialism, taking control of possessions and the physical body rather than being possessed by them.

Saturn in the Third House
Trials that are often experienced because of brothers or sisters, or because of the lack of any siblings, are meant to be coped with. The lesson to be learned is to communicate with others using one's mental and vocal capacities to the full. Perhaps the need is to accept with equanimity the responsibility for a relative should it prove necessary.

Saturn in the Fourth House
The true value of the home has to be learned and the parents should be valued and respected. Difficulties may well be encountered through the parents or the lack of a parental figure. The lesson to be learned is not to see the home as a trial or liability, but to love it for its own sake and also to acquire a sense of being part of the family rather than its keeper or its servant.

Saturn in the Fifth House
Because of a tendency to take emotional matters too seriously, and to set so much store by Perfect Love, innumerable hurts may be endured. Unhappiness caused by children or even the lack of children is possible. Gambling or investments may well mean losses unless care is exercised. The lesson to be learned is to simply live enjoying life, beauty and feeling, for their own sake without seeking any kind of reward.

Saturn in the Sixth House
Care must be taken where the health is

concerned to avoid or mitigate potential health problems in later life. While it may be necessary to work hard, the rewards that come from having used one's energy wisely can be enormous but they may not take a material form. Colleagues may prove difficult but one's own attitude should be examined before stones are cast. The life lesson is to understand the meaning of physical suffering whether it is through one's own or in helping others to ease their pain.

Saturn in the Seventh House
The partner may be dour or restrictive in some way. It is necessary to learn to cope with emotional relationships and to counteract any emotional cowardice in oneself. Legal matters may be problematic and there may be a tendency to attract rivalry. The lesson is to learn to live in harmony with self and others.

Saturn in the Eighth House
There may well be a tendency to mask feelings through the easier involvement with material issues. Money must be earned the hard way through one's own resources of time and energy. Life is unlikely to be cushioned by monies gained through others such as inheritance or legacy. However, it is possible to make a good living through handling other peoples' goods or monies. The lesson to be learned is to respect and trust the feeling nature, making it possible to deal openly and honestly with oneself and others.

Saturn in the Ninth House
Attempting to live up to one's family's expectations can prove burdensome, particularly since the elusive area of intelligence is under scrutiny. A sense of inadequacy concerning intellectual capabilities can delay studies in the earlier part of the life. Yet such factors often conspire to persuade one to continue, or even commence, studies late in life. Foreign travel prospects may be uncertain and suffer delays. The lesson to be learned is to recognize the need to acquire a spiritual philosophy or belief system that provides moral certitude.

Saturn in the Tenth House
Strongly concerned with the attainment of a particular position in life so that all resources are devoted to a single purpose. There are instances where the successful attainment of a goal is followed by a reversal or loss of position. The lesson here is to acquire trust in the power of good that is in mankind so that there is no need to fear that one's position may be threatened or in jeopardy.

Saturn in the Eleventh House
Before progress can truly be made, disappointment and the frustration of ambitions must be accepted and understood, for it is essential to acquire a true purpose to the life. Friendships may be difficult, with differences and disillusionment likely. The lesson is to work towards achieving ideals and to discover the real value of true friendship which must be initiated by oneself.

Saturn in the Twelfth House
Indefinable frustrations tend to occur because of negative attitudes and by allowing oneself to be influenced by the thoughts and ideas of others. The lesson to be learned is to love one's own self, for the Kingdom of Heaven lies within. The emphasis must be on the acquisition of spiritual awareness that then reaches out from self to touch others.

The Exaltations of the Planets

According to traditional astrology, a planet is said to be *dignified* in its own sign, for the energy flows in a wholly natural manner, and at a disadvantage, its *detriment*, when in the sign opposite that which it rules. In the sign of its *exaltation*, a planet is said to be expressed at its most constructive. Conversely, in the sign opposite that of its exaltation, i.e., its *fall*, it is believed to function least well.

The idea of ascribing strength or weakness to the planets in this manner has largely fallen into disuse because there seems to be no mathematical sequence or astronomical basis for such assumptions. Such demarcations are too rigid, hinting at dogma, which is at variance with the flexible attitude favoured by modern astrologers. Nevertheless, there is a sound reason for the exaltations which can prove useful in judging the potential of the individual to be creative. Because the system is based upon meaning, it defies the possibility of measurement by the usual scientific methods. Resting upon the framework of the Seven Naked Eye Planets, the exaltations trace the capacity of the human being to develop the life force as ultimate creative expression. They refer to the beauty of the human spirit.

PLANET	Dignity	Detriment	Exaltation	Fall
SUN ☉	♌	♒	♈	♎
MOON ☽	♋	♑	♉	♏
MERCURY ☿	♊ ♍	♐ ♓	♍	♓
VENUS ♀	♉ ♎	♏ ♈	♓	♍
MARS ♂	♈ ♏	♎ ♉	♑	♋
JUPITER ♃	♐ ♓	♊ ♍	♋	♑
SATURN ♄	♑ ♒	♋ ♌	♎	♈

Without the Sun there could be no life upon the Earth. The Sun assumes prime significance in the symbolic system of the exaltations representing the intrinsic life force. In Aries, the Sun is individualized, expressing the inspiration that initiates the true creative act. The desire, now clear, must be executed with the same purity of spirit that the child brings to its play. Enthusiasm must be tempered by dedicated perseverance and channelled by concentration as shown by Mars, ruler of Aries, in its exaltation in Capricorn.

Saturn, the ruler of Capricorn, is exalted in Libra, lending line, discipline and form to any creative endeavour. It is not sufficient to desire or to have the ability to be creative, there must be an actual result that can be appreciated by others.

Venus, natural ruler of Libra, is exalted in Pisces signifying the capacity of the human soul to be enlivened, enriched and exhilarated by beauty. The harmony of the spheres is brought to reality for all to hear through music and the sound of the human voice; it is seen in the colour and composition of works of art and in the co-ordination of the movement of the human body. The age-old argument of materialism versus the creative arts continues unabated, yet without faith, hope and trust in the ability of man to attune to the perfection and beauty of the human soul, there is little to tempt the survival instinct. Mere existence is not enough! As the traditional ruler of the sign of Faith, Pisces, Jupiter exalted in Cancer reveals the motivating force that nurtures creative expression as the power that drives the Universe. Here is the confidence in the divine purpose of actions, in the belief that inspiration stems directly from the source of the Greater Whole.

The ruler of Cancer is the Moon, which has its exaltation in Earthy Taurus, the sign that represents manifested form. Creative endeavour must have actual tangible results. Its ultimate goal is the creative expression of the life force upon this planet for the greater enrichment of its peoples. It is the joy of being alive!

Apparently outside, yet actually an integral part of this scheme, Mercury has its exaltation in Virgo. All three Earth signs are venerated as the perennial acknowledgement of the beauty of this planet and the commitment man has to use it creatively and wisely. The involvement of all four Cardinal signs places the onus to be actively creative on man.

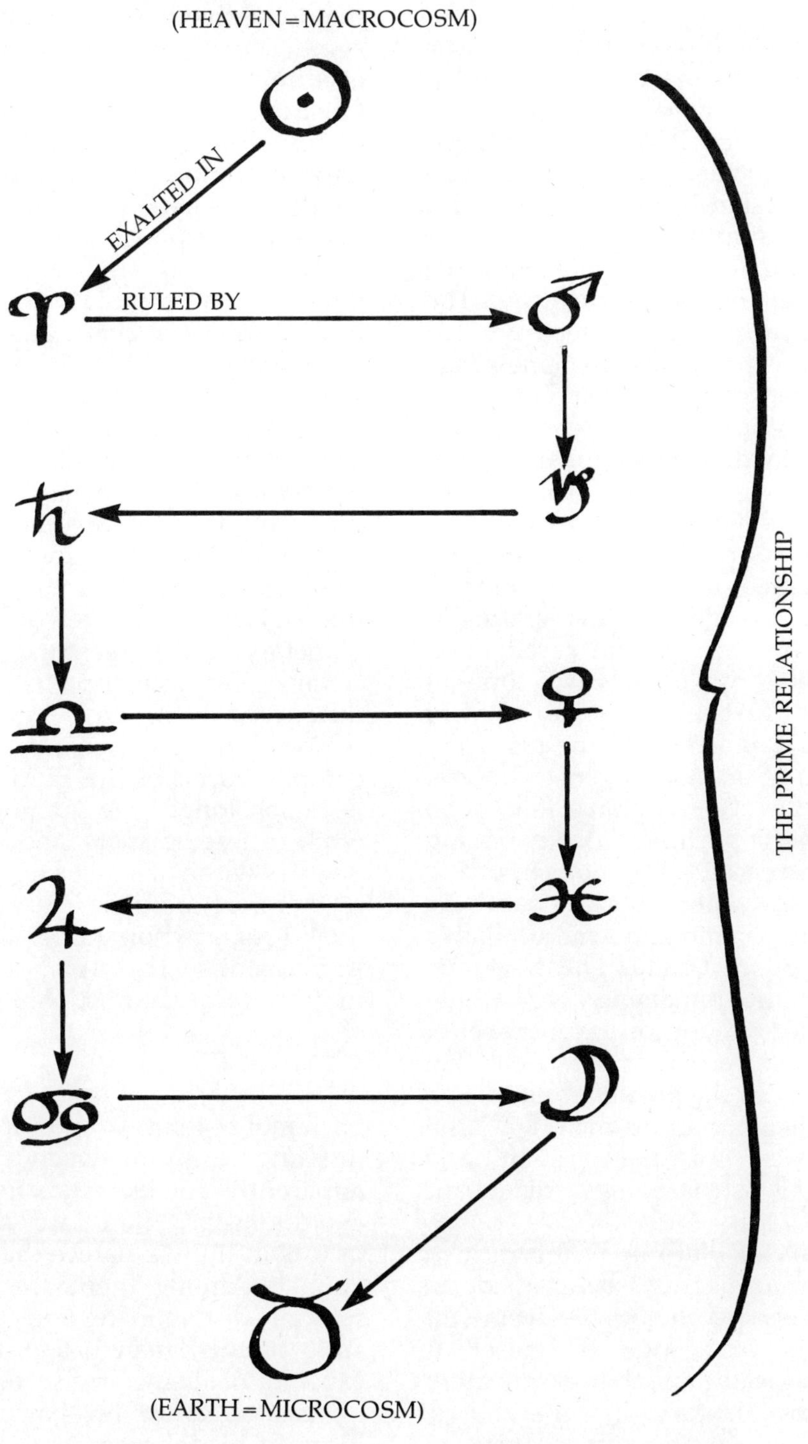

Figure 26 The Exaltations

In Virgo, Mercury the Messenger signifies that it is the search for perfection that opens up the pathway to supreme consciousness.

In the birth charts of those notable in the world of the arts or who display a marked sense of creativity in their lives, the exaltations are often significant. There may be an interchange of the planets and signs or houses. For example, Saturn in Venus — ruled Taurus, Mars in tenth, Moon conjunct Jupiter, and so forth.

The Extra-Saturnian Planets

Although it is easy to scoff at the simplistic interpretations that have been handed down to us from those astrologers who used only the Seven Naked Eye Planets, their findings coincided with man's limited ability to understand the natural world around him. Without an optical device it is not possible to see beyond Saturn's boundaries, 740 million miles away. The telescope that is needed to measure the positions of the extra-Saturnian planets may well be the symbolic psychological microscope required by astrologers, psychologists, medical practitioners *et al* to examine the complexities of the human nature in today's detailed manner.

The discovery of planets beyond the orbit of Saturn seemed to provide astrology's critics with an easy means of denigrating it. The magical, mystical system based upon the Seven Naked Eye Planets was thought to be flawed, first by the discovery of Uranus in 1781, and then by the discovery of Neptune in 1846. Astrologers, who are, often from necessity, adaptable folk, soon appreciated the opportunity to expand and refine the existing system, not simply to embrace the newcomers, but to enable the Sun and Moon to command a more suitably prominent position. Uranus and Neptune, together with the remaining five, would then account for the appropriate number of seven planets. In retrospect it is clear that this coincided with the greater emphasis on man as an individual, in his own right, and paved the way for the growth and development of astrology as a diagnostic tool.

The discovery of Pluto in 1930 coincided with the enormous strides being made in the realms of psychology. Twentieth-century man's knowledge of himself is escalating at a greater rate than at any other time in recorded history. In spite of this, little is really known about man's psychological make-up. It is acknowledged that a great deal of research has still to be done. For similar reasons astrologers are constantly revising and devising new methods in order to gain greater comprehension of the meaning of the three extra-Saturnian planets and the now enlarged scheme of ten planets. In Pythagorean thinking, the number ten has always been of enormous significance. It is the more highly evolved strata of number one. The symbolism of the number 1 next to the circle of infinity, 0, expresses, 'I am one with the Greater Whole', or universal oneness. Clearly, the extra-Saturnian planets must have profound significance with far more subtle connotations of the nature of man and his purpose. Not unnaturally, the meanings associated with these planets tend to have a more psychological inference in the individual chart, and are particularly pertinent where they are *strong*. That is, if the planet in question is the ruler of the chart — of the Ascendent, angular, or the ruler of the Sun or the Moon. Unless the extra-Saturnian planets are emphasized in this way, it is advisable not to endow their sign and house positions with too much significance. Note that this will also apply to the aspects which interconnect these three planetary bodies (see page 135).

Since their orbital paths lie at such great distances from the Sun, their orbital periods, the time taken to perform a complete orbit of the Sun, will necessarily be much longer. Generations will be born while these planets move only a few degrees within a single sign of the zodiac. It is, therefore, possible to examine the overall quality of a whole generation or series of generations through the correlating movement of Uranus, Neptune and Pluto.

Uranus ♅

For more than a hundred years, the 'missing link' between man and his apparently ape-like ancestors has puzzled evolutionists. There are some profound factors in human nature that supersede the animal. Among them are the abilities to reason, discriminate and to perceive. In spite of this, man has proved that he is capable of being more bestial than the lowliest creature on Earth, especially in terms of his inhumanity to man. There is a subjective side to human nature which is concerned with values, morality and conscience that elevates the spiritual qualities in the personality beyond the practical and the mundane. In spite of this there is an emphasis on materialism that seeks to denigrate the natural inclination to worship or to have faith in a Greater Power. Although knowledge of the irrational as opposed to the rational or physical nature of man is as yet in its infancy, it can be seen that the denial of a balance between matter and spirit can lead to deep unhappiness which can be expressed variously, depending upon the individual and his circumstances; from a complete withdrawal from society to a determination to destroy or to hurt as compensation for the agony experienced within.

The discovery of Uranus in 1781 by William Herschel (1738-1822) has heralded a key period in man's evolution in which the right to question who he is, his life and environment has gradually become the prerogative of the majority in Western society. Uranus symbolizes the breaking down of those barriers that have held man Earthbound, resulting in man-made flight and space travel. Modern methods of communication and education have effectively reduced the size of the Earth, paving the way for the ideal goal of dismantling the barriers that exist between the countries and races of the world.

Man may be maturing at an extremely rapid rate but the transformation from ignorance to enlightenment is far from complete. Uranus expresses the impact of earthly experience on the consciousness, the awakening to reality through the understanding of what is taking place on both the physical and the spiritual levels. Man is undergoing the process of learning to become aware of how closely life upon Earth is a reflection of the nature of the universe. In time the cosmic rule that 'Movement is Life' will come to be acknowledged. Regardless of the yearning for the security of known boundaries and the type of order signified by Saturn, no-one is exempt from the compulsion to progress. To become complacent or cling too rigidly to any particular set of values denies the possibility of perfecting the nature. The developmental journey through life must continue. To this end change has to be encountered and accepted as evidence of the necessary metamorphosis that opens up the soul to enlightenment and general well-being. Change may occur in many ways — through external circumstances, social pressures, as an antedote to boredom, or due to the inner promptings of the soul. While the love of change and variety may be professed, it is controllable, dictated change that is meant. Change that disrupts the whole life with unexpected suddenness is that which most people fear or find difficult to cope with. Should there be resistance to change, the effect upon the psyche or physical well-being can be devastating. We look to the quality of Uranus in the birth chart shown by sign, house and aspects with other planetary bodies to indicate the individual capacity to accept and cope with change.

Uranus aids comprehension of some of the conflicts to which collective and individual man is exposed. Most problems arise when we are not true to ourselves; and yet discovering who we are presents our greatest challenge. There is a factor in human nature that desires oneness with the rest of humanity without relinquishing that unique force which is recognized as true individuality. However, everyone is familiar with the feeling of being out of step with everyone else, which is, at times, interpreted as 'man versus society'. Thus Uranus is often prominent in the birth charts of the notoriously eccentric or unusual who have periods in their lives when they have encountered tremendous opposition or resentment from others. Even though there is often an overt dislike of anyone who is too different, such people, nevertheless, provide an endless source of fascination and inspiration for those who would wish to emulate such open individuality but lack the courage and audacity to flout convention. While there are rare individuals who seem to have been especially born to alter the whole direction of society, there are those who anarchistically view society's rules and regulations as something that should be overthrown regardless of their obvious usefulness for someone else. Nevertheless, everyone experiences feelings of rebellion at some point. We all know how overt authoritarianism can easily be interpreted as an act of aggression by officialdom, arousing feelings of resentment and rebellion in the breast of the mildest soul.

For the most part such feelings are carefully controlled or concealed. In general, society demands sameness, for no matter how democratic or liberal it purports to be, every social system depends upon order. The individual attempts to conform to this expectation adopting an outwardly sober appearance but so often feels trapped by routine and expectations which seem self-instigated. But should the pressure to conform to a particular ideal or way of life prevent independence of spirit or genuine growth, the psyche will revolt, usually manifesting as rebellious behaviour that may or may not be directed against the root cause. Thus, Uranus may be used to describe your 'flash-point' and that quality of energy that sets you apart from everyone else.

Just as refraction revealed light to be not simply white but comprised of the whole spectrum, so Uranus governs elements of human life that are sometimes taken for granted or deemed beyond the bounds of comprehension. Electricity, which has instigated modern technology, yet defies real explanation, is ruled by Uranus. We all have a magnetic field of energy or aura which alters in colour and intensity according to shifts in mood or states of health. There is also that inexplicable chemistry or physical magnetism that attracts people to one another.

Many astrologers consider Uranus to be the 'higher octave' of Mercury (see page 98). Indeed, the initial step towards truth is perception. It is an altruistic, inventive type of intelligence that compels the true scientist to seek solutions and determine causes, together with an ability to analyse a minor detail without losing sight of the whole. It is the capacity to allow the intuition free rein to sift and sort information from the Collective Intelligence which is seen in the highly-strung nervous system so often associated with intellectual brilliance. Uranus' rulership of astrology stems from the capacity to gain insight into the panorama of life seen against the over-view of past, present and future. It is the symbol of Universal Mind.

It is fitting that Uranus is the only known planet in our solar system that appears to spin on its axis in the opposite direction to all the other planets. This is due to the almost horizontal tilt of Uranus' north and south poles to the ecliptic, an inclination of 98°.

Guide to the Interpretation of Uranus Through the Zodiac

Uranus in Aries (those born 1927–1934)
This is a generation not born for complacency. The emphasis is on the power and willingness of the individual to come to the aid of those weaker than themselves, to care for the good of humanity. The individual is likely to be motivated by sudden flashes of inspiration. Idealistic and zealous if fired by a cause, there is often the demand for change. However, this is not necessarily deemed as a prerequisite for self!

Uranus in Taurus (those born 1934–1942)
An eminently resourceful generation that is capable of living with marked fluctuations in material values. It seems born to live through many changes in the social order. The individual often has the ability to apply thinking on a large scale and to see another's point of view, especially if Venus is strong. Can be unyielding and implaccable unless able to understand the need for change and disruption.

The Orbital Planes of Earth and Uranus

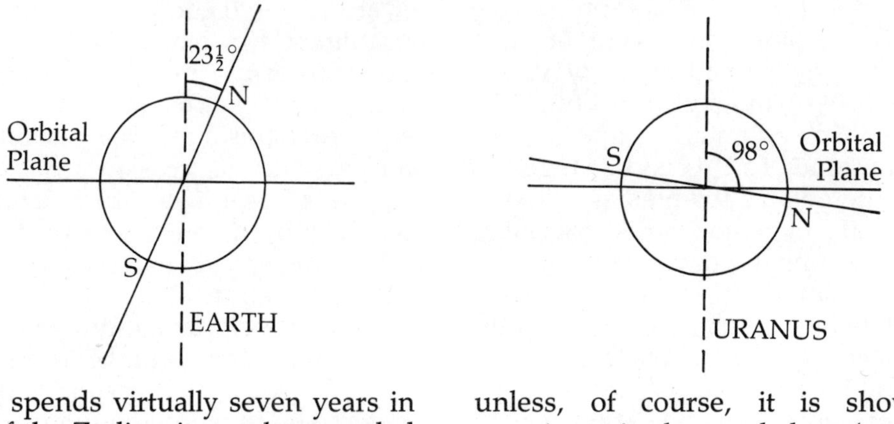

As Uranus spends virtually seven years in each sign of the Zodiac, it may be regarded as indicative of the quality of the generation unless, of course, it is shown to be prominent in the natal chart (see page 84).

Uranus in Gemini (those born 1941–1948)
In need of constant stimulation, this is a generation whose fickle tastes cannot be satisfied and yet it is capable of such ingenuity. The individual is often highly intelligent but requires mental discipline to lend purpose and challenge to life. Speech can be sloppy and there may well be a liking for easy answers. In time, the reality is discovered: there are none!

Uranus in Cancer (those born 1948–1956)
There is a seemingly endless need for instant sensual gratification so this is the 'fast-food' generation. Any device that can make life simpler or assuage the mounting tension in society is welcomed. The individual can easily become a seeker after palliatives, yet is capable of understanding the very nature of life itself. Perhaps this is the underlying reason for intensity and predilection to stress.

Uranus in Leo (those born 1955–1962)
This might well be called the 'gimme' generation, for the 'cult of self' is especially prominent. To demand that one's own needs must take priority is a form of self-protection so that the individual is not lost or overlooked among the teeming mass of humanity on this planet. In the personal chart this can indicate an individual who wishes to be recognized as such, yet is desirous of improving society for the good of all. There can be no reform without recognition!

Uranus in Virgo (those born 1961–1968)
A generation of enormous expectations which cannot be realized due to the great and extremely sudden social changes that have a particular bearing on work and health. During these years, Pluto was also in Virgo (see page 96) correlating with the generation that has grown up in the 1980s which has to understand the harsh reality of mass unemployment and the increasing menace of glue-sniffing and hard drugs that destroy the nervous system. The individual must often learn the hard way to have greater respect for the physical body so that interest in pursuing a healthful regime for self or for others may well become a prominent factor later on.

Uranus in Libra (those born 1968–1975)
The emphasis with this generation is on liberty and civil rights. Until the reality of extremism is understood and polarized with spiritual growth, relationships with authority may well prove endlessly, and often needlessly, disruptive. The individual is usually well aware of the need of freedom for all, but places even more emphasis on the right to choose associates and life-styles according to his own standards.

Uranus in Scorpio (those born 1974–1981)
A generation capable of exerting an extremely powerful influence which may or may not be welcomed by society. Prone to be affected subversively and capable of suppressing many slights or injustices which are bound to surface at some stage. The individual is capable of gaining true understanding, possibly arising through some searing life experiences. Can be very demanding and finds it difficult to maintain self-control at times.

Uranus in Sagittarius (those born 1897–1904 and 1981–1988)
Marked changes in social order and the founding of new styles of living indicate a generation in a perpetual state of transition. Generally motivated by a restless need to find something or someone to believe in, these are generations capable of breaking down man-made barriers or religious differences to remind humanity that we are all earthlings. The individual is capable of gaining insight into the reason for being, deriving an enormous sense of optimism that can be passed on to others.

Uranus in Capricorn (those born 1904–1912 and 1988–1996)
On the heels of largess and a period in which there is a blatant disregard for convention, comes the need to be reminded of the earthly substance of life. Sudden reminders of austerity and the basic needs of society can become prominent. The individual has to strike a balance between the erratic and the conventional, for the general good of society must prevail. There may well be a capacity for profound insight or a gift for creating original ideas, art forms or designs which can be of practical value.

Uranus in Aquarius (those born 1912–1919 and 1995–2003)
With Uranus in its own sign, these generations can be more inclined towards the humanities, with an emphasis on equality for all. Such idealism is invariably accompanied by the remnants of the old order that refuses to give way to the new. Often ahead of his time, the individual can sometimes be thought too far-sighted and revolutionary for comfort, even in the most mundane areas of life. A sense of lonely frustration could hinder development until it is learned that no group can ever dominate the true individual.

Uranus in Pisces (those born 1919–1927)
A generation who learned that world suffering is the concern of every individual, emerging to contribute to the betterment of society, often in the most unthought of ways. The individual may well have a gift to heal others through unusual means and is, therefore, willing to adopt alternative medical practice when conventional methods have been found wanting. Whether on a personal level or on the grand scale, this is a committed personality mindful of having a particular purpose or mission in life.

Guide to the Interpretation of Uranus Through the Houses

Uranus in the First House
A creature of his own generation with a ready empathy for contemporaries. Rebellious and can be cantankerous, so behaviour is often unpredictable. Wilfully pursues his own way of being, regardless of how others may think (or feel!) Often autocratic yet capable of exhibiting fine leadership qualities ... if desired!

Uranus in the Second House
Financial matters can become complex, undergoing marked fluctuations. Personality is likely to undergo drastic changes at certain stages in life, which has a direct bearing on attitudes to material possessions (and vice versa!). Finances should be carefully structured to avoid unexpected losses. At some stage, it is likely that the sense of security could be quite suddenly undermined.

Uranus in the Third House
Outspoken and independent in thought and manner with a tendency to analyse the consequences later. Ideas tend to be altruistic rather than realistic. May well have an unslakeable thirst for knowledge yet be unwilling to do more than superficially examine a never-ending stream of subjects, unless mental discipline is acquired.

Uranus in the Fourth House
With unbearable standards to live up to, the inclination is to constantly kick over the traces. Changes in residence are likely or the home proves to be a disruptive environment by being in a perpetual state of flux contributing to an unsettled and stressful mien. The individual is also likely to be extremely stubborn and resistant to anything that is not self-engendered.

Uranus in the Fifth House
Highly original and often extremely creative with very modern and unusual tastes or style. Children are likely to be very intelligent but also possibly unruly and difficult to rear. Emotional problems likely through a tendency to be too changeable. There may be separations or a feeling of alienation from loved ones so there is little continuity.

Uranus in the Sixth House
The capacity to cope with irregular hours or work schedules attracts unusual types of occupations. Usually more than one occupation or interest is pursued simultaneously for each stimulates and creates energy for the other(s). Anything that provides more energy is welcomed, hence the likely adoption of good dietary and exercise habits.

Uranus in the Seventh House
A free, open attitude to relationships where the legalities may well be disregarded. Attraction for the 'different' partner who might easily shock or dismay parents. Partner may pursue an unusual career, perhaps one of the sciences, psychology or astrology, with a need to be recognized in his/her own right. Separations may be due to own or partner's career.

Uranus in the Eighth House
Capable of sudden insights into the

meaning of life and the nature of death. Very often having the ability to tune in to the Collective Unconscious and to empathize with the pressure of modern life. There is an inclination to adopt a career in the humanities. A liking to be self-employed together with disinterest in material matters, inclines income to be spasmodic requiring careful husbanding and structured insurance.

Uranus in the Ninth House
The world citizen who does not believe in any form of restrictions physically, mentally or emotionally. May have a sense of not really belonging anywhere yet being part of all things. Often anti-establishment and eccentric with a wilful disregard for convention. Far-flung and sometimes outrageous ideas have to be contained and harnessed if they are to be of value.

Uranus in the Tenth House
Often strongly career-orientated with a liking for an unusual occupation. At some stage, the career direction may alter dramatically, and a hobby may eventually become a new career. Two or more simultaneous career lines are preferred where possible. There may be a strong pull to be of service or to do work that can benefit the community.

Uranus in the Eleventh House
Change is preferred, often for the sake of it. Unusual people are sought as friends because they are invariably intelligent, pursue diverse interests and make some sort of contribution, even if it is simply to stimulate a facet of this personality. Driven by the desire to know why relationships can be so painfully trying, the quest to know what it is that makes people tick can become a virtual disease.

Uranus in the Twelfth House
Although there may be a strong sense of not being in contact with own inner resources as if afraid of the very idea of self-sufficiency, this individual is invariably perfectly capable of functioning in this way. This is the quiet eccentric who goes his own way regardless of others' opinions; the philanthropist who does good work without seeking recognition. Generally reclusive tendency preferring own company and yet able to organize groups, perhaps at home, for occult or healing work.

Neptune ♆

Once change has forced us to move beyond the confines of known territory, we are instantly confronted with that most chilling prospect, the Unknown. There is no way of knowing what change will mean to our lives and so we shirk the very idea of it. Change that is not self-engendered seems to demand that one should be a victim of circumstance. The in-roads that technology and the modern scientific approach have made on our lives tend to deny the individual the right to be free to make decisions for himself, yet society maintains that we are responsible for our actions, and therefore, our lives. This dichotomy can be very bewildering, for the responsibility to ensure survival as individuals is meant to be our own, and yet collective survival is so unsure.

Emphasis has been laid on the logical, rational mind over matter. The emotional side of human nature has steadily been denigrated but it is not possible to deny that man is an emotional creature who requires the nurturing of very ordinary human emotions such as those generated by faith, optimism, dreams, ideals and love. The denial that these emotions are valid has robbed mankind of sufficient outlet for them. The steady erosion of religion in the last two hundred and fifty years has meant that these emotions have been unfed and left unsatisfied. They have been replaced by negativity and the fear that there seems nothing to believe in. Anyone who persists in maintaining religious views is usually thought of as a crank, eccentric or cohort of an exlusive clique that seems to be dependent upon a quasi herd instinct as if the group can protect the individual from the derision of others. Recent events have shown that an over-emphasis on any belief system can be disastrous. Witness the desperate suicide by the Jones sect in Guyana, or the disruptive force in the Middle East stemming from the resurgence of orthodox Muslim religion that seems so repressive to liberal Western minds. Such extremes should not be regarded as so strange considering how far removed the majority have come from treating religion as the norm. It should not be surprising that there is over-zealousness when there is little experience of the consequences. These happenings together with the continuing emergence of new religious sects and the adoption of Eastern religions are symptomatic of the need that man has to believe in something greater than himself, to inspire him and lend purpose to his waking life.

It is too early for a valid assessment of the impact of modern life on the progress of mankind. Historians may not be able to examine it fully until the whole century can be seen in retrospect. Nevertheless, there is growing evidence that apathy and lack of caring are major problems stemming from the emphasis on the increasing isolation of the individual. Society may purport to benefit the individual but any cry for the sanctity of individuality is usually interpreted as man versus society. Afforded with our over-view, astrologers are able to assess this period as a mixture of both the Uranian and the Neptunian principles recognizing it is part of man's natural evolution. We are possibly witnessing the commencement of a real breakdown in human and social values in order that a true sense of individuality emerges and survives.

For most students of astrology, the planet Neptune presents an enigma. Perhaps because it forces a confrontation with those issues that we prefer not to discuss too openly. It both fascinates and confounds because it rules those issues that should be discussed openly. Neptune in the natal chart will describe the individual capacity to believe in self, society and in the Unknown. It is easier to understand this when considering society and the need for a belief system; it is more difficult to cope with the idea of belief in self since it immediately conjures up those deep-rooted fears that seek to deny such a whole-hearted acceptance of self.

The irony of life is that we do not necessarily appreciate that which we have and only become aware of certain needs or attributes when they are withheld or denied. To acquire belief in self means that it is necessary to experience that lack of belief which most of us are familiar with as lack of self-confidence. There are all manner of emotions that can stand between lack of belief and belief in self. Various forms of self-deception, fears, fancies or phobias can prevent the belief that you too are worthy of the gift of life. To use that gift to its fullest extent, committing that life to the good of all, creates a purpose for existing. It is founded upon the capacity to live in close harmony with one's own self enjoying the openness of spirit that allows for ready self-examination and genuine love of self that is completely unselfish. Thus, the quality of Neptune seen in the natal chart by sign, house and aspects will describe the multi-various shades and nuances of illusion, deception or gullibility that prevent open honesty with self and life in general.

Since Neptune relates to the inner self, it also rules the finer qualities and vibrations of the soul which are most readily discerned in any artistic endeavour. It is for this reason that Neptune is seen esoterically as the higher octave of Venus. It is understandable that those who have a particular talent for creative self-expression need to know the other side of that coin. Most actors who are willing to portray someone other than themselves in front of vast audiences are notoriously shy in private life. Every writer, composer and artist knows the awful periods of depression that can prove to be the gestation period of their most creative work. Every dancer and singer knows the feeling of never being able to attain the ultimate goal of perfect control over their very human instrument. Perhaps it is the price that must be paid for such artistry.

It is interesting that even with the use of the largest telescopes, little can be discerned of Neptune's surface. Neptune was discovered in 1846 after observations of the irregularities in Uranus' orbit showed that they did not depend exclusively upon the gravitational pull of Jupiter and Saturn. Astronomers think of Uranus and Neptune as twin planets since they are similar in size, although Neptune is slightly larger, more dense and bluish in colour rather than green. Astrologers regard them as closely linked in meaning for in order to gain the state of consciousness depicted by Uranus, it is essential to rid oneself of any fears of reaching into the centre of self, for it is that part of every human being that relates directly to the greater whole. This is the supposed 'Unknown' that should not be feared for it is the soul's natural abode.

Neptune's orbital period of approximately

165 years means that it spends about fourteen years in each of the signs of the zodiac. Because it moves so slowly it must be regarded as another indicator of the quality of a whole generation. You will observe in the following dates, when Neptune changes zodiacal signs during the course of the twentieth century, certain significant years: for example, the year 1914 when Neptune entered Leo, synonymous with the commencement of the First World War; the change from Leo to Virgo which correlates with the period of the financial collapse of Wall Street and the ensuing depression of the 1930s; or the period when Neptune moved from Virgo to Libra when virtually all the nations of the world were drawn into combat in the Second World War, and so on. The symbolism of astrological principles tallies so closely with terrestrial happenings that it is easy to think that the planets have caused such events. However, this merely endorses the accuracy of the mirror image, the macrocosm and the microcosm. It is through our ability to look into the Mirror of Time that it becomes possible to understand the alterations that have taken place in peoples' feelings about themselves, and how illusions have been shaped over the years as successive events have altered the concept of life.

Guide to the Interpretation of Neptune in the Signs from Gemini to Aquarius

Neptune in Gemini (1888–1902)
The desire to find an answer or a solution to anything and everything caused an explosion of invention founding an era of gadgetry. In becoming aware of man's ingenuity, life took on an excitement that seemed to clearly presage a better world.

Neptune in Cancer (1901–1915)
Neptune entered Cancer coincident with the death of Queen Victoria. With her passing, an era, and ultimately an empire, came to an end. Thanks to the inventiveness of the previous years, the reality grew that a reasonable standard of living could be within reach of everyone. Those born during these years had to learn how to re-create a home, a nation and a world after the devastation of the First World War. It was their task to build a new life.

Neptune in Leo (1914–1929)
Those born during these years became 'The Glamour Generation' producing the performers and the audiences for the new revolution, the cinema. To wish for some means of escape from the drab austerity of the depression years was not surprising. The strongest influence came from the new gods and goddesses of the factory of illusion, Hollywood. New images of behaviour and life-style shaped the quality of the desire to want much more.

Neptune in Virgo (1928–1943)
Expectations of what life should provide rather than what it did or could provide began to escalate. Dreams and illusions were supposed to become reality. Yet, from this generation has emerged a greater consciousness for the need to increase longevity and make the physical body more dependable. The tendency has become a need to nurture and protect the physical body rather than chase after shadows. This is the generation that has instigated the greater need for health awareness.

Neptune in Libra (1942–1957)
As Neptune changed sign, America was drawn into the vortex of the Second World War. Those born during these years were to become the 'Flower People' of the 1960s, susceptible to the temptations of others who preyed upon their weaknesses. Their dream to 'make love, not war' was shattered by drugs. At the same time medical practitioners and chemical manufacturers encouraged the taking of pills for everything. Some failed to test their wares fully, with predictable results.

Neptune in Scorpio (1955–1970)
From austerity to the extreme of 'conscience money': the young are given money, toys or anything that their hearts desire, in place of love and open affection. The result is a generation which can never find complete satisfaction. Consumerism has imbued its children with the illusion that the material world is all.

Neptune in Sagittarius (1970–1984)
The inventiveness of Neptune's Geminian period at the turn of this century reaches a new dimension. The children born during the period 1970 to 1984 are the Hi-Tech

generation who respond as readily to a computer as their parents did to the telephone. The majority of them have entered a world in which belief systems have been distorted, eroded or destroyed altogether. The need will grow for a balance between earthly, mundane values and spiritual understanding. They are a generation of hope for the future.

Neptune in Capricorn (1984–1998)
Neptune is 'earthed' in Capricorn and much disillusionment with society is likely to take place. While there may be evidence of anarchy and social unrest, the children who shall be born during this period should come to understand the importance and need for social order. Eventually a better society can emerge.

Neptune in Aquarius (1998–2011)
Will there be disillusionment with social systems that attempt to alienate the individual, or will the individual take heart in the knowledge that it is society's illusion that it can reduce mankind to a common denominator? What of the super-bright generation of children born during these years? Shall the sixth sense be as normal as the other five?

Guide to the Interpretation of Neptune Through the Houses

Neptune in the First House
Highly sensitive to atmospheres, which can cause moods to fluctuate. Easily swayed and influenced by others and often subject to fears that are not always self-engendered. Invariably has to work hard at maintaining self-confidence and goals in life. The latter may take some time to realize.

Neptune in the Second House
The tendency to be vague or absent-minded often expresses itself in material terms by muddled accounts and carelessness where possessions are concerned. Care must be exercised to protect oneself against the draining of one's emotions and energies. It is important to maintain own image of self-worth and to be true to oneself.

Neptune in the Third House
Fertile imagination should be given a creative outlet, especially through the written word, poetry, songs, etc., otherwise a potentially undisciplined mind can give way to foolish fears and fancies. There may be the possibility of some mystery or scandal where a brother or sister is concerned. Also the likelihood of a debilitating dilemma or illness at some stage.

Neptune in the Fourth House
There is usually a sense of being 'at sea' regardless of the situation. A feeling of not being sure of one's origins or of not truly belonging, which can be self-defeating. One belongs to oneself! Mother or even both parents could be very ill at some stage and there is a possibility that the child may be brought up by someone other than the real parents.

Neptune in the Fifth House
A highly creative position but there is also a tendency to harbour illusions about oneself. There may be a fluctuating sense of inflated importance so that capabilities do not always measure up to expectation, concurrent with phases of being overly modest belying actual aptitude. Father may possibly be absent around the period of the birth, perhaps pursuing a career associated with Neptune such as the sea, oil, films, etc.

Neptune in the Sixth House
A weak Neptune can indicate a tendency to pick up infections or diseases easily. Illnesses can also occur psychosomatically yet it is also possible for the ability to heal to be developed. Energy levels must be guarded and there may well be the tendency to pursue work in a Neptunian field such as, the arts, the healing professions, or in institutions or welfare organizations.

Neptune in the Seventh House
There is a tendency to attract a partner with a weakness or problem that may initially be difficult to diagnose. In common with the First House, there may be the habit of 'projecting' feelings and thoughts onto the partner, blaming them for behaviour which is actually self-engendered. The partner may well follow a career associated with an area ruled by Neptune.

Neptune in the Eighth House
With the tendency to feel the woes of the

world, there may be the sensitivity to actually hear the world scream. Energy may be channelled into a helping profession, often after following a course of similar help for oneself. Financial matters and joint responsibilities can become burdensome through muddle and unthought-of difficulties. It is wiser to seek professional help to deal with either emotional or financial matters.

Neptune in the Ninth House
Can over-compensate for failings and justify actions in the belief that one is governed by a divine right. Unless Neptune is strongly aspected, studies may peter out through lack of self-discipline; plans are rarely made or adhered to; travel can be difficult but, perhaps, ocean voyages prove the exception! Travel documentation should be checked regularly.

Neptune in the Tenth House
Difficulties may arise in the attainment of aspirations if there is not sufficient purpose, for it is often hard to maintain belief in self since there is an ever-accompanying feeling of not really knowing who one is. The first priority is to 'Know Thyself'. The glamour professions can be extremely successful, for imagination allied with practicality can prove beneficial partners. Misunderstandings can occur with those in authority.

Neptune in the Eleventh House
Often subject to disillusionment where personal values are concerned, they may have to be seriously amended at some stage. Much interest may be expressed in groups involved in welfare, health or healing, but it pays to be discerning and to guard against gullibility. Friends are usually found in creative areas and prove highly stimulating.

Neptune in the Twelfth House
A highly tuned psychic gift can be utilized for the good of others, especially in encouraging them to grow closer to the centre of being. However, psychic energy can be easily drained. Situations can become very confused until they seem impossible to deal with. With such a giving nature, it is possible to be preyed upon by others' weaknesses and to arouse jealousy in others.

Pluto ♇ ⯓

Although a very small planet, Pluto is thought to be of a density powerful enough to exert sufficient gravitational pull to cause the inexplicable perturbations in the orbits of both Uranus and Neptune that led to its first sighting in 1930. Forty-eight years later, Pluto's satellite, *Charon* was found. Pluto's diameter is approximately 3,000km and Charon's is 1,300km. At a distance of only 1,950km apart, Pluto and Charon are the nearest to a double planet yet discovered.

Astrologers must have intuitively recognized the binary nature of Pluto, for it has optional symbols, ⯓ and ♇ . Variations of the former symbol, such as ⯔ or ⯕ reflect subtle differences in interpretation of this, as yet, very recent discovery. Information regarding the nature of the energies associated with the principle of Pluto is constantly being gathered. Whether the Circle of Superconsciousness is connected to the Cross of Matter has relevance in this search for more knowledge. When unconnected it can symbolize the need for the unconscious to continue gathering earthly experience in preparation for the next vital step on the journey to perfection. As if with arms outstretched, it reflects a yearning for superconsciousness.

The second symbol is based upon the initials of its discoverer, Percival Lowell. Perhaps less popular (although my preference) because of its association with a man, this symbol may be thought to lack true spiritual significance. However, when a number is inverted, it does not lose its meaning but can relate even more closely with the subtleties of the inner being. Inverted, the number 7 becomes the letter L retaining all the connotations of the vertical and horizontal lines (see page 23) in readiness for spiritual unfolding. In keeping with the regenerative quality of Pluto, it is also indicative of the beginning and ending of a cycle. The semi-circle depicting the unconscious mind and storehouse of memory is on the right, masculine side, signifying initiatory force. In this symbol is expressed the need to deliberately formulate the decision to descend to the very depths of the unconscious mind until enlightenment and understanding can be attained, for it is only then that the soul is ready to undertake the journey towards attaining a state of superconsciousness.

It is possible that the discovery of Charon in 1978 heralded a period in which a breakthrough in understanding the psychology of man can begin to emerge. Perhaps a case might eventually be proven for the creation of a symbol that suggests a unified Pluto and Charon, such as ♇ , in which the ellipse depicts the combining of both sides of the psyche as well as an image of world consciousness.

Astrologers do not view the naming of the planets or, indeed, any of the celestial bodies, as coincidence. It is believed that the names emanate from the Collective Soul and are the archetypes that gave rise to the ancient myths found in every culture.

In Graeco-Roman mythology, it was the duty of Charon as ferryman to usher the Souls of the Dead across the waters of the Styx and Acheron to the infernal regions presided over by Pluto, God of the Underworld. In payment, Charon received an obulus for each soul. It was an old Roman custom to place an obulus (a coin) in the mouth of a corpse before interment. Sometimes referred to as Hades, Pluto was the son of Saturn and the brother of Jupiter and Neptune. He was usually depicted seated upon his black throne, with the dog Cerberus lying at his feet.

Probably the most powerful legend to be handed down to us is that of Hercules (or Herakles, Greek) and his Twelve Labours. On consulting the oracle of Apollo at Adelphi, Hercules was commanded to serve Eurystheus for twelve years (an orbital period of Jupiter) during which time he was honour-bound to perform the Twelve Labours. The Labours trace the growth of the human soul seen against the background of the twelve signs of the zodiac. The teacher to whom Hercules refers for guidance concerning how to undertake each task represents the Sun. Each Labour contains its own incisive wisdom symbolically describing the capacity for the human soul to develop as it acquires experience and understanding of its nature. Authorities may vary concerning the order in which the Labours were performed but seem to agree that the Slaying of Cerberus is the most difficult (See Appendix, page 167). The reason for this particular Labour was revealed to Hercules in a vision seen through his Third Eye. His task was to rescue Prometheus, whose cries for help went unheeded in the depths of the infernal regions, and bring him to the light. (See also page 68.)

To reach Hades, Hercules called upon Charon to ferry him across the Waters of the Dead. Charon was so frightened by Hercules' determination that he forgot to exact his usual fee. Hercules then stood before Pluto who said that he might release Prometheus so long as Hercules slew Cerberus with his bare hands. Having given permission for the power struggle to commence, Pluto stood aside and waited. Confronting the three-headed monster dog, Hercules grasped its central throat and grappled with it until Cerberus ceased his writhings. Hercules was then able to find Prometheus, break the chains that held him prisoner and lead him out of the perpetual dark of the Underworld.

This purely allegorical tale explains that although the Third Eye might be opened up to reveal insight into superconsciousness, it is necessary for man, bound by his physical universe, to make a conscious struggle with those areas of the unconscious that prevent access to complete awareness. Cerberus, Guardian of the Mysteries, must only be fought with bare hands, for there are no tools or weapons that can be used other than one's own along the pathway to complete self-mastery. Through confrontation, one's own private hell can be overcome, for the torment or trauma experienced during the life-time is for a purpose. The liberation of Prometheus explains that by freeing the self from memories of past personal torment, the capacity to raise consciousness to a supernal level can be released. Hercules' act of leading Prometheus to the light tells us that knowledge is not meant for self alone but should be freely given to the rest of the world; for pure, unfettered communication of Truth is Mercury's ultimate goal.

As the tenth planetary factor in the birth chart, Pluto exemplifies the perfection-seeking element of the life force, signifying not only the desire to live, but also the love of life. Reminiscent of the energy of Spring following Winter, it is associated with phases of beginning and ending, of Birth and Death mentally, emotionally and physically. Any brush with death immediately arouses a greater awareness of what it means to be alive. Some people are so open to this that they feel life coursing through every part of their being. Many are more fearful of its consequences and seek ways, consciously and unconsciously, to protect themselves from too much exposure to it. There are as many reasons why free-flowing self-expression may be hindered as there are people on this planet. However, the psyche seems to have its own safety-valve. Akin to the way that poison in the physical body will erupt in the form of a boil, there are periods in life that must be encountered when the psyche revolts against suppression of any kind. Like the vital force seen in fresh, young shoots that persist in growing from the most mutilated remains of a tree, the human psyche is remarkably resilient. Even after enduring the most exacting trauma, it is possible to begin again and build a new life. Often able to be more appreciated in retrospect, such periods can transform the whole life, for the individual has been forced to come to terms with certain information regarding himself. There can be no escape from the necessity to 'know thyself'. Interest in psychology is very often reflected in the birth chart by a strongly placed Pluto, for the desire and ability to delve into the recesses of the mind are the frequent results of attempts to understand the complexities of one's own nature.

Having once stepped on the other side of consciousness, the personality is strengthened, yet it is a gentle strength for it emanates from the central column of self. Almost as a side-effect, those who have still to understand this vital force can find such strength disturbing. There is an instinctive tendency to feel threatened by anything that is of an unknown quantity, and so the usual means of defence is aggression.

There seems to be a factor in man's nature whereby he seeks to destroy the very spark that can make him truly creative. Perhaps it is the desire to remain in control, in command of oneself, that manifests as attempts to assume superiority and see the other person squirm. The mass of evidence accumulated down through the ages does not lessen man's apparent inhumanity to man. Witch-hunts against those who prefer to practise a different religion or pursue another set of ideals persist. So the devils of the unconscious become devils in reality.

For a very short period in its extremely eccentric orbit, Pluto comes three million miles closer to the Sun than Neptune. In 1978, the year of Charon's discovery, the orbital planes of Neptune and Pluto intersected. Because of its inclination, Pluto cannot collide with Neptune. (See diagram below). Pluto will be at its nearest point to the Sun and to Earth in 1989.

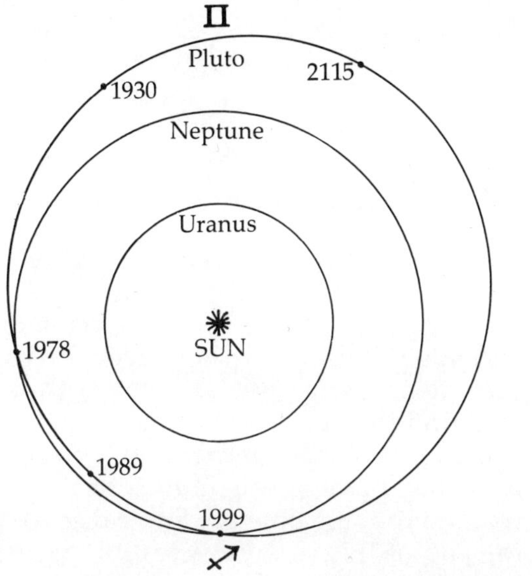

Figure 27 The orbits of Uranus, Neptune and Pluto

American astrologer, Dane Rudhyar* considers such a period, 'a cosmic fecundation in which the Plutonian seeds are deposited within the orb of Neptune'. We should take heart in the thought that these twenty-one years, from 1978 to 1999, could well see the beginning of a new phase in the world's history in which we can learn to reach towards a greater sense of consciousness with growing confidence and a lessening of the fears that have led to so many negative confrontations between individuals and nations.

No matter how insular or personalized we might believe our lives to be, not one of us is exempt from the collective experience. While it is not possible to make a full study of historical events without studying the inter-relationships by aspects of the planets one with another (see Chapter 6), we can formulate a picture of the feeling of those

* *New Mansions For New Men* by Dane Rudhyar, published by David McKay Company, Washington Square, Philadelphia, USA, 1946.

times through examination of the slower-moving planets according to the signs of the zodiac.

Because Pluto is so far from the Sun its rate of motion is exceedingly slow. It is used to mirror the subtle, yet often ultimately dramatic changes in consciousness experienced by the general population over considerably long periods. The eccentricity of its orbit means that it will seem to spend widely differing lengths of time in each of the zodiacal signs (see Figure 27). Discovered in Cancer in 1930, it will be moving at its fastest speed during the remainder of this century through the signs of long ascension. At the commencement of the twentieth century, Pluto was in Gemini and will be in Sagittarius at its close. This means that although taking fewer years to pass through these six signs, they will take longer to rise over the eastern horizon in the individual birth chart (see page 56). This is coincident with the current period in mankind's history in which the individual is being forcibly made more conscious of what is taking place in all four corners of the world. From the time of Pluto's discovery to the end of this century is seventy years (10 × 7), three score and ten. There is growing evidence that it is the period in man's history in which he is meant to 'grow up'. Stage by stage we are being raised to Collective Consciousness. By the time Pluto is in Sagittarius, the twenty-first century should presage an era of peace and prosperity both materially and spiritually.

The most prominent phases in Pluto's cycle are those when this planet appears to change from one zodiacal sign to another. While the change from Taurus to Gemini lasted two years, in 1995 the change from Scorpio to Sagittarius will take only, rather appropriately, ten months. It is impossible not to relate Pluto's increasing speed to the gathering momentum of the modern pace of life.

Guide to the Interpretation of Pluto Through the Signs of Long Ascension

Pluto in Gemini (1882–1914)
(Changing from Taurus to Gemini from 1882 to 1884.)
The individual has been given the opportunity to question what he sees, hears and believes through the benefits of improved communication and widening possibilities in education.

Pluto in Cancer (1912–1939)
(Changing from Gemini to Cancer from 1912 to 1914.)
The individual has to experience the total upheaval of home, family and national values in order to appreciate their meaning on a personal level. The very depths of being have to be disturbed to test the measure of humanity.

Pluto in Leo (1937–1958)
(Changing from Cancer to Leo from 1937 to 1939.)
The commitment to be seen to be an individual has to be made in spite of the growing urge towards totalitarian societies. The revolution in individual consciousness must begin and ultimately end with self.

Pluto in Virgo (1956–1972)
(Changing from Leo to Virgo from 1956 to 1958.)
The individual has to make a conscious effort to be useful and of service to others. Without a sense of real purpose, life becomes meaningless. Knowledge is available to those who seek the Truth.

Pluto in Libra (1971–1984)
(Changing from Virgo to Libra from 1971 to 1972.)
Consciousness of the right of every human being to be treated justly releases the freedom to relate on equal terms as individuals and, ultimately, collectively. One rule for all, 'honour thy neighbour'.

Pluto in Scorpio (1983–1995)
(Changing from Libra to Scorpio from 1983 to 1984.)
Materialism has to be understood according to the value it has for mankind and the individual, not vice versa. The beauty that lies within the darkest emotion and experience has to be recognized. Everyone and everything must be seen as being of significance.

Pluto in Sagittarius (1995–2008)
(Changing from Scorpio to Sagittarius in 1995.)
Faith, hope and trust have to be earned before the way can be clearly seen for a new

era and way of being to commence. The individual must become aware of compassion for self and for the world.

Guide to the Interpretation of Pluto Through the Houses

Pluto in the First House
The necessity to learn to cope with disappointments and problems engenders inner power and strength of purpose. Often extremely self-conscious, difficulties can arise through stubborn wilfulness that can make it hard for self and others to comprehend actions and behaviour.

Pluto in the Second House
Personal and collective sufferings are invariably internalized creating a build-up of pressure and tension. The dam has to burst in order to clear the way for the next stage in the life. Financial upheavals can occur often due to matters outside an individual's control. Yet it is usually possible to begin again.

Pluto in the Third House
Although capable of harbouring very strong opinions, these are seldom voiced. Can become preoccupied with certain ideas to the exclusion of everything else. Petty slights or hurts often revolve around in the mind, which can mask the innermost needs to delve and seek new information which will lead to greater consciousness.

Pluto in the Fourth House
There is often a temptation to dwell upon family injustices. Parents, particularly the mother, may well be seen as a domineering influence from whom there seems no escape until the decision is made to move far away either mentally or physically. Much inner growth must take place before the real strength of character may be discerned, usually through some painful experiences.

Pluto in the Fifth House
The depth of emotion can sometimes be so overwhelming that there may well be the tendency to switch off from it as if it doesn't exist at all. Yet, once that energy is harnessed creative expression can be exceptionally dynamic. The father, or one's offspring, may seem to exert a dominant influence. Concentration upon self-interests cannot protect one from the stream of life.

Pluto in the Sixth House
A dedicated, zealous worker with an aptitude for research. The work situation is liable to external changes and upheavals so that it is wise to be flexible about conditions and type of work preferred. The healing professions may well provide essential job-satisfaction. Internalized tension can become a real health hazard unless mitigated by some form of regular relaxation.

Pluto in the Seventh House
Obsessive, jealous feelings for, or by, the partner clearly make hard work of the relationship. There is a tendency to feel drawn together as if by forces unseen. Equally, there is a reluctance to admit defeat in spite of any problems or difficulties that may be encountered.

Pluto in the Eighth House
Feelings can run so deep that they are thought better left unrevealed. Usually happier when able to deal with others' problems, or a feeling nature with a liking for psychology or involvement in those areas concerned with this earth — geology, archaeology, etc. Preference is expressed for only one partner to be dominant in any relationship.

Pluto in the Ninth House
To be at peace with oneself is the prime requisite, yet the search to attain this end may never cease during the life-time. Insight concerning the reason for being may suddenly flood the conscious. It does not appease the lust to know more but merely whets the appetite for yet another revelation. Will study with concentrated intensity if truly interested or if the subject has a useful application.

Pluto in the Tenth House
Dedication to an ideal that can be of general benefit can prove indefatigably all-consuming. Conversely, there may well be the belief that society has to prove to serve the individual before it is trusted. The 'loner' who is capable of making a vast contribution, or who can become a destructive element, most essentially to self.

Pluto in the Eleventh House
Deep desires which may or may not be realized during the life-time. Tends to view life very seriously in spite of superficial light-heartedness. Life is subject to frequent severe changes in direction that are not always self-instigated. The values placed upon society may be transient but those upon self and loved ones must endure regardless.

Pluto in the Twelfth House
The need to create a life that has meaning can inspire extraordinary acts of charity and endurance. A finely-tuned, feeling nature that may seem unacceptable in the early part of the life, depends upon a rich life experience in order to be of value to the community. It is not to be feared or denied but held up as an example for others.

The Extra-Saturnians, The Higher Octaves

The existence of planets beyond the boundaries of the naked eye is thought to have been known by the ancients. The rediscovery of Uranus, Neptune and Pluto seems to echo new dimensions in the development of human consciousness. There is the possibility that man has already walked along a similar path, perhaps in an earlier civilization. It is conceivable that he did not successfully learn to polarize spirit and matter, but as the Wheel of Life turns, perhaps the opportunity to do so has presented itself once more.

Any planets additional to the first seven (including Sun and Moon) are judged as signifying a new sequence or level of energy expression. As the 'awakeners' of consciousness, Uranus, Neptune and Pluto are generally deemed the *higher octaves* of Mercury, Venus and Mars respectively. The powers of thought, understanding and action are elevated, allowing for a more ideal realization of wisdom, love and will. It follows that every human being both individually and collectively has within him the potential to attune his behaviour accordingly.

The Extra-Saturnians, The Exaltations

The exaltations of the planets beyond Saturn have been attempted by various authorities but mainly with scant regard for the underlying spiritual import of this system. It is possible that Uranus, like the Moon is exalted in Taurus, for in order to ensure the progress of the human condition, there has to be the capacity to alter the pattern from that which has gone before. From the deep sense of insecurity that has to be endured before a new direction in life can take place, a fresh appraisal of self can emerge. Neptune, the higher octave of Venus, ruler of Taurus, is most probably exalted in Aries, the sign associated with courage and self-honesty. It is these attributes that enable a relatively easy confrontation that gives access to at-one-ment with the Greater Whole.

At the time of its discovery, Pluto was thought the possible co-ruler of Virgo but the bulk of astrological opinion agreed that the co-rulership of Scorpio is more appropriate. There does, however, appear to be a strong connection between Pluto and Mercury, especially in consideration of the Promethean legend, for it is the god Mercury who conducts the souls of the dead to Hades. With his magical staff, the caduceus, he held the power to raise the dead. Originally, in common with Cerberus, the caduceus was three-headed, representing Enlightenment, Desire and Wisdom. By grasping Cerberus' central throat, Hercules subjugated his animal nature, relinquishing all worldly constraints that might hinder the development of consciousness. The caduceus was later adopted by the medical profession as the symbol of healing.

Without the application of thoughtful intelligence, self-knowledge has no meaning and cannot be made useful. The ultimate goal of creative force is to be of service to mankind as exemplified by Virgo. Out of the perfect union (immaculate conception) between the life force (Heaven) and the Earth (Virgo, sign of the virgin) a child (mankind) was conceived (creativity), called Adonis or Tammuz (Babylonia), Mithra (Persia), Quetzalcoatl (Aztec), Buddha (Buddhist), Krishna (Hindu), Jesus (Christian) or Prometheus, who was sacrificed as the Saviour taking away the sins of mankind (through the opposite sign, Pisces) so that the Sun might be born again

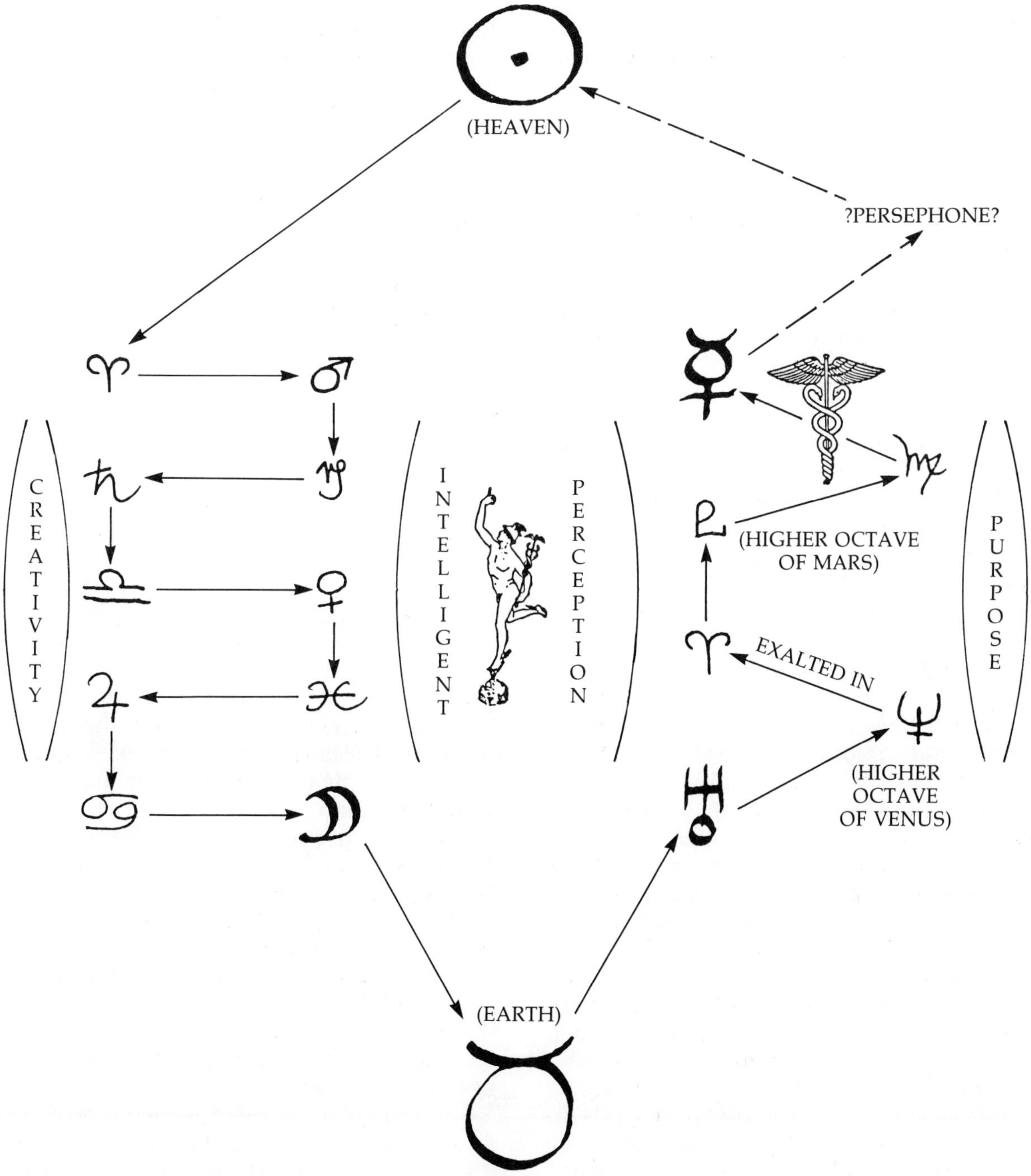

Figure 28 The Exaltations: the path to enlightenment

(at the Spring Equinox). Such intensely spiritual connotations infer the likelihood that Pluto, as the higher octave of Mars, Ruler of Aries, shares the exaltation of Virgo in common with Mercury.*

The system of exaltations may not yet be final. The discovery of any planet or planets beyond Pluto could allow for the summation of the circle commencing and culminating with the Sun. The discovery of such a planet is imminent. Astronomers already refer to it as Persephone. In Greek mythology, Persephone was stolen from her mother, Demeter (Ceres in Roman mythology) Goddess of the Produce of the Earth, by Pluto to rule Hades as his Queen. So great was Demeter's wrath that she caused a famine throughout the land. Pluto

* It should be noted that the proposed exaltations of the extra-Saturnian planets are those made by the author and are not in general use.

allowed Persephone to return on condition that she ate no food in Hades. Because she ate a forbidden pomegranate seed she was forced to spend a third of each year in the Underworld, and so became Goddess of the Spring.

Guide to the General Meaning of the Planets

Since the Sun, Moon, Mercury and Venus are all associated with the factors most immediately pertinent to self-understanding, they are the planets of *Consciousness*.

Mars, Jupiter and Saturn show how we acquire understanding of our behaviour through actual events and are therefore called the planets of *Experience*.

Uranus, Neptune and Pluto can aid understanding of the reasoning for so many of our thoughts, actions and ideals and are the planets of *Purpose*.

Although it was announced by Russian observers in 1974 that two extra-Plutonian planets had been discovered, until recently no further information verifying their existence has been made. Chiron (not to be confused with Pluto's satellite, Charon) has an orbital plane that lies between those of Saturn and Uranus and may possibly be regarded as a new planet. Discovered in 1977, it is not yet known what Chiron is. It may be a large asteroid or a body that does not actually belong to our solar system. Its extremely erratic orbit crosses Saturn's path when nearest to Earth, and Uranus' orbital path when most distant from Earth. Research concerning the astrological significance of Chiron is being conducted. An ephemeris for Chiron is available, as well as ephemerides for various asteroids, from CAO Times, Box 75, New York, NY 10011. Please supply SAE for details of prices.

While Voyager 2 continues on its mission supplying new information concerning our solar system, the Infra-Red Astronomical Satellite was launched in 1983 to survey any objects radiating infra-red energy. It is already relaying a mass of new information that will take many years to assess, but it seems that there is a possibility that new planets in our solar system will be discovered. Astrology has proved itself sufficiently flexible to encompass any such findings. Concurring with the reality that life is movement, it is able to keep pace with any significant developments in our evolution. It is entirely possible that the discovery of any new planets will correlate with our eventual capacity to fully appreciate the meaning of existence becoming the planets of *Enlightenment*.

Calculating the Position of the Planets at Birth

Planetary movement is usually monitored by astronomers using the measurements Right Ascension and Declination, which are akin to terrestrial longitude and latitude extended to the Celestial Sphere. For astrological work the positions of the planets will be found in an ephemeris given in *Celestial Longitude*, which is determined according to the Tropical Zodiac commencing each year at the Spring Equinox, 0° Aries. It is an arbitrary matter which system of measurement is used, for the position of the planets will be the same. Most ephemerides also provide the corresponding Celestial Latitude as well as the positions of the planets by Right Ascension and Declination.

With the more advanced work, Progressions and Transits, it is essential to become very familiar with the various features of an ephemeris. John Filbey has devoted an extremely lucid chapter to understanding the contents of an ephemeris in his *Natal Charting*. However, to simply determine the position of the planets for a specific birth-time, only Celestial Longitude need be employed.

Since the planets are in perpetual motion, inexorably maintaining their orbital paths, their positions can be pin-pointed at any moment in time, either back in history or forward into the future. While there are computer programmes that cover 10,000 years, ephemerides in book form such as *Raphael's* are available for single years from 1860 to the current year. It is more convenient and economical to invest in an ephemeris covering a number of years, apportioned from 1850 to 2050, such as *The Concise Planetary Ephemeris* (Hieratic), *The American Ephemeris* (Astro-Calculating Service) or *The World Ephemeris for the Twentieth Century* (Para Research). These ephemerides are calculated either in universal time (GMT) or ephemeris time (ET). See pages 100–104. The correction from universal time to ephemeris time given in ephemerides for the appropriate year is as follows:

1900	minus 4 seconds
1910	plus 10 seconds
1920	plus 20 seconds
1930	plus 23 seconds
1940	plus 24 seconds
1950	plus 29 seconds
1960	plus 33 seconds
1970	plus 41 seconds
1980	plus 51 seconds

To convert universal time to ephemeris time add the interval to the birth time at GMT. For example, in 1975 the birth time at 3.15 p.m. GMT would be 3.15.46 secs or 3.16 p.m. ET. It should be noted that this conversion is only necessary when great accuracy is desired as in the instance of the timing of Progressions and Transits. For natal work it may be disregarded.

The bewildering array of symbols and numbers in an ephemeris can seem daunting at first but, as with everything, it really is easy when one knows how. The signs of the zodiac given at the head of each

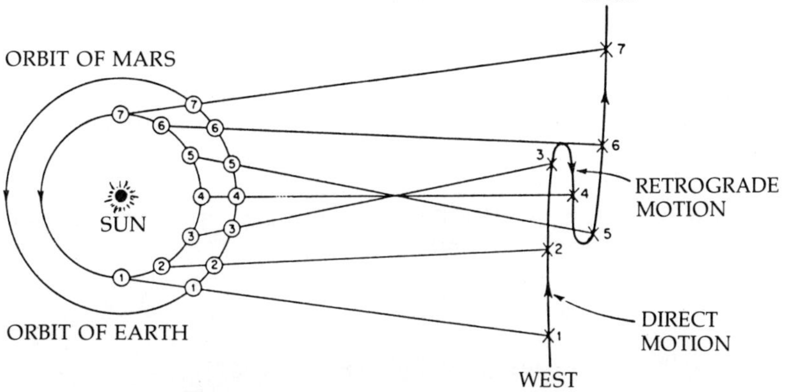

Figure 29a Retrograde motion

DAY	MARCH ♂	APRIL ♂	MAY ♂	JUNE ♂	1952 DAY
	° ′	° ′	° ′	° ′	
1	15 ♏ 12.7	18 ♏ 12.5	10 ♏ 38.7	1 ♏ 43.6	1
2	15 27.3	18 R 7.1	10 R 16.6	1 R 36.6	2
3	15 41.5	18 1.1	9 54.4	1 30.3	3
4	15 55.1	17 54.2	9 32.2	1 25.0	4
5	16 8.3	17 46.6	9 10.0	1 20.4	5
6	16 20.9	17 38.2	8 47.9	1 16.7	6
7	16 33.0	17 29.1	8 25.9	1 13.8	7
8	16 44.6	17 19.2	8 4.1	1 11.7	8
9	16 55.7	17 8.6	7 42.5	1 10.4	9
10	17 6.2	16 57.2	7 21.1	1 9.9	10
11	17 16.1	16 45.1	7 .1	1 D 10.2	11
12	17 25.4	16 32.3	6 39.4	1 11.3	12
13	17 34.1	16 18.8	6 19.0	1 13.2	13
14	17 42.2	16 4.6	5 59.0	1 15.8	14
15	17 49.8	15 49.6	5 39.4	1 19.2	15
16	17 56.6	15 34.1	5 20.4	1 23.4	16
17	18 2.9	15 17.8	5 1.8	1 28.3	17
18	18 8.5	15 1.0	4 43.8	1 34.0	18
19	18 13.4	14 43.5	4 26.3	1 40.4	19
20	18 17.7	14 25.5	4 9.5	1 47.6	20
21	18 21.2	14 6.9	3 53.3	1 55.5	21
22	18 24.1	13 47.8	3 37.8	2 4.1	22
23	18 26.2	13 28.2	3 22.9	2 13.4	23
24	18 27.7	13 8.1	3 8.8	2 23.4	24
25	18 28.4	12 47.7	2 55.4	2 34.0	25
26	18 28.4	12 26.9	2 42.8	2 45.4	26
27	18 R 27.6	12 5.7	2 30.9	2 57.3	27
28	18 26.1	11 44.3	2 19.8	3 10.0	28
29	18 23.8	11 22.6	2 9.5	3 23.3	29
30	18 20.8	11 .7	2 .1	3 37.2	30
31	18 17.0		1 51.4		31

Figure 29b Retrograde motion in the ephemeris. The retrograde and direct motion of Mars shown in the top diagram is duplicated by the degrees and minutes of Scorpio as they decrease and increase. Mars begins to retrograde on 27 March returning to direct motion on 11 June. Note that minutes are given to tenths of a minute.

column signify the position reached by a planet in its orbit in relation to the zodiacal band. The numbers are the degrees and minutes of that sign expressing the distance travelled by a planet in each twenty-four hour period either from midnight *at the start of the day*, or at noon. *Raphael's Astronomical Ephemeris* gives the positions of the planets at noon each day in a single year whereas the collections of ephemerides for several years are available for midnight or noon. It is a matter of personal preference which is used.

The planets' motion through the zodiac can be traced by following their daily positions over several months. Although the planets pursue constant forward motion in their orbits, their motion does appear to change direction, moving forward (direct motion) or backwards (retrograde motion) since their speeds differ from that of the Earth. All the planets, with the exception of the Sun and the Moon will at some time appear to retrograde. In the columns of the ephemeris, retrograde motion is noted as ℞ , and direct motion as D. The shifting degrees show the alterations in the speed of motion with a noticeable slowing down until it appears to stand still (stationary, which is noted as STA) prior to turning retrograde or direct.

The calculation to determine the positions of the planets at a particular time of birth is not difficult. Two methods are given. The first, performed manually, uses Proportional Logarithms (see page 106). The second requires a basic electronic calculator that incorporates a memory function. In both instances, examples of the methods of calculation will employ both a Midnight and a Noon ephemeris.

Pluto's positions are available in separate ephemerides, as in the example in Figure 32, which is an extract from *Pluto Ephemeris 1773–2000* (Omega), given at ten-day intervals. Pluto's daily positions are included in the collections of ephemerides such as *The Concise Planetary Ephemeris* and *The American Ephemeris.*

Planetary Positions for Midnight GMT

DECEMBER 1949

Day	Sid. T.	Sun	Moon	Merc.	Venus	Mars	Jup.	Saturn	Uranus	Nept.	Pluto	N.Node
1	4:38: 4	8 Sg 28 0	17 Ar 32	13 Sg 31	25 Cp 15	18 Vi 40	0 Aq 2	18 Vi 40	3 Cn 58 R	16 Li 42	18 Le 10 R	13 Ar 45
2	4:42: 1	9 28 49	29 20	15 5	26 10	19 10	0 14	18 43	3 56	16 43	18 10	13 42
3	4:45:58	10 29 39	11 Ta 12	16 39	27 5	19 39	0 25	18 46	3 54	16 45	18 10	13 39
4	4:49:54	11 30 31	23 12	18 12	28 0	20 8	0 36	18 49	3 52	16 46	18 9	13 36
5	4:53:51	12 31 23	5 Ge 21	19 46	28 53	20 37	0 48	18 51	3 49	16 49	18 9	13 33
6	4:57:47	13 32 16	17 42	21 19	29 46	21 6	1 0	18 54	3 47	16 49	18 8	13 29
7	5: 1:44	14 33 10	0 Cn 15	22 53	0 Aq 39	21 34	1 12	18 57	3 44	16 51	18 8	13 26
8	5: 5:41	15 34 6	13 0	24 27	1 30	22 3	1 23	18 59	3 42	16 52	18 7	13 23
9	5: 9:37	16 35 2	25 56	26 0	2 21	22 31	1 35	19 2	3 40	16 53	18 7	13 20
10	5:13:34	17 36 0	9 Le 4	27 33	3 12	22 59	1 47	19 4	3 37	16 55	18 6	13 17
11	5:17:30	18 36 59	22 24	29 7	4 1	23 26	2 0	19 6	3 35	16 56	18 6	13 13
12	5:21:27	19 37 58	5 Vi 56	0 Cp 40	4 49	23 54	2 12	19 8	3 32	16 57	18 5	13 10
13	5:25:23	20 38 59	19 41	2 14	5 37	24 21	2 24	19 10	3 30	16 58	18 4	13 7
14	5:29:20	21 40 1	3 Li 40	3 47	6 24	24 48	2 36	19 12	3 27	17 0	18 4	13 4
15	5:33:17	22 41 4	17 52	5 20	7 10	25 15	2 49	19 13	3 25	17 1	18 3	13 1
16	5:37:13	23 42 8	2 Sc 17	6 53	7 55	25 42	3 1	19 15	3 22	17 2	18 2	12 58
17	5:41:10	24 43 13	16 51	8 26	8 38	26 8	3 14	19 17	3 20	17 3	18 2	12 54
18	5:45: 6	25 44 19	1 Sg 30	9 58	9 21	26 34	3 27	19 18	3 17	17 4	18 1	12 51
19	5:49: 3	26 45 25	16 8	11 30	10 3	27 0	3 39	19 19	3 15	17 5	18 0	12 48
20	5:52:59	27 46 33	0 Cp 36	13 2	10 43	27 26	3 52	19 21	3 12	17 6	17 59	12 45
21	5:56:56	28 47 40	14 48	14 32	11 22	27 51	4 5	19 22	3 9	17 7	17 58	12 42
22	6: 0:53	29 48 48	28 38	16 3	12 0	28 17	4 18	19 23	3 7	17 8	17 58	12 39
23	6: 4:49	0 Cp 49 57	12 Aq 3	17 32	12 37	28 41	4 31	19 23	3 4	17 9	17 57	12 35
24	6: 8:45	1 51 6	25 3	19 0	13 12	29 6	4 44	19 24	3 2	17 10	17 56	12 32
25	6:12:42	2 52 14	7 Pi 40	20 27	13 46	29 30	4 57	19 25	2 59	17 11	17 55	12 29
26	6:16:39	3 53 23	19 56	21 52	14 19	29 54	5 10	19 25	2 57	17 12	17 54	12 26
27	6:20:35	4 54 32	1 Ar 57	23 15	14 50	0 Li 18	5 23	19 26	2 54	17 12	17 53	12 23
28	6:24:31	5 55 41	13 48	24 36	15 19	0 42	5 37	19 26	2 51	17 13	17 52	12 19
29	6:28:28	6 56 49	25 36	25 54	15 46	1 5	5 50	19 26	2 49	17 14	17 51	12 16
30	6:32:25	7 57 58	7 Ta 24	27 9	16 12	1 28	6 3	19 26	2 46	17 15	17 50	12 13
31	6:36:21	8 59 7	19 19	28 20	16 36	1 50	6 17	19 26R	2 44	17 15	17 49	12 10

Figure 30 Example of the postions given in The World Ephemeris for the Twentieth Century.

Pluto's positions are given on page 39 of ephemerides from 1940 until 1979. Thereafter they are included with the entries for all other planets.

Planetary Positions for Noon GMT.

New Moon—December 19, 6*h*. 55*m*. 29*s*. *p.m.*

24 **DECEMBER, 1949** [*RAPHAEL'S*

D M	Neptune. Lat.	Neptune. Dec.	Herschel. Lat.	Herschel. Dec.	Saturn. Lat.	Saturn. Dec.	Jupiter. Lat.	Jupiter. Dec.	Mars. Lat.	Mars. Declin.	Mars. Declin.
	° ′	° ′	° ′	° ′	° ′	° ′	° ′	° ′	° ′	° ′	° ′
1	1N34	5 S 8	0N16	23N39	1N52	6N12	0 S 34	20 S 41	2 N 1	6N14	6 N 4
3	1 34	5 9	0 16	23 39	1 53	6 10	0 34	20 36	2 3	5 53	5 43
5	1 34	5 10	0 16	23 39	1 53	6 8	0 34	20 31	2 5	5 32	5 22
7	1 34	5 11	0 16	23 40	1 54	6 7	0 34	20 26	2 6	5 11	5 1
9	1 34	5 12	0 16	23 40	1 54	6 5	0 34	20 21	2 8	4 51	4 40
11	1 34	5 13	0 16	23 40	1 55	6 4	0 34	20 16	2 10	4 30	4 20
13	1 34	5 13	0 16	23 40	1 55	6 3	0 34	20 10	2 12	4 10	4 1
15	1 35	5 14	0 16	23 40	1 56	6 2	0 34	20 4	2 14	3 51	3 41
17	1 35	5 15	0 16	23 40	1 56	6 1	0 34	19 59	2 16	3 32	3 22
19	1 35	5 16	0 16	23 41	1 57	6 1	0 35	19 53	2 18	3 13	3 3
21	1 35	5 16	0 16	23 41	1 58	6 1	0 35	19 47	2 20	2 54	2 45
23	1 35	5 17	0 16	23 41	1 58	6 0	0 35	19 41	2 22	2 36	2 28
25	1 35	5 17	0 16	23 41	1 59	6 0	0 35	19 34	2 24	2 19	2 10
27	1 35	5 18	0 16	23 41	1 59	6 1	0 35	19 28	2 26	2 2	1 54
29	1 35	5 18	0 16	23 41	2 0	6 1	0 35	19 21	2 28	1 45	1 37
31	1 35	5 19	0 16	23 41	2 0	6 2	0 35	19 15	2 30	1 29	

D M	D W	Sidereal Time.	⊙ Long.	⊙ Dec.	☽ Long.	☽ Lat.	☽ Dec.	MIDNIGHT ☽ Long.	MIDNIGHT ☽ Dec.
		H. M. S.	° ′ ″	° ′	° ′ ″	° ′	° ′	° ′ ″	° ′
1	Th	16 40 3	8 ♐ 58 25	21 S 48	23 ♈ 25 41	0 N 43	9 N 46	29 ♈ 19 45	12 N 23
2	F	16 43 59	9 59 14	21 57	5 ♉ 15 0	1 44	14 55	11 ♉ 11 50	17 19
3	S	16 47 56	11 0 5	22 6	17 10 37	2 42	19 33	23 11 39	21 36
4	𝔖	16 51 53	12 0 57	22 14	29 15 10	3 32	23 27	5 ♊ 21 22	25 3
5	M	16 55 49	13 1 49	22 22	11 ♊ 30 24	4 14	26 22	17 42 21	27 22
6	Tu	16 59 46	14 2 43	22 30	23 57 16	4 44	28 2	0 ♋ 15 10	28 21
7	W	17 3 42	15 3 38	22 37	6 ♋ 36 4	5 1	28 17	12 59 54	27 51
8	Th	17 7 39	16 4 34	22 43	19 26 41	5 2	27 2	25 56 22	25 50
9	F	17 11 35	17 5 31	22 49	2 ♌ 28 57	4 49	24 18	9 ♌ 4 26	22 26
10	S	17 15 32	18 6 29	22 55	15 42 50	4 20	20 16	22 24 13	17 49
11	𝔖	17 19 28	19 7 28	23 0	29 8 39	3 36	15 8	5 ♍ 56 13	12 16
12	M	17 23 25	20 8 28	23 5	12 ♍ 47 2	2 39	9 13	19 41 12	6 1
13	Tu	17 27 22	21 9 30	23 9	26 38 46	1 32	2 44	3 ♎ 39 48	0 S 36
14	W	17 31 18	22 10 32	23 13	10 ♎ 44 16	0 18	3 S 58	17 52 5	7 19
15	Th	17 35 15	23 11 36	23 16	25 3 3	0 S 58	10 36	2 ♏ 16 54	13 45
16	F	17 39 11	24 12 40	23 19	9 ♏ 33 10	2 11	16 44	16 51 20	19 30
17	S	17 43 8	25 13 46	23 22	24 10 43	3 15	21 59	1 ♐ 30 31	24 7
18	𝔖	17 47 4	26 14 52	23 24	8 ♐ 49 54	4 7	25 51	16 7 54	27 9
19	M	17 51 1	27 15 59	23 25	23 23 36	4 43	27 59	0 ♑ 36 4	28 20
20	Tu	17 54 58	28 17 6	23 26	7 ♑ 44 27	5 0	28 12	14 48 0	27 37
21	W	17 58 54	29 18 14	23 27	21 46 3	4 58	26 35	28 38 11	25 11
22	Th	18 2 51	0 ♑ 19 22	23 27	5 ♒ 24 2	4 39	23 26	12 ♒ 3 30	21 24
23	F	18 6 47	1 20 31	23 26	18 36 34	4 6	19 9	25 3 25	16 42
24	S	18 10 44	2 21 40	23 26	1 ♓ 24 20	3 21	14 6	7 ♓ 39 43	11 24
25	𝔖	18 14 40	3 22 48	23 24	13 50 5	2 27	8 37	19 56 1	5 48
26	M	18 18 37	4 23 57	23 23	25 58 8	1 28	2 57	1 ♈ 57 6	0 6
27	Tu	18 22 33	5 25 6	23 20	7 ♈ 53 39	0 26	2 N 44	13 48 28	5 N 32
28	W	18 26 30	6 26 15	23 17	19 42 16	0 N 37	8 16	25 35 44	10 57
29	Th	18 30 27	7 27 24	23 14	1 ♉ 29 34	1 37	13 31	7 ♉ 24 24	15 59
30	F	18 34 23	8 28 33	23 11	13 20 50	2 34	18 18	19 19 25	20 27
31	S	18 38 20	9 29 42	23 6	25 20 39	3 25	22 25	1 ♊ 24 57	24 9

First Quarter—December 27, 6*h*. 31*m*. 18*s*. *a.m.*

Full Moon—December 5, 3*h*. 13*m*. 21*s*. *p.m.*

EPHEMERIS] **DECEMBER, 1949** 25

D M	Venus. Lat.	Venus. Declin.	Venus. Declin.	Mercury. Lat.	Mercury. Declin.	Mercury. Declin.	☽ Node.
	° ′	° ′	° ′	° ′	° ′	° ′	° ′
1	2 S 53	23 S 50	23 S 37	1 S 24	23 S 55	24 S 10	13 ♈ 44
3	2 46	23 23	23 8	1 34	24 25	24 38	13 37
5	2 39	22 54	22 39	1 43	24 50	25 0	13 31
7	2 31	22 23	22 7	1 52	25 9	25 17	13 25
9	2 22	21 51	21 35	1 59	25 23	25 28	13 18
11	2 12	21 18	21 1	2 5	25 32	25 34	13 12
13	2 1	20 44	20 26	2 10	25 34	25 34	13 6
15	1 49	20 9	19 51	2 13	25 31	25 27	12 59
17	1 36	19 33	19 15	2 15	25 22	25 15	12 53
19	1 21	18 57	18 38	2 15	25 7	24 57	12 46
21	1 5	18 20	18 2	2 12	24 46	24 33	12 40
23	0 48	17 43	17 25	2 8	24 18	24 3	12 34
25	0 30	17 6	16 48	2 0	23 46	23 27	12 27
27	0 11	16 30	16 11	1 50	23 8	22 47	12 21
29	0 N 10	15 53	15 36	1 36	22 26	22 3	12 15
31	0 32	15 18		1 19	21 40		12 8

Mutual Aspects.

1. ☿ P ♀, ♂ ☌ & P ♄.
2. ☿ ∠ ♃, ♀ P ♅.
3. ☿ ✱ ♆, △ ♇.
4. ☿ □ ♄, ♀ P ♇. 5. ☿ □ ♂.
6. ⊙ P ♀. 7. ♀ ☌ ♃, ♂ P ♆.
8. ☿ ⊥ ♃.
9. ⊙ ∠ ♃, ✱ ♆, ☿ ⊥ ♀.
10. ⊙ △ ♇, ☿ Q ♆, ♀ ∇ ♅.
11. ⊙ □ ♄, ♀ ⚼ ♄.
12. ⊙ ∠ ♀ ♂ ⊥ ♇.
13. ⊙ P ♇, ☿ ⊻ ♃, ☍ ♅, □ ♇.
15. ♀ P ♃.
17. ☿ ⊻ ♀, ♀ ± ♅, ♃ ∇ ♅.
19. ⊙ □ ♂, ☿ ± ♇.
20. ⊙ ⊥ ♃.
21. ⊙ Q ♆.
22. ☿ □ ♆, ♃ ⚼ ♄.
23. ☿ ∇ ♇.
24. ☿ △ ♄, ♀ ± ♄.
25. ⊙ ☍ ♅, ⚼ ♇, ☿ P ♅.
26. ⊙ P ☿.
27. ⊙ ⊻ ♃, ☿ P ♇.
28. ⊙ P ♇, ♅ ∠ ♇.

D M	♆ Long.	♅ Long.	♄ Long.	♃ Long.	♂ Long.	♀ Long.	☿ Long.	Lunar Aspects ⊙	♇	♆	♅	♄	♃	♂	♀	☿
	° ′	° ′	° ′	° ′	° ′	° ′	° ′									
1	16 ♎ 43	3 ♋ 57	18 ♍ 42	0 ♒ 8	18 ♍ 55	25 ♑ 43	14 ♐ 19	⚼	△						□	
2	16 45	3 ℞ 55	18 45	0 19	19 24	26 38	15 53				✱	⚼	□	⚼		⚼
3	16 46	3 52	18 48	0 31	19 54	27 33	17 27		□		∠	△		△		
𝔖	16 48	3 50	18 50	0 42	20 23	28 27	19 0			⚼	⊻		△		△	
5	16 49	3 48	18 53	0 54	20 52	29 20	20 34	☍		△			⚼		⚼	
6	16 50	3 45	18 56	1 6	21 20	0 ♒ 13	22 7		✱			□		□		☍
7	16 52	3 43	18 58	1 18	21 49	1 5	23 41		∠		☌					
8	16 53	3 40	19 1	1 30	22 17	1 56	25 14		⊻	□		✱		✱		
9	16 54	3 38	19 3	1 42	22 45	2 47	26 48	⚼			⊻	∠	☍	∠	☍	
10	16 56	3 36	19 5	1 54	23 13	3 37	28 21	△	☌	✱	∠	⊻				⚼
𝔖	16 57	3 33	19 7	2 6	23 40	4 26	29 54			∠	✱			⊻		△
12	16 58	3 31	19 9	2 18	24 8	5 14	1 ♑ 28		⊻	⊻		☌	⚼			
13	17 0	3 28	19 11	2 30	24 35	6 1	3 1	□	∠		□		△	☌	⚼	
14	17 1	3 26	19 13	2 43	25 2	6 47	4 34			☌					△	□
15	17 2	3 23	19 15	2 55	25 29	7 32	6 7	✱	✱			⊻		⊻		
16	17 3	3 21	19 16	3 8	25 55	8 17	7 40	∠			△	∠	□	∠	□	✱
17	17 4	3 18	19 18	3 20	26 22	9 0	9 13	⊻	□	⊻	⚼	✱		✱		∠
𝔖	17 5	3 16	19 19	3 33	26 48	9 42	10 45			∠			✱		✱	⊻
19	17 6	3 13	19 20	3 46	27 14	10 23	12 17	☌	△	✱		□	∠	□	∠	
20	17 7	3 10	19 21	3 59	27 39	11 3	13 48		⚼		☍		⊻		⊻	☌
21	17 8	3 8	19 22	4 12	28 4	11 42	15 18			□		△		△		
22	17 9	3 5	19 23	4 25	28 29	12 19	16 48	⊻				⚼	☌			
23	17 10	3 3	19 24	4 38	28 54	12 55	18 17	∠	☍	△	⚼			⚼	☌	⊻
24	17 11	3 0	19 25	4 51	29 19	13 30	19 44	✱		⚼	△		⊻			∠
𝔖	17 12	2 58	19 25	5 4	29 43	14 3	21 10					☍			⊻	
26	17 12	2 55	19 26	5 17	0 ♎ 7	14 34	22 34						∠	☍	∠	✱
27	17 13	2 52	19 26	5 30	0 30	15 5	23 56	□	⚼		□		✱			
28	17 14	2 50	19 26	5 44	0 54	15 33	25 16		△	☍					✱	
29	17 15	2 47	19 26	5 57	1 17	16 0	26 32				✱	⚼	□			□
30	17 15	2 44	19 26	6 10	1 39	16 25	27 45	△	□		∠			⚼	□	
31	17 16	2 42	19 26	6 24	2 2	16 48	28 54	⚼				△				△

Last Quarter—December 13, 1*h*. 47*m*. 54*s*. *a.m.*

Figure 31 Example page from Raphael's Astronomical Ephemeris

If a birth time occurs at either the precise stroke of Midnight or Noon GMT, the planetary positions may be taken as read from the appropriate ephemeris. In all other instances, any variant from the positions given in a Midnight or Noon ephemeris must be calculated.

Chart forms for this calculation are available from stockists of astrological books. Alternatively, you may copy the method outlined on page 107 of *The Astrology Workbook.*

The calculation for the positions of the planets at a particular birth time depends upon the accurate determination of the planets' Daily Motion (or Diurnal Motion), which is the distance, for astrological purposes, in Celestial Longitude, travelled by a planet in a twenty-four hour period. This preparatory step is always performed manually before proceeding with the calculations either by proportional logarithms or an electronic calculator. Alternatively, there are tables available in

1949	LONG		LAT		DEC		1950	LONG	
	°	′	°	′	°	′		°	′
JAN 4	16	4 R	7 N	46	23 N	26	JAN 9	17	39 R
JAN 14	15	52	7	48	23	31	JAN 19	17	26
JAN 24	15	39	7	49	23	36	JAN 29	17	12
FEB 3	15	25	7	50	23	41	FEB 8	16	58
FEB 13	15	10	7	51	23	47	FEB 18	16	44
FEB 23	14	57	7	51	23	50	FEB 28	16	30
MAR 5	14	44	7	51	23	54	MAR 10	16	17
MAR 15	14	32	7	51	23	58	MAR 20	16	7
MAR 25	14	23	7	50	23	59	MAR 30	15	58
APR 4	14	16	7	48	24	0	APR 9	15	51
APR 14	14	11	7	47	24	1	APR 19	15	47
APR 24	14	9	7	46	24	0	APR 29	15	46 D
MAY 4	14	10 D	7	45	23	58	MAY 9	15	48
MAY 14	14	13	7	43	23	56	MAY 19	15	52
MAY 24	14	19	7	42	23	53	MAY 29	15	59
JUN 3	14	28	7	41	23	49	JUN 8	16	
JUN 13	14	39	7	40	23	45	JUN 18	16	
JUN 23	14	52	7	39	23	40	JUN 28	16	
JUL 3	15	7	7	38	23	35	JUL 8	16	
JUL 13	15	23	7	38	23	30	JUL 18	17	
JUL 23	15	40	7	38	23	25	JUL 28	17	
AUG 2	15	58	7	38	23	20	AUG 7		
AUG 12	16	16	7	39	23	14	AUG 17		
AUG 22	16	34	7	40	23	10	AUG 27		
SEP 1	16	52	7	41	23	6	SEP 6		
SEP 11	17	9	7	43	23	2	SEP 16		
SEP 21	17	24	7	45	23	0	SEP 26		
OCT 1	17	38	7	47	22	57	OCT 6		
OCT 11	17	50	7	49	22	55	OCT 16		
OCT 21	18	0	7	52	22	56	OCT 2		
OCT 31	18	6	7	55	22	56	NOV		
NOV 10	18	11	7	58	22	57	NOV		
NOV 20	18	12 R	8	1	23	0	NOV		
NOV 30	18	10	8	4	23	3	DEC		
DEC 10	18	6	8	7	23	7	DEC		
DEC 20	17	59	8	9	23	12	DEC		
DEC 30	17	50	8	11	23	17	JAN		
APR 26	STAT. DIRECT						APR		
NOV 20	STAT. RETRO.						NOV		

Figure 32 Pluto ephemeris

book form, such as the *Tables of Diurnal Planetary Motion* published by the American Federation of Astrologers.

Daily Motion varies throughout the year since the orbital paths of the planets are elliptical, so they move faster or slower relative to their distance from the Sun. Daily Motion is measured according to the Earth's axial rotation, and its annual elliptical orbit can be traced via the Sun's Daily Motions which vary from 57′ 11″ at the Summer Solstice, and 1° 01′ 12″ in Winter. Because Daily Planetary Motion can vary from day to day, most noticeably with the faster-moving planets, it is necessary to select the Daily Motion *nearest to the birth time* to pin-point the planetary positions with accuracy.

It is important to remember that planetary positions are usually given in Universal or Ephemeris Time, *thus the birth time must first be converted (if necessary) to Universal Time (GMT).*

To Determine the Daily Motion for an A.M. Birth

Example Data: 6.58 a.m., GMT, 22 December 1949

Using a Midnight Ephemeris

The nearest twenty-four hour period to the birth time lies between Midnight (0 hours on the morning of) 22 December and Midnight (0 hours on the morning of) 23 December. It is, therefore, necessary to *subtract* the positions of all the planets for the 22nd *from* those for the 23rd. For example: See page 102, Planetary Positions for Midnight GMT. Under the column headed ☉

Sun's Longitude 23 Dec. 0° 49′ 57″ ♒
− 22 Dec. 29° 48′ 48″ ♑

Equals the Sun's Daily Motion = 1° 01′ 09″

The *interval* of time between the nearest Midnight (22 December) and the birth time is an additional (Plus) 6 hours 58 minutes.

Using a Noon Ephemeris

The nearest twenty-four hour period to the birth time lies between Noon (12 hours) 21 December and Noon 22 December. It is then necessary to *subtract* the positions of all the planets for the 21st from those for the 22nd. For example: see page 103 Planetary Positions for Noon GMT. Under the column headed ☽ Long.

Moon's Longitude 22 Dec. 5° 24′ 02″ ♒
− 21 Dec. 21° 46′ 03″ ♑

Equals Moon's Daily Motion = 13° 37′ 59″

The *interval* of time from the birth time, 6.58 a.m., *to* the nearest noon (22 December) is 5 hours 02 minutes.

To Determine the Daily Motion for a P.M. Birth

Example data: 8.33 p.m. G.M.T. 8 December 1949

Using a Midnight Ephemeris
The nearest twenty-four hour period to the birth time lies between Midnight (0 hours on the morning of) 8 December and Midnight, 9 December. Therefore, *subtract* the positions of all the planets given for 8 December from those for 9 December. For example: see page 102, Planetary Positions for Midnight GMT. Under the column headed ☿ Long.

Mercury's Longitude	9 Dec.	26° 00′ ♐
	– 8 Dec.	24° 27′ ♐
Equals Mercury's Daily Motion	=	1° 33′

The *interval* between the birth time, 8.33 p.m., and the nearest Midnight (9 December) is an additional 3 hours 27 minutes. That is, Midnight *minus* a p.m. birth time.

Using a Noon Ephemeris
The nearest twenty-four hour period to the birth time, 8.33 p.m., lies between Noon on 8 December and Noon on the 9th. To gain the Daily Motion, *subtract* the positions of all the planets for the 8th from those for the 9th. For example: see page 103, Planetary Positions for Noon GMT. Under the column headed ♃ Long.

Jupiter's Longitude	9 Dec.	1° 42′ ♒
	– 8 Dec.	1° 30′ ♒
Equals Jupiter's Daily Motion	=	0° 12′

The *interval* from Noon on 8 December to the birth time is an additional (*plus*) 8 hours 33 minutes.

Method for Using Proportional Logarithms

Invented by John Napier (1550–1617) for his astrological computations, logarithms simplify division of time (in Hours and Minutes) to find the corresponding proportion of angular units (in Degrees and Minutes), or vice versa. For example, if the Moon travels 13° 37′ 59″ in twenty-four hours, how far has it moved by 6.58 a.m.?

Working in Hours/Degrees and Minutes *only*, if more than 30″, round up to the nearest minute.

Therefore, Moon's Daily Motion = 13° 38′

Using the table of Proportional Logarithms for locating the planets' positions, trace down the column (Hours/Degrees) headed 13 until 38 minutes (far left or right hand columns) is reached. (See page 106.)

Logarithm of Daily Motion = 2456

The distance in *time* between the birth time and the nearest Noon is 5 hours 02 minutes. Trace down the column (Hours/Degrees) headed 5, until 2 minutes (left hand column) is reached.

Logarithm of Interval (5 hrs 02mins) = 6784

Regardless whether an a.m. or a p.m. birth, always *add* these two logarithms together.

Addition of Logarithms equals 9240

Using the table of Proportional Logarithms, find the *nearest* number to 9240 (which is 9228) then read off the numbers, firstly at the top of the column (Hours/Degrees), 2 , and then at the side column (Minutes), 52 . This is known as the *anti-log*. The distance *in degrees* travelled by the Moon in 5 hours 02 minutes equals 2° 52′.

As this is an a.m. birth, it is necessary to *subtract* this amount from the Noon position of the Moon given in the ephemeris. The difference in time is shown by the difference in distance of the planet in question.

The Moon's Longitude (position) at Noon on 22 December 1949	= 5° 24′ 02″	
Difference in distance in 5 hours 02 minutes	= 2° 52′	*subtract*
Moon's position at birth (6.58 a.m.)	= 2° 32′	

The Pitfalls of Calculating Planets' Positions

The most able mathematician is capable of making errors, especially when calculating the planets' positions. The temptation to

TABLE OF PROPORTIONAL LOGARITHMS FOR LOCATING PLANETS' POSITIONS

HOURS or DEGREES

MINUTES	0	1	2	3	4	5	6	7	8	9	10	11	12	13	14	15	MINUTES
0	3.1584	1.3802	1.0792	9031	7781	6812	6021	5351	4771	4260	3802	3388	3010	2663	2341	2041	0
1	3.1584	1.3730	1.0756	9007	7763	6798	6009	5341	4762	4252	3795	3382	3004	2657	2336	2036	1
2	2.8573	1.3660	1.0720	8983	7745	6784	5997	5330	4753	4244	3788	3375	2998	2652	2330	2032	2
3	2.6812	1.3590	1.0685	8959	7728	6769	5985	5320	4744	4236	3780	3368	2992	2646	2325	2027	3
4	2.5563	1.3522	1.0649	8935	7710	6755	5973	5310	4735	4228	3773	3362	2986	2641	2320	2022	4
5	2.4594	1.3454	1.0614	8912	7692	6741	5961	5300	4726	4220	3766	3355	2980	2635	2315	2017	5
6	2.3802	1.3388	1.0580	8888	7674	6726	5949	5289	4717	4212	3759	3349	2974	2629	2310	2012	6
7	2.3133	1.3323	1.0546	8865	7657	6712	5937	5279	4708	4204	3752	3342	2968	2624	2305	2008	7
8	2.2553	1.3258	1.0511	8842	7639	6698	5925	5269	4699	4196	3745	3336	2962	2618	2300	2003	8
9	2.2041	1.3195	1.0478	8819	7622	6684	5913	5259	4690	4188	3738	3329	2956	2613	2295	1998	9
10	2.1584	1.3133	1.0444	8796	7604	6670	5902	5249	4682	4180	3730	3323	2950	2607	2289	1993	10
11	2.1170	1.3071	1.0411	8773	7587	6656	5890	5239	4673	4172	3723	3316	2945	2602	2284	1989	11
12	2.0792	1.3010	1.0378	8751	7570	6642	5878	5229	4664	4164	3716	3310	2938	2596	2279	1984	12
13	2.0444	1.2950	1.0345	8728	7552	6628	5866	5219	4655	4156	3709	3303	2933	2591	2274	1979	13
14	2.0122	1.2891	1.0313	8706	7535	6614	5855	5209	4646	4149	3702	3297	2927	2585	2269	1974	14
15	1.9823	1.2833	1.0280	8683	7518	6600	5843	5199	4638	4141	3695	3291	2921	2580	2264	1969	15
16	1.9542	1.2775	1.0248	8661	7501	6587	5832	5189	4629	4133	3688	3284	2915	2575	2259	1965	16
17	1.9279	1.2719	1.0216	8639	7484	6573	5820	5179	4620	4125	3681	3278	2909	2569	2254	0960	17
18	1.9031	1.2663	1.0185	8617	7467	6559	5809	5169	4611	4117	3674	3271	2903	2564	2249	1955	18
19	1.8796	1.2607	1.0153	8595	7451	6546	5797	5159	4603	4109	3667	3265	2897	2558	2244	1950	19
20	1.8573	1.2553	1.0122	8573	7434	6532	5786	5149	4594	4102	3660	3258	2891	2553	2239	1946	20
21	1.8361	1.2499	1.0091	8552	7417	6519	5774	5139	4585	4094	3653	3252	2885	2547	2234	1941	21
22	1.8159	1.2445	1.0061	8530	7401	6505	5763	5129	4577	4086	3646	3246	2880	2542	2229	1936	22
23	1.7966	1.2393	1.0030	8509	7384	6492	5752	5120	4568	4079	3639	3239	2874	2536	2223	1932	23
24	1.7781	1.2341	1.0000	8487	7368	6478	5740	5110	4559	4071	3632	3233	2868	2531	2218	1927	24
25	1.7604	1.2289	0.9970	8466	7351	6465	5729	5100	4551	4063	3625	3227	2862	2526	2213	1922	25
26	1.7434	1.2239	0.9940	8445	7335	6451	5718	5090	4542	4055	3618	3220	2856	2520	2208	1917	26
27	1.7270	1.2188	0.9910	8424	7318	6438	5706	5081	4534	4048	3611	3214	2850	2515	2203	1913	27
28	1.7112	1.2139	0.9881	8403	7302	6425	5695	5071	4525	4040	3604	3208	2845	2509	2198	1908	28
29	1.6960	1.2090	0.9852	8382	7286	6412	5684	5061	4516	4032	3597	3201	2839	2504	2193	1903	29
30	1.6812	1.2041	0.9823	8361	7270	6398	5673	5051	4508	4025	3590	3195	2833	2499	2188	1899	30
31	1.6670	1.1993	0.9794	8341	7254	6385	5662	5042	4499	4017	3583	3189	2827	2493	2183	1894	31
32	1.6532	1.1946	0.9765	8320	7238	6372	5651	5032	4491	4010	3577	3183	2821	2488	2178	1890	32
33	1.6398	1.1899	0.9737	8300	7222	6359	5640	5023	4482	4002	3570	3176	2816	2483	2173	1885	33
34	1.6269	1.1852	0.9708	8279	7206	6346	5629	5013	4474	3995	3563	3170	2810	2477	2168	1880	34
35	1.6143	1.1806	0.9680	8259	7190	6333	5618	5003	4466	3987	3556	3164	2804	2472	2164	1875	35
36	1.6021	1.1761	0.9652	8239	7174	6320	5607	4994	4457	3979	3549	3157	2798	2467	2159	1871	36
37	1.5902	1.1716	0.9625	8219	7159	6307	5596	4984	4449	3972	3542	3151	2793	2461	2154	1866	37
38	1.5786	1.1671	0.9597	8199	7143	6294	5585	4975	4440	3964	3535	3145	2787	2456	2149	1862	38
39	1.5673	1.1627	0.9570	8179	7128	6282	5574	4965	4432	3057	3520	3139	2781	2451	2144	1057	39
40	1.5563	1.1584	0.9542	8159	7112	6269	5563	4956	4424	3949	3522	3133	2775	2445	2139	1852	40
41	1.5456	1.1540	0.9515	8140	7097	6256	5552	4947	4415	3942	3515	3126	2770	2440	2134	1848	41
42	1.5351	1.1498	0.9488	8120	7081	6243	5541	4937	4407	3934	3508	3120	2764	2435	2129	1843	42
43	1.5249	1.1455	0.9462	8101	7066	6231	5531	4928	4399	3927	3501	3114	2758	2430	2124	1838	43
44	1.5149	1.1413	0.9435	8081	7050	6218	5520	4918	4390	3919	3495	3108	2753	2424	2119	1834	44
45	1.5051	1.1372	0.9409	8062	7035	6205	5509	4909	4382	3912	3488	3102	2747	2419	2114	1829	45
46	1.4956	1.1331	0.9383	8043	7020	6193	5498	4900	4374	3905	3481	3096	2741	2414	2109	1825	46
47	1.4863	1.1290	0.9356	8023	7005	6180	5488	4890	4365	3897	3475	3089	2736	2409	2104	1820	47
48	1.4771	1.1249	0.9330	8004	6990	6168	5477	4881	4357	3890	3468	3083	2730	2403	2099	1816	48
49	1.4682	1.1209	0.9305	7985	6975	6155	5466	4872	4349	3882	3461	3077	2724	2398	2095	1811	49
50	1.4594	1.1170	0.9279	7966	6960	6143	5456	4863	4341	3875	3455	3071	2719	2393	2090	1806	50
51	1.4508	1.1130	0.9254	7947	6945	6131	5445	4853	4333	3868	3448	3065	2713	2388	2085	1802	51
52	1.4424	1.1091	0.9228	7929	6930	6118	5435	4844	4324	3860	3441	3059	2707	2382	2080	1797	52
53	1.4341	1.1053	0.9203	7910	6915	6106	5424	4835	4316	3853	3435	3053	2702	2377	2075	1793	53
54	1.4260	1.1015	0.9178	7891	6900	6094	5414	4826	4308	3846	3428	3047	2696	2372	2070	1788	54
55	1.4180	1.0977	0.9153	7873	6885	6081	5403	4817	4300	3838	3421	3041	2691	2367	2065	1784	55
56	1.4102	1.0939	0.9128	7854	6871	6069	5393	4808	4292	3831	3415	3035	2685	2362	2061	1779	56
57	1.4025	1.0902	0.9104	7836	6856	6057	5382	4799	4284	3824	3408	3028	2679	2356	2056	1774	57
58	1.3949	1.0865	0.9079	7818	6841	6045	5372	4789	4276	3817	3401	3022	2674	2351	2051	1770	58
59	1.3875	1.0828	0.9055	7800	6827	0633	5361	4780	4268	3809	3395	3016	2668	2346	2046	1765	59
	0	1	2	3	4	5	6	7	8	9	10	11	12	13	14	15.	

rush through them in order to get on to the more interesting work of setting up the birth chart should be resisted. It is far more frustrating to find later on that the birth chart is not correct, that a planet has been entered in the wrong sign or house, for example. Errors tend to occur in the following instances:

Addition and subtraction in general, particularly since sexagesimal and decimal sums are necessary.

Calculation of the correct Daily Motion. The listed Daily Motions of the Planets on pages 26–28 of *Raphael's Ephemerides* sometimes contain errors and should only be used as a cross-check.

Selection of the correct interval from or to Midnight and to or from Noon.

Copy Errors, in transferring one set of figures to another area or page or in copying positions from the ephemeris correctly.

Planetary positions calculated by Proportional Logarithms are reasonably accurate. Certainly, if the birth time is not known precisely, they are perfectly adequate. However, at times it does occur that there is a discrepancy of a minute if using both a Midnight and a Noon ephemeris as a cross-check. Refer to the position of the Sun in the following examples on pages 108 and 109. Unless absolute accuracy is required, as in the instance of Progressions, Transits or Harmonics, it is optional which position to take. Of course, this quandary can be solved by resorting to an electronic calculator or computer which allow for calculations of the Sun and Moon to the second, or planetary positions to tenths of a minute.

Procedure for Calculating the Positions of the Planets at Birth Using an Electronic Calculator

The *algorithms* (formulae for electronic calculators) given in *The Astrology Workbook* are suitable for the average calculator that incorporates a memory function. With practice, the positions of the planets can be tapped out very quickly. It is possible to purchase a calculator that allows for conversion to angular units, or hours, minutes and seconds, at the touch of a button. If using a calculator with a sexagesimal conversion, it is not necessary to convert degrees, hours, minutes and seconds to decimals as given in the algorithms on page 110.

Procedure for Calculating the Positions of the Planets at Birth
Using Proportional Logarithms

Interval *from* or *to* Midnight ____________ Interval *to* or *from* Noon ____________

PLANET (Insert Zodiacal Sign)	☉	☽	☿	♀	♂	♃
MOTION in 24 Hour Period						
Log of Daily Motion						
Log of INTERVAL (Always) PLUS						
Addition of Logs						
USING MIDNIGHT EPHEMERIS LONGITUDE at MIDNIGHT						
a.m.(PLUS)/p.m.(MINUS)*						
USING NOON EPHEMERIS LONGITUDE at NOON						
a.m.(MINUS)/p.m.(PLUS)*						
PLANET'S POSITION AT BIRTH GMT						
Birth Data						

* Reverse PLUS or MINUS if Planet is Retrograde

LIST OF PLANETS IN ZODIACAL AND DEGREE ORDER											
♈	♉	♊	♋	♌	♍	♎	♏	♐	♑	♒	♓

PROCEDURE FOR CALCULATING THE POSITIONS OF THE PLANETS AT BIRTH USING PROPORTIONAL LOGARITHMS FOR AM BIRTHS

Using a Midnight Ephemeris

Interval *from* or *to* Midnight *6hrs 58mins* Interval *to* or *from* Noon

PLANET (Insert Zodiacal Sign)	☉ ♐ ♑	☽ ♑ ♒	☿ ♑	♀ ♒	♂ ♍	♃ ♒
MOTION in 24 Hour Period	1° 01′	13° 25′	1° 29′	0° 37′	0° 25′	0° 13′
Log of Daily Motion	1.3730	2526	1.2041	1.5902	1.7604	2.0444
Log of INTERVAL (Always) PLUS	5372	5372	5372	5372	5372	5372
Addition of Logs	1.9102	7898	1.7413	2.1274	2.2976	2.5816
USING MIDNIGHT EPHEMERIS LONGITUDE at MIDNIGHT 22nd	° ′ 29 49	° ′ 28 38	° ′ 16 03	° ′ 12 00	° ′ 28 17	° ′ 4 18
a.m.(PLUS)/p.m. (MINUS)	0 18	3 54	0 26	0 11	0 07	0 04
USING NOON EPHEMERIS LONGITUDE at NOON						
a.m. (MINUS)/p.m. (PLUS)						
PLANET'S POSITION AT BIRTH GMT	0° 07′	2° 32′	16° 29′	12° 11′	28° 24′	4° 22′
Birth Data: 22/12/1949 at 6.58am						

Using a Noon Ephemeris

Interval *from* or *to* Midnight Interval *to* or *from* Noon *5hrs 02mins*

PLANET (Insert Zodiacal Sign)	☉ ♑	☽ ♒	☿ ♑	♀ ♒	♂ ♍	♃ ♒
MOTION in 24 Hour Period	1° 01′	13° 38′	1° 30′	0° 37′	0° 25′	0° 13′
Log of Daily Motion	1.3730	2456	1.2041	1.5902	1.7604	2.0444
Log of INTERVAL (Always) PLUS	6784	6784	6784	6784	6784	6784
Addition of Logs	2.0514	9240	1.8825	2.2686	2.4388	2.7228
USING MIDNIGHT EPHEMERIS LONGITUDE at MIDNIGHT	° ′	° ′	° ′	° ′	° ′	° ′
a.m. (PLUS)/p.m. (MINUS)						
USING NOON EPHEMERIS LONGITUDE at NOON 22nd	0 19	5 24	16 48	12 19	28 29	4 25
a.m.(MINUS)/p.m. (PLUS)	0 13	2 52	0 19	0 08	0 05	0 03
PLANET'S POSITION AT BIRTH GMT	0° 06′	2° 32′	16° 29′	12° 11′	28° 24′	4° 22′
Birth Data: 22/12/1949 at 6.58am						

LIST OF PLANETS IN ZODIACAL AND DEGREE ORDER

♈	♉	♊	♋	♌	♍	♎	♏	♐	♑	♒	♓
			♅ 3°06′ ℞	♇ 17°57′ ℞	♄ 19°23′	♆ 17°08′			☉ 0°07′	☽ 2°32′	
					♂ 28°24′				☿ 16°29′	♃ 4°22′	
										♀ 12°11′	

PROCEDURE FOR CALCULATING THE POSITIONS OF THE PLANETS AT BIRTH USING PROPORTIONAL LOGARITHMS FOR PM BIRTHS

Using a Midnight Ephemeris

Interval *from* or *to* Midnight *3hrs 27mins*   *Interval to* or *from* Noon

PLANET (Insert Zodiacal Sign)	☉ ♐	☽ ♋	☿ ♐	♀ ♒	♂ ♍	♃ ♒
MOTION in 24 Hour Period	1° 01′	12° 56′	1° 33′	0° 51′	0° 28′	0° 12′
Log of Daily Motion	1.3730	2685	1.1899	1.4508	1.7112	2.0792
Log of INTERVAL (Always) PLUS	8424	8424	8424	8424	8424	8424
Addition of Logs	2.2154	1.1109	2.0323	2.2932	2.5536	2.9216
USING MIDNIGHT EPHEMERIS LONGITUDE at MIDNIGHT 9th	° ′ 16 35	° ′ 25 56	° ′ 26 00	° ′ 2 21	° ′ 22 31	° ′ 1 35
a.m. (PLUS)/p.m.(MINUS)	0 09	1 51	0 13	0 07	0 04	0 01
USING NOON EPHEMERIS LONGITUDE at NOON						
a.m. (MINUS)/p.m. (PLUS)						
PLANET'S POSITION AT BIRTH GMT	16° 26′	24° 05′	25° 47′	2° 14′	22° 27′	1° 34
Birth Data: 8/12/1949 at 8.33pm						

Using a Noon Ephemeris

Interval *from* or *to* Midnight   Interval *to* or *from* Noon *8hrs 33mins*

PLANET (Insert Zodiacal Sign)	☉ ♐	☽ ♋	☿ ♐	♀ ♒	♂ ♍	♃ ♒
MOTION in 24 Hour Period	1° 01′	13° 02′	1° 34′	0° 51′	0° 28′	0° 12′
Log of Daily Motion	1.3730	2657	1.1852	1.4508	1.7112	2.0792
Log of INTERVAL (Always) PLUS	4482	4482	4482	4482	4482	4482
Addition of Logs	1.8212	7139	1.6334	1.8980	2.1594	2.5274
USING MIDNIGHT EPHEMERIS LONGITUDE at MIDNIGHT	° ′	° ′	° ′	° ′	° ′	° ′
a.m. (PLUS)/p.m. (MINUS)						
USING NOON EPHEMERIS LONGITUDE at NOON 8th	16 05	19 27	25 14	1 56	22 17	1 30
a.m. (MINUS)/p.m.(PLUS)	0 22	4 38	0 33	0 18	0 10	0 04
PLANET'S POSITION AT BIRTH GMT	16° 27′	24° 05′	25° 47′	2° 14′	22° 27′	1° 34′
Birth Data: 8/12/1949 at 8.33pm						

For details of calculations using an Electronic Calculator refer to page 110.

SUN'S POSITION USING ELECTRONIC CALCULATOR

INTERVAL 3 hours 27 minutes

27 ÷ 60 + 3 ÷ 24 = M + (0.14375)

DAILY MOTION 1° 00′ 56″ (or 60′ 56″)

56 ÷ 60 + 60 × MR = 8.75916[R]

− 8 (MINUS 8 minutes) × 60 = 45.549[R]

which is 8 minutes 46 seconds

SUN at MIDNIGHT (9th) p.m. (MINUS)	16° 35′ 02″ 8′ 46″
SUN at 8.33p.m.	16° 26′ 18″

LIST OF PLANETS IN ZODIACAL AND DEGREE ORDER

♈	♉	♊	♋	♌	♍	♎	♏	♐	♑	♒	♓
			♅ 3° 40′ ℞	♇ 18°07′	♄ 19°02′	♆ 16°53′		☉ 16°26′		♃ 1°34′	
			☽ 24°05′		♂ 22°27′			☿ 25°47′		♀ 2°14′	

SUN'S POSITION USING ELECTRONIC CALCULATOR

INTERVAL 8 hours 33 minutes

33 ÷ 60 + 8 ÷ 24 = M + (0.35625)

DAILY MOTION 1° 00′ 57″ (or 60′ 57″)

57 ÷ 60 +60 × MR = 21.7134375

− 21 (MINUS 21 minutes) × 60 = 42.80625

which is 21 minutes 43 seconds

SUN at NOON (8th) p.m. (PLUS)	16° 04′ 34″ 21′ 43″
SUN at 8.33p.m.	16° 26′ 17″

PROCEDURE FOR CALCULATING THE POSITIONS OF THE PLANETS AT BIRTH USING AN ELECTRONIC CALCULATOR WITH MEMORY FUNCTION

(Example: 6.58 a.m. 22 December 1949)

USING A MIDNIGHT EPHEMERIS

Based upon the INTERVAL FROM MIDNIGHT $\frac{\text{6 hours 58 minutes}}{\text{24 hours}}$,
commit the following bracketed formula to the calculator's MEMORY:

[58 (minutes) DIVIDE BY 60 PLUS 6 (hours) DIVIDE BY 24 (hours) EQUALS MEMORY PLUS]
(in symbols) [58 ÷ 60 + 60 ÷ 24 = M + (0.29027 etc.)]

SUN's Daily Motion 1° 01′ 09″ (Convert to Minutes) (i.e. 61 minutes 09 seconds)

9 (seconds) DIVIDE BY 60 PLUS 61 (minutes) MULTIPLIED BY MEMORY RECALL EQUALS (17.750 etc. minutes)
MINUS 17 (minutes) MULTIPLIED BY 60 EQUALS (45.029 etc. seconds) (round up)
(in symbols) 9 ÷ 60 + 61 × MR = (17.75) − 17 (mins) × 60 = (45.02) or 45 (secs)

SUN's Longitude at MIDNIGHT	29° 48′ 48″
INTERVAL *PLUS*	17° 45″
SUN's Longitude at 6.58 a.m.	0° 06′ 33″ *(0° 07′♑)*

MOON's Daily Motion 13° 25′

25 (minutes) DIVIDE BY 60 PLUS 13 (Degrees) MULTIPLIED BY MEMORY RECALL EQUALS (3.894 etc. Degrees)
MINUS 3 (Degrees) MULTIPLIED BY 60 EQUALS (53.673 etc. minutes) (round up)
(in symbols) 25 ÷ 60 + 13 × MR = (3.89) − 3 (degs) × 60 = (53.67) or 54 (mins)

MOON's Longitude at MIDNIGHT	28° 38′♑
INTERVAL *PLUS*	3° 54′
MOON's Longitude at 6.58 a.m.	2° 32′♒

MERCURY's Daily Motion 1° 29′ (Convert to minutes (i.e. 89 minutes)

89 (minutes) MULTIPLIED BY MEMORY RECALL EQUALS
(in symbols) 89 × MR = (25.834 etc. minutes) or 26 minutes

MERCURY's Longitude at MIDNIGHT	16° 03′♑
INTERVAL PLUS	26′
MERCURY's Longitude at 6.58 a.m.	16° 29′♑

Re Decimal Places for calculations involving MINUTES only. If less than 0.5 use existing whole number. If more than 0.5, round up to next whole figure.

USING A NOON EPHEMERIS

Based upon the INTERVAL TO NOON $\frac{\text{5 hours 02 minutes}}{\text{24 hours}}$,
commit the following bracketed formula to the calculator's MEMORY:

[2 (minutes) DIVIDE BY 60 PLUS 5 (hours) DIVIDE BY 24 (hours) EQUALS MEMORY PLUS]
(in symbols) [2 ÷ 60 + 5 ÷ 24 = M + (0.2097 etc.)]

SUN's Daily Motion 1° 01′ 08″ (Convert to Minutes) (i.e. 61 minutes 08 seconds)

(Refer to example for MIDNIGHT EPHEMERIS)
(in symbols) 8 ÷ 60 + 61 × MR = (12.8210 etc.) (use whole numbers only) − 12 (minutes × 60 = (49.2611 etc.) or 49 (seconds)

SUN's Longitude at NOON	0° 19′ 22″
INTERVAL MINUS	12′ 49″
SUN's Longitude at 6.58 a.m.	0° 06′ 33″ *(0° 07′♑)*

MOON'S Daily Motion 13° 37′ 59″

(in symbols) 59 (seconds) ÷ 60 + 37 (minutes) ÷ 60 + 13 (degrees) × MR = (2.8591 etc.) − 2 (degrees) × 60 = (51.5492 etc.) − 51 (minutes) × 60 = (32.9569 etc.) or 33 (seconds)

MOON'S Longitude at NOON	5° 24′ 02″
INTERVAL *MINUS*	2° 51′ 33″
MOON'S Longitude at 6.58 a.m.	2° 32′ 29″ *(2° 32′♒)*

MERCURY's Daily Motion 90 minutes
(in symbols) 90 × MR = (18.87 etc.) (19 minutes)

VENUS' Daily Motion	0° 37′ minutes 37 × MR = (7.75 etc.) (0° 08 minutes)
MARS Daily Motion	0° 25′ minutes 25 × MR = (5.24 etc.) (0° 05 minutes)
JUPITER Daily Motion	0° 13′ minutes 13 × MR = (2.72 etc.) (0° 03 minutes)

SATURN, URANUS, NEPTUNE and PLUTO move so slowly that their rate of motion in relation to the birth time can be calculated in one's head.

COMPARE PLANETARY POSITIONS WITH THOSE CALCULATED BY PROPORTIONAL LOGARITHMS

Using the List of Planets in Zodiacal and Degree Order, enter the planets around the chart as below (see Chapter 4, page 42) and Finding the Local Sidereal Time to Determine Ascendant and Descendent (see page 57).

LIST OF PLANETS IN ZODIACAL AND DEGREE ORDER

♈	♉	♊	♋	♌	♍	♎	♏	♐	♑	♒	♓
			♅ 3° 06′ ℞	♇ 17° 57′ ℞	♄ 19° 23′	♆ 17° 08′			☉ 0° 07′	☽ 2° 32′	
					♂ 28° 24′				☿ 16° 29′	♃ 4° 22′	
										♀ 12° 11′	

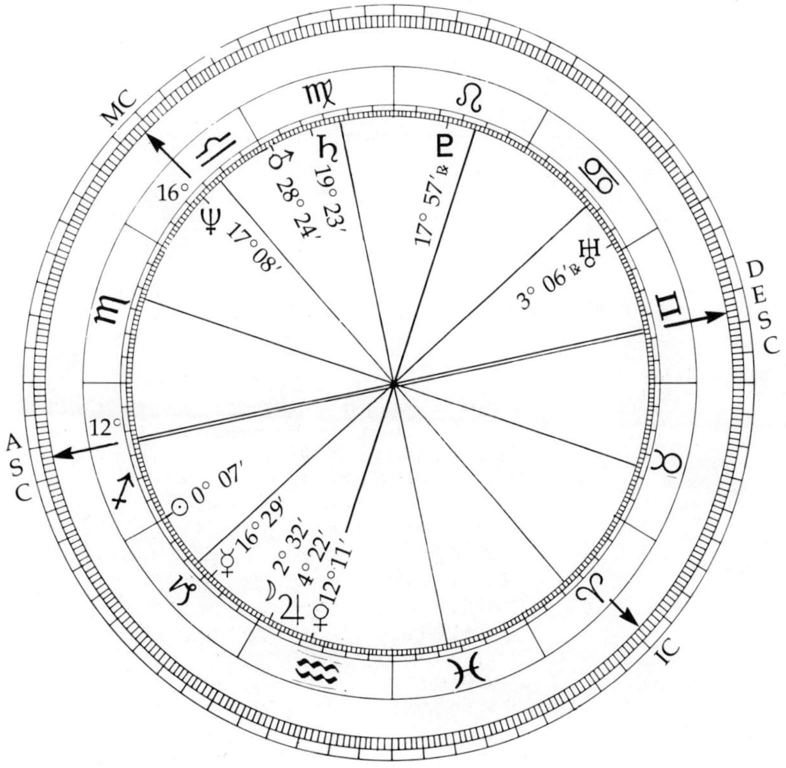

Figure 33 An example chart

Figure 34 shows an example of a computerized birth chart (*reduced in size*). Note that the computer has not been programmed to show the Midheaven on the chart form according to the Equal House system. However, it is listed at the bottom of the column giving the Planet's positions. A slight disparity can be observed in the positions for the planets amounting to a minute, as in the instance of the Moon, between those given in the previous examples. While it does depend upon how accurately the computer has been programmed, the computer offers greater precision than the ephemeris. However, such precision is only required for advanced work. Not all computer print-outs provide a list of the planet's Daily Motions such as that shown in Figure 33.

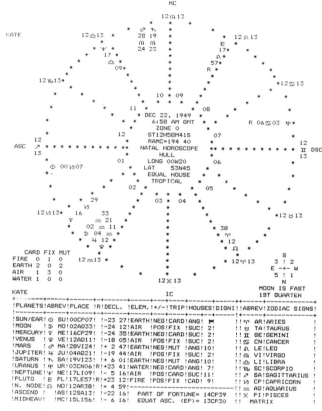

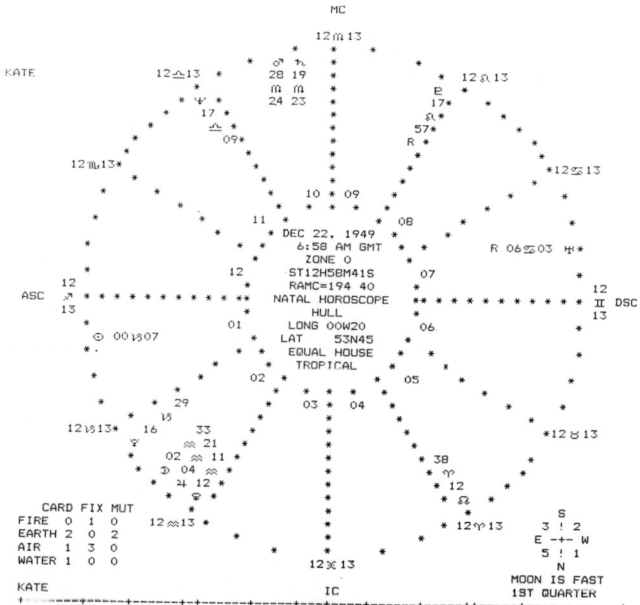

KATE

PLANETS	ABREV	PLACE	R	DECL.	ELEM.	+/-	TRIP	HOUSES	DIGNI
SUN/EAR	☉ SU	00CP07		-23 27	EARTH	NEG	CARD	ANG	[illegible]
MOON	☽ MO	02AQ33		-24 12	AIR	POS	FIX	SUC	2
MERCURY	☿ ME	16CP29		-24 35	EARTH	NEG	CARD	SUC	2
VENUS	♀ VE	12AQ11		-18 05	AIR	POS	FIX	SUC	2
MARS	♂ MA	28VI24		+ 2 47	EARTH	NEG	MUT	ANG	10
JUPITER	♃ JU	04AQ21		-19 44	AIR	POS	FIX	SUC	2
SATURN	♄ SA	19VI23		+ 6 01	EARTH	NEG	MUT	ANG	10
URANUS	♅ UR	03CN06	R	+23 41	WATER	NEG	CARD	ANG	7
NEPTUNE	♆ NE	17LI09		- 5 16	AIR	POS	CARD	SUC	11
PLUTO	♇ PL	17LE57	R	+23 12	FIRE	POS	FIX	CAD	9
N. NODE	☊ NO	12AR38		+ 4 59					
ASCEND	AS	12SA13		-22 16	PART OF FORTUNE= 14CP39				
MIDHEAV	MC	15LI56		- 6 16	EQUAT ASC. (EP)= 13CP30				

ABREV	ZODIAC SIGNS
♈ AR	ARIES
♉ TA	TAURUS
♊ GE	GEMINI
♋ CN	CANCER
♌ LE	LEO
♍ VI	VIRGO
♎ LI	LIBRA
♏ SC	SCORPIO
♐ SA	SAGITTARIUS
♑ CP	CAPRICORN
♒ AQ	AQUARIUS
♓ PI	PISCES
MATRIX	

Figure 34 A computerized birth chart (Reduced in size)

CHART DATA-SCOPE FOR KATE

ASPECTS PER PLANET

CODE	PLANET NAME	R	DAILY MOTION	£
SU	00CP07		1 01 07	6
MO	02AQ33		13 18 10	5
ME	16CP29		1 29 25	5
VE	12AQ11		36 56	7
MA	28VI24		24 56	6
JU	04AQ21		12 59	4
SA	19VI23		00 52	3
UR	03CN06	R	02 35	5
NE	17LI09		00 55	7
PL	17LE57	R	00 52	8
NO	12AR38		03 00	7
AS	12SA13		00 00	5
MC	15LI56		00 00	6

HOUSES

PLANETS PER HOUSE	
01=12SA13	1
02=12CP13	4
03=12AQ13	0
04=12PI13	0
05=12AR13	1
06=12TA13	0
07=12GE13	1
08=12CN13	0
09=12LE13	1
10=12VI13	2
11=12LI13	1
12=12SC13	0

Figure 35 A computer print-out of birth data

Chapter 6
Visual Energies

The aspects are the angular relationships of the planets to one another. They are of enormous significance in astrological interpretation for they serve to indicate the most subtle alterations in the quality of the principles symbolized by the planets and, therefore, the smallest differences discernible in the individual personality. It is usual practice to draw in the aspects on the birth chart, linking up those planets which are said to be 'in orb' with one another. This creates a mass of interweaving, interlocking lines which illustrate the most subtle factors of the human personality.

Since everything in astrology is based upon relationship, the fact that an aspect links one planet with another reveals something concerning the *quality* of those individual planets. In traditional astrology we have been taught that certain aspects like certain planets are malefic, 'difficult', or benefic, 'easy', whereas modern astrology maintains that if a single aspect is said to symbolize a facet of personality then no aspect, as such, can possibly be all good or all bad.

In view of the revolutionary character of harmonics, it is surprising that many astrologers still believe that the division of aspects into major and minor means that major aspects are more important and stronger, while minor aspects are less important or 'weaker'. Major aspects are not more significant than minor aspects but are evocative of the different kinds of energy that it is possible to sense about an individual just as it is possible to hear the changes from the major to minor keys in music. The aspects can be likened to music or light, for they are also of a wave formation.

John Addey's work on harmonics has shown us pictorially the wave formation of the aspects that are used in astrology. In time to come, it may be possible that the wave formation depicted by Kirlian photography can also be linked with the differing aspects that reflect the energy of the personality, for they both provide visual means of assessing the unique manner in which the individual expresses the Life Force.

The many different kinds of aspects used in astrology tell of the *quality of energy* between the planetary bodies involved. It is understood today that the whole universe is a vast field of energy that dilates and contracts. Astrophysicists and astronomers are still undecided whether or not the universe is expanding and, in fact, know little concerning the vastness, shape or the origins of our universe. Nevertheless, it is possible to understand it in certain terms even though its vastness can be beyond our comprehension. The enormous size of our galaxy shrinks by comparison with a hypergalaxy comprising approximately 10,000 such galaxies. The phenomenon of expansion and contraction was first recognized in 1841 by Christian Doppler and became known as the 'Doppler Effect'.

The Doppler Effect applies to both sound and light, or indeed anything which has any kind of wave motion. As a sound comes nearer to us, it is more easily recognized as a high pitch because of the short sound waves it emits, while long waves are sensed at a low pitch. Hence the sound changes according to distance. The same yardstick applies to light and is studied more particularly by astrophysicists, who have observed that an object moving away from us shows a reddish glow whereas one moving towards us shows its light as shifting towards violet. This is known as the 'Red Shift'.

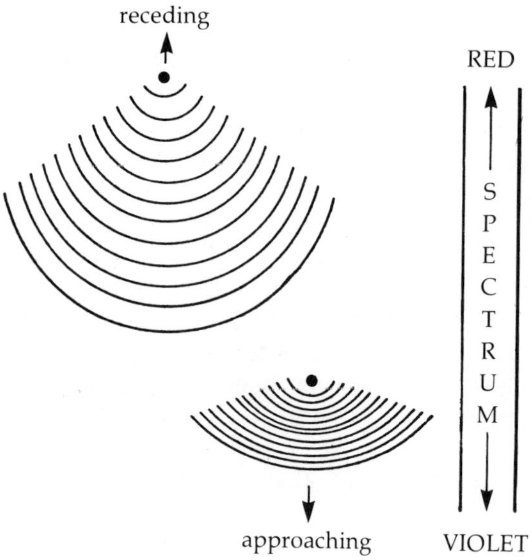

The Doppler Effect

As science moves closer to the esoteric concept that everthing in the universe is formulated of the same matter, evidence is being accumulated of the reality of Oneness. It is well known that the patterning of atoms and molecules in our physical bodies closely resemble the solar system. If there is, indeed, an integral relationship between all things in the universe, and our solar system can be described as the means of relating to and comprehending the quality and character of the universe, it follows that any alterations in the distances of the planets in our solar system as their orbits take them closer or further away from one another could also be linked to the Doppler Effect shifting from one end of the spectrum to the other. Contemplated as visual energies, in terms of wave formations or seen against the background of the spectrum vis à vis the Doppler Effect, the various qualities of energy depicted by the aspects can become more comprehensible.

If the Life Force is movement it may be understood to be either expanding, that is moving away from us, which according to the Doppler Effect shows that the frequency of light waves per second will have lessened and the lines of the spectrum have shifted towards the red end, or, be contracting, moving towards us, which would be a similar shift towards the violet end of the spectrum. We can also visualize that whatever may be seen to be expanding or contracting between any of the planetary bodies will create different kinds of qualities of energies. We can then visualize that the energy fields lying between the planetary bodies must be either expanding or contracting.

On the strength of a report by an astronomer (he refused to be named) who had rejected the statistics without actually having seen them, the discoveries of electrical engineer John H. Nelson were subjected to a great deal of ridicule by professional astronomers. As a result of their attitude no astronomical journal would publish his findings. Nelson had found that radio disturbance caused by magnetic storms usually occurred when two planets were in conjunction, opposition or square aspect to the Sun. He also found that disturbance-free periods were formed when planets were in either sextile or trine aspect to the Sun. This unquestionably concurs with the traditional view that the aspects could be seen to be either 'malefic' — difficult, disharmonious, or 'benefic' — easy, harmonious. Unfortunately, newcomers to astrology have always found it extremely difficult to comprehend the aspects according to these terms. It is a fact that the bulk of astrological references and principles can only be truly understood in the light of practical experience, but this means that many potentially fine astrologers give up further work confronted with so little really clear guidance. Perhaps some further light might be shed by visualizing the aspects as a system of understanding energy according to how much it expands or contracts.

The orbiting planets are constantly forming aspects one to another as they move from the beginning of the cycle at conjunction (0°) to the completion of the cycle at the following conjunction. Using a computer to trace the patterning of the planets' orbits in relation to one another, a ten minute film was created called *Patterns of Existence,* in which the complex orbits revealed divinely simple symbols which we take for granted in our daily lives. The orbit of the Earth in relation to the planet Venus produces a perfect heart shape. The joint orbits of Jupiter and Uranus create the six-pointed Star of David among many other familiar patterns. Such formations naturally take many years to accomplish, particularly those involving the slower-moving planets of Saturn through to Pluto.

Reminiscent of the Doppler Effect is the ebb and flow of the various aspects in the birth chart. Planetary movement towards the point when an aspect is 'exact', is described as 'applying'; once exactitude has been reached, the planets begin to move apart, referred to as 'separating'. At exactitude (allow 1° orb) an aspect is at its most powerful, but, it is generally accepted that an applying aspect is stronger than when separating. Planets approaching conjunction of any of the Four Angles, in an anti-clockwise direction, are similarly noted as being stronger than when separating.

Such usage of the aspects has been empirically established during the past 5,000 years or so and is now being borne out by the researches of metallurgist Nick Kollerstrom.

A planet is said to be 'angular' when within 8° orb (10° for Sun or Moon) of one of the Four Angles. The quality of energy signified by such a planet can dominate the birth chart and is correspondingly found to be a noticeable feature of the personality.

TABLE OF ASPECTS

Divisions of 360° circle	Symbol	Name of Aspect	Degree of Arc	Orb Allowance	
1	☌	Conjunction	0°	8°	MAJOR ASPECTS (INC ⚹)
2	☍	Opposition	180°	8°	
3	△	Trine	120°	8°	
4	□	Square	90°	8°	
5	Q	Quintile	72°	2°	MINOR ASPECTS (APART FROM ⚹)
2/5	BQ	Bi-quintile	144°	2°	
6	⚹	Sextile	60°	4°	
7	1/7	Septile	51°26′	1°	
8	∟	Semi-square	45°	2°	
3/8	⚼	Sesquiquadrate	135°	2°	
9	N	Novile	40°	1°	
10	1/10	Decile	36°	1°	
111	1/11	Undecile	32°43′	1°	
12	⚺	Semi-sextile	30°	2°	
5/12	⚻	Quincunx	150°	2°	

For major aspects involving the Sun and Moon allow 10° orb

For minor aspects involving the Sun and Moon allow 3° orb

For sextile aspects involving the Sun and Moon allow 6° orb

It is useful to record on the aspect grid of the birth chart the following:

a for applying;
s for separating;
e for exact;
w where the orbs' allowance is at its widest.

Orbs' allowances for planetary aspects merely provide a guideline, but it is agreed amongst astrological practitioners that there can be no rigid demarcation of when an aspect begins or ends its influence, for the cycles are like all things in nature and never clearly defined. It is not unusual for an astrologer to accept a much wider orb in certain instances because that astrologer 'feels' it is there. By the same token, astrologers may be 'mean' when it comes to certain other aspects.

A table is provided citing the main aspects in use today but you will have to understand their fluidity in the light of your own experience. The orbs cited are those most commonly recognized in this country.

Harmonics

The aspects and the lines drawn in on the birth chart are our means of seeing the initial vibration of the human soul. The warp and woof of the pattern gives us a dimension of the reality of that potential; yet consistent work with the birth chart causes the astrologer to reflect that we are in a sense simply scratching the surface and there is an awareness that there is a need to examine the vibrations of the chart more particularly. That is not to say that only very little can be gained from examining the birth chart, for when an astrologer refers to the 'scratching the surface' s/he is nevertheless probably capable of examining the human personality in finer detail than by any other means available at this time.

Human nature, being what it is, inspires the astrologer to delve even further and to continually perfect his art. At least that is how it should be! Until the last ten years in astrology's history, we have been forced to accept certain methods because there did not appear to be any other. The major breakthrough came with John Addey's work on harmonics and we are fortunate that in spite of his ailing health, he was able to publish his illuminating work *Harmonics in Astrology* in 1976.

Essentially a mystic, John Addey sought to integrate spiritual values with modern scientific methods and while in pursuit of testing the veracity of traditional astrological values, had the sagacity to truly appreciate and comprehend what the mass of accumulated statistical data really implied. Twenty years of research produced the dawning of a new era in astrology. With his typical modesty John Addey was aware of the privilege he was afforded in being able to initiate this most vital stage in astrology's evolution.

It is true to say that many astrologers veer sharply away from the study of harmonics in the belief that it is overly scientifically orientated. This is mostly because they look at the vast statistical work which paved the way for John Addey's discoveries. There is also the false impression that harmonics is complex. While harmonic charts and the whole inference of harmonic periods initially sounds daunting, it is truly no more difficult than to attune one's ear to appreciate differing forms of music. For music of the soul is what we are actually able to witness in the form of related harmonic charts. In a manner akin to that of the pathologist who is able to examine the condition of the physical body by peering at a smear of blood under a microscope, so the astrologer can further refine his understanding of the human soul by analysing any series of harmonic charts that he might wish.

In ancient times there was no separation between philosophy, the physical body, music and mathematics, or indeed, anything in nature or in Man. The knowledge that is said to have been handed to Pythagoras from Apollo and Orpheus contained the fundamental unity of number in the belief that music is the expression of number in sound. We no longer see any rift between the harmonies in music and mathematics, especially when it is becoming usual practice for the musician to compose using computer programmes incorporating the scales' twelve tones. However, while this connection can be appreciated, it was John Addey who recognized the need to return to the fundamental science of numbers in all its symbolism for, in essence, this is harmonics and astrology.

The Pythagorean view of beauty involved the perfect proportions between differing parts and a relationship between those parts and the whole form. This directly links with our knowledge of astrology in which each part is an intrinsic sequence pertaining to the whole. By the same token this yardstick may be attributed to any involvement of the mind, body or spirit in the arts or sciences.

John Addey's researches treat astrological concepts as having one common theme. He describes any of the fundamental circles, the zodiac, the houses and the planetary cycles, as 'Cosmic Periods'. The traditional system of defining the angular distances of the planets as the aspects stems from *divisions* of the 360° circle by two, three, four, five, and so forth. Addey saw that by *multiplying* the 360° circle by two, three, four, five, and so forth, the birth chart is made to *vibrate to a particular number*.

Multiplying all the features of the birth chart by a particular number creates a resulting harmonic chart which bears the quality of that number. It means that this chart can be interpreted according to the symbolism of that number. Fascinatingly, the chart will also relate to the corresponding year in the life. For example, the multiplication of the whole birth chart (which is the first harmonic), including all its parts, the angles and planetary positions, by two creates a second harmonic chart in which any planets that were in opposition (180° apart) will be seen as being in conjunction (0°). It will also refer to the quality of the second year in life. Multiplication by three will produce the similar effect with trine aspects (120° apart) appearing as conjunctions (0°) and correspond to the third year. Multiplication by four does the same with squares (90° apart) corresponding to the fourth year, by five with the quintiles (72° apart) and so forth. In this manner the respective aspects are magnified so that their intensity, or emphasis, in the birth chart or the individual personality can be seen as if examining them under a microscope.

By combining the knowledge of number with astrology, the likely nature of any year in the life may be examined. The interpretation of the higher harmonics can be aided by adopting the numerological principle of reducing the number to absolutes (1 to 9). For example, the 36th harmonic will describe the quality of the number 36, which is a multiple of the creative number 3 as follows: 36 in which the digits can be added, 3 + 6 equalling 9, together with the factors surrounding the meaning of the number 4 since 4 × 9 equals 36. This shows that the 36th year would be a time in which any creative potential will find actual expression and outlet. The 36th harmonic chart would reveal the details of this according to the individual personality.

Many astrologers use such harmonic charts to endorse and refine their work. Hindu astrology has long used a similar system of sixteen subdivision charts, known as Shodasavargas, which concentrate mainly on the Navamsa or ninth-harmonic chart. Until the nature of the birth chart is fully appreciated, it is unwise to make use of harmonic charts. There are now two books which the keen student should acquire when ready to embark on this specialized area, John Addey's *Harmonics in Astrology*, and David Hamblin's *Harmonic Charts*.

The circle or 0 (zero) is without beginning or end, for it is timelessly eternal, complete unto itself. At zero the circle commences in accord with the commencement of the circle of the zodiac at 0° ♈. The aspect of *conjunction* expresses this concept of being everything yet timelessly perfect; with the coming together of two or more planets in the same area of the zodiac, they adopt the same quality and symbolism associated with the starting point, zero becoming a focal point from which energy must stem. As a neutral aspect the conjunction, involving two or more planets, will be amended by aspects with other planetary bodies.

Constructed as it is from the time and place of birth, the birth chart is the first division of the 360° circle and, therefore, may also be termed the first harmonic (see page 30). Taking its cue from the symbolic starting point of the zodiac, 0° ♈, when energy expression is said to be at its peak (see page 29), the first harmonic in principle, expresses the quality of the first year and the potential for the entire life-span. In scientific and medical circles there is an increasing acceptance that the first year of our lives is of vital importance in the creation of the conditions what will colour the personality for the remainder of our life-span. The influence and the power of the first harmonic is clear. In numerology the number one expresses the creative principle as the Idea, for it is from this that the first movement of life is generated. The self-conscious mind in the form of a human being has been created with the readiness to live out the life experience according to that individual's needs.

PROCEDURE FOR CALCULATING HARMONIC POSITIONS USING AN ELECTRONIC CALCULATOR WITH MEMORY FUNCTION

When performing the calculations for a *single* Harmonic chart the Memory need not be used. Calculate each position independently as follows:

For example: 7th HARMONIC
MERCURY 16° 29′ CAPRICORN equals 286° 29′ in Absolute Longitude

29 (minutes) DIVIDE BY 60 PLUS 286 (degrees) DIVIDE BY 360
(gives position according to proportion of 360° circle)
MUTLIPLY BY 7 (7th Harmonic)
EQUALS 5.570, etc.

MINUS whole Numbers 5 (circles) MULTIPLY BY 360
(remainder's proportion of 360° circle)
EQUALS 205.383, etc.

MINUS 205 (degrees) MULTIPLY BY 60 EQUALS 22.999, etc. (minutes)
THEREFORE 205° 23′ (Absolute Longitude) EQUALS *25° 23′ LIBRA*

(in symbols) 29 ÷ 60 + 286 ÷ 360 × 7 = (5.570, etc.)
−5 × 360 (circles) = (205.383, etc.)
−205 (degrees) × 60 = (22.999, etc. minutes)
205° 23′ or *25° 23′ LIBRA*

The 7th Harmonic Chart is set up in the usual way commencing from the 7th Harmonic Ascendant. As given in the example below (Figure 36) using the data from p. 111

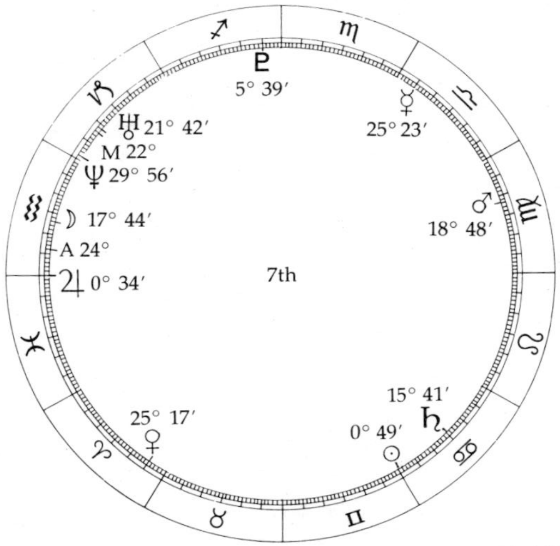

Figure 36 A harmonic chart

Harmonic afficionados who wish to set up a series of Harmonic charts may well find it saves time to calculate a *run* of Harmonic positions by making use of the Electronic Calculator's Memory as follows:

JUPITER 4° 22′ AQUARIUS equals 304° 22′ in Absolute Longitude

Commit the following bracketed formula to the calculator's Memory:

[22 (minutes) DIVIDE BY 60 PLUS 304 (degrees) DIVIDE BY 360 (proportion of 360 circle) EQUALS MEMORY PLUS]
(in symbols) [22 ÷ 60 + 304 ÷ 360 = M+ (0.84546, etc.)]

Jupiter's 3rd Harmonic
3 (Harmonic Number) TIMES MEMORY RECALL EQUALS 2.536, etc.

MINUS 2 (whole numbers ie circles) TIMES 360 (proportion or circle)
EQUALS 193.099, etc.

MINUS 193 (degrees) TIMES 60 EQUALS 5.999, etc. (minutes) 193° 06′
(Absolute Longitude or 13° 06′ Libra

(in symbols) 3 × MR = 2.536, etc.
−2 × 360 = 193.099, etc.
−193 × 60 = 5.999, etc.
193° 06′ or 13° 06′ Libra

Jupiter's 4th Harmonic 4 × MR = 3.381, etc.
−3 × 360 = 137.466, etc.
−137 × 60 = 27.9r
137° 28′ or 17° 28′ Leo

Jupiter's 8th Harmonic 8 × MR = 6.763, etc.
−6 × 360 = 274.93r
−274 × 60 = 55.9r
274° 56′ or 4° 56′ Capricorn

Jupiter's 35th Harmonic 35 × MR = 29.591, etc.
−29 × 360 = 212.833, etc.
−212 × 60 = 49.9r
212° 50′ or 2° 50′ Scorpio

and so forth

CONVERSION TABLE FOR ABSOLUTE LONGITUDE

°	♈	♉	♊	♋	♌	♍	♎	♏	♐	♑	♒	♓	°
0	0	30	60	90	120	150	180	210	240	270	300	330	0
1	1	31	61	91	121	151	181	211	241	271	301	331	1
2	2	32	62	92	122	152	182	212	242	272	302	332	2
3	3	33	63	93	123	153	183	213	243	273	303	333	3
4	4	34	64	94	124	154	184	214	244	274	304	344	4
5	5	35	65	95	125	155	185	215	245	275	305	335	5
6	6	36	66	96	126	156	186	216	246	276	306	336	6
7	7	37	67	97	127	157	187	217	247	277	307	337	7
8	8	38	68	98	128	158	188	218	248	278	308	338	8
9	9	39	69	99	129	159	189	219	249	279	309	339	9
10	10	40	70	100	130	160	190	220	250	280	310	340	10
11	11	41	71	101	131	161	191	221	251	281	311	341	11
12	12	42	72	102	132	162	192	222	252	282	312	342	12
13	13	43	73	103	133	163	193	223	253	283	313	343	13
14	14	44	74	104	134	164	194	224	254	284	314	344	14
15	15	45	75	105	135	165	195	225	255	285	315	345	15
16	16	46	76	106	136	166	196	226	256	286	316	346	16
17	17	47	77	107	137	167	197	227	257	287	317	347	17
18	18	48	78	108	138	168	198	228	258	288	318	348	18
19	19	49	79	109	139	169	199	229	259	289	319	349	19
20	20	50	80	110	140	170	200	230	260	290	320	350	20
21	21	51	81	111	141	171	201	231	261	291	321	351	21
22	22	52	82	112	142	172	202	232	262	292	322	352	22
23	23	53	83	113	143	173	203	233	263	293	323	353	23
24	24	54	84	114	144	174	204	234	264	294	324	354	24
25	25	55	85	115	145	175	205	235	265	295	325	355	25
26	26	56	86	116	146	176	206	236	266	296	326	356	26
27	27	57	87	117	147	177	207	237	267	297	327	357	27
28	28	58	88	118	148	178	208	238	268	298	328	358	28
29	29	59	89	119	149	179	209	239	269	299	329	359	29
°	♈	♉	♊	♋	♌	♍	♎	♏	♐	♑	♒	♓	°

Use right or left-handed columns nearest to zodiacal Sign in question. Minutes are not affected. For example:

15° 23′ Scorpio = 225° 23′ Absolute Longitude

28° 59′ Pisces = 358° 59′ Absolute Longitude

Interpretation of the Aspects

All aspects are angular units of the fundamental zodiacal circle. There are twelve aspects, which is most appropriate in view of the twelve signs of the zodiac. However, we have found, thanks to John Addey's work on harmonics, that the circle of 360° may be subdivided 359 times and, in time, there may be a review of the number of aspects used, and indeed, a reassessment of how they shall be used in future. As we are currently in the transition stage of utilizing the best that has come to us by tradition and examining the principles of astrology in the light of its inherent harmonics, we should examine the known aspects in the context of our knowledge of the 360° circle.

Major aspects tend to be more dynamically obvious whereas minor aspects reflect the more subtle qualities in the nature. It is as if the shorter, or more numerous, number of waves in the 360° circle, created by minor aspects, serve to indicate the higher frequencies in the nature, so that it is the more highly strung or more highly tuned type of personality that has a chart with more minor aspect prevalent or noticable by virtue of their exactitude.

The aspects may be more readily understood by relating their distribution according to the signs of the zodiac around the birth chart. For instance, the *square* aspect may be more easily appreciated by contemplating the kind of energy between Aries and Cancer; the *trine* aspect through the energy between Leo and Sagittarius: the *sextile* through the compatibility between Scorpio and Capricorn (Water and Earth). And with the minor aspects the tension of the *quincunx*, for instance, can be understood through the quality of energy between Cancer and Aquarius.

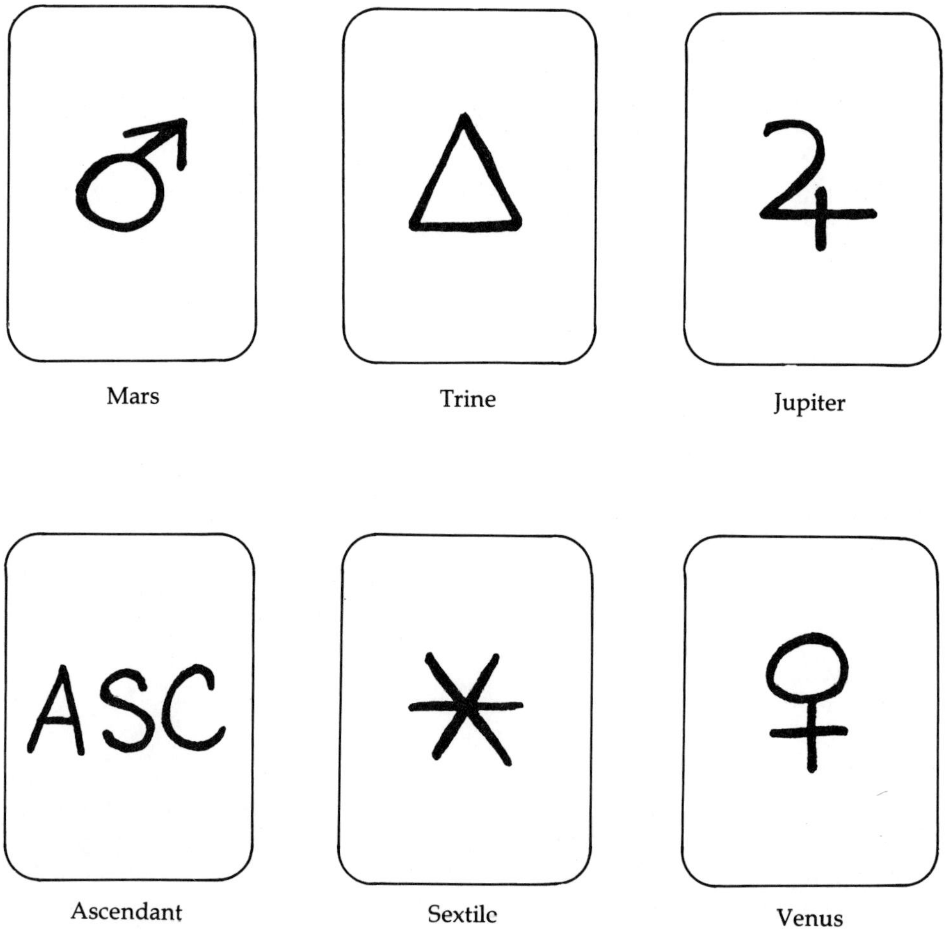

Figure 37 The Card System of Learning

The system of using the symbols of the planets and signs together with numbers for the houses, drawn on index cards (see p.25) can now be enlarged to embrace the symbols for each of the twelve aspects. While reading and learning about the aspects the card bearing the appropriate symbol should be propped up within your sight-line. When contemplating any combination of planets, place the relevant cards before you, for this will help to train your mind to allow your natural, intuitive processes to draw upon the knowledge you have already acquired, arranging it automatically in context with all that you are now attempting to assimilate. The cards may be laid-out as shown in Figure 37.

1. ☌ **Conjunction** 0°

The principle of Oneness and unity is reflected in the spirit of the expression of zero, for this connects with the spiritual starting point of the whole zodiac at the Spring equinox at 0° Aries. When two or more planets are conjunct there is a coming together of the principles involved by those planets and they are said to function as one. Although creating a focus or focal point in the birth chart, the conjunction is to be regarded as neutral and should be judged according to the aspects it forms with other planetary bodies. (See pages 29 and 30.)

2. ☍ **Opposition** 180°

Embodied in the aspect of opposition is the principle of polarity in which the extremes must logically be encountered (see page 30). The number one represents the masculine spirit, the number two representing the feminine principle of the soul and unconscious mind.

Number one is the starting point of all measurements and its purest division or multiplication is that when it halves or multiplies itself to become the number two. By becoming two the Creative Principle emerges as both spirit and matter. In order to fully test the extremes and partake of the full value signified by the planets involved in any opposition, the individual will invariably find that the first half of the life will be beset by the need to live out the problems and difficulties as fully as possible in order to touch the extremes that they imply. With growing maturity, the capacity to utilize the full strength of these energies constructively can be realized so that there may be every opportunity of attaining harmony and wisdom that can only come from encountering such a full life experience, drawing, as it does, upon the opposing sides of the zodiac. The opposition effectively creates an axis across the birth chart.

3. △ **Trine** 120°

The triangle was considered by the alchemists as the symbol for the element Fire, being the aspiration towards spirituality. Its three corners indicate the Trinity, being the Supernal Triangle relating its parts to the number three (see 'Triplicities', pages 31–33). It also relates to the feeling nature of Man and it is perhaps in this context that we can appreciate the historical shifts in understanding of the trine aspect of 120° which divides the 360° circle by 3. In times past the trine aspect was held to be synonymous with the easy usage of energy and, therefore, regarded as 'fortunate'. With the passage of time, good fortune without serious application has been thought less worthy and with the more materialistic approach to life of modern times, the square aspect of 90°, which divides the 360° circle by 4, is thought of as more valuable. As with all areas of astrology, balance must rule paramount and understanding of the subtleties involved with the different aspects clearly expresses this same principle. In essence, the triangle and the trine aspect symbolize our capacity to attain spirituality. Most of us attune readily to the understanding of creativity as allied with the number three but a little contemplation reveals that the feeling associated with creativity and the concept of creation is our access to pure spirituality. The association is with the Supernal Triangle and the Holy Trinity, man, the father and woman, the mother, combining to create a child which is Man's prerogative — the child being the image of God.

The general ease of use of energies implies the likelihood of taking such matters for granted. Nevertheless, it is possible, especially should there be strong supporting aspects such as the *square* or *opposition*, to gain exceptional momentum utilizing the best of oneself in the most positive and creative manner. The quality of energy implied is that naturally exuberant spirit associated with those signs in trine aspect to 0° Aries: Leo and Sagittarius (also see 'the Grand Trine' page 33).

4. □ **Square** 90°

The number four and the symbol of the four-cornered square indicate the concretization of the Life Force on the earthly plane (see also 'Quadruplicities', pages 33–34). The square aspect is often related to *challenge* for the simple reason that the individual is inevitably confronted with life, as in the instances of the Dilemmas (see pages 34–36), and is obliged to literally 'square up' to it. In keeping with the actual shape of the symbol for the square □ the individual very often tends to feel 'boxed in' and seemingly cannot escape from his own vicissitudes.

This aspect is often seen as a very positive factor particularly in modern times because the individual must accept the challenge and fight the good fight, thus, in many instances, overcoming negative factors in his nature and achieving a great deal in life. Since all numbers of Manifestation are based upon the number two, being four, eight, sixteen, etc., it is often found that the charts of those capable of being self-made or deemed successful contain several so-called 'hard' aspects — oppositions (division by 2), squares (division by 4), sesquiquadrates (division by 8), etc.

Whereas the trine aspect infers the capacity and the potential to give vent freely to the creative power of the Life Force in the true spirit of the number three, the square aspect reflects the need for thorough worldly experience. It is not possible to maintain that life should be simple or easy, for then the challenge to progress would be removed and there would be little point or purpose for existence on this planet. Unless we are confronted with the full impact of life we may not utilize the potential inherent in our natures. For this reason no chart contains only one type of aspect, but a healthy mixture of them all according to the needs of the individual personality.

Upon the numbers, one, two, three and four are based all other numbers. Their symbolic principles are the roots of any ensuing numbers.

5. **Q, BQ Quintile Series** 72°, 144°

The number five is often described as the number of Man for it relates to his capacity to be and to do. In keeping with the division of the 360° circle by 5 being quintile (72°) or biquintile (144°) and the fifth-harmonic, we seek to understand the talents inherent in the nature. It is through our five senses that we experience life directly and since these are our natural gifts, the principle of the gift is that it should be used and so the talents, and all of which we are capable, must be brought to fruition. The qualities of the planets in quintile aspect to one another are taken to describe the particular gifts of the individual. However, unless supported by the more challenging aspects of Manifestation it is possible that the talents may not be realized to any great extent. It is the power of Mind and self-discipline which enables talents to be used to their full — hence the association very often of Mercury with the quintile aspects.

6. ⚹ **Sextile** 60°

The six-pointed star symbolizes the human soul and the union of spirit and matter. It is formed from the Fire and Earth areas of the chart which indicate the power of the mind and inspiration (see 'the Triplicities', pages 31–32). This symbol is more familiar as the Star of David and is often seen contained within the Circle of Totality, expressing universal love and the capacity to depend and link with the inner self which is part of the Greater Whole. The number six tells of our decisive function and capacity to bring an action to completion; thus the sextile aspect expresses the ability to recognize and to attract opportunities that they may be utilized. Currently the sextile aspect is being less highly regarded, possibly because its opportunistic attitudes are not truly understood. The trine differs from the sextile in that such chances to fully express the self tend to be rather taken for granted until the point is reached when the reservoir of openings eventually dries up. The sextile aspect can be seen as a useful barometer of the individual's capacity to take advantage of whatever he or she may have as a human being, in other words, the capacity to recognize beauty in one's own soul and in life in general. Perhaps the sextile is not viewed nowadays in a good light simply because we have lost, or seem to have lost, our knowledge of how to appreciate that which we have. However, it is fair to say that energy of any kind that is misdirected can get out of control and thus become destructive.

7. 1/7, 2/7, 3/7 **Septile Series** From 51° 26′

The septile series of aspects, notably the septile of 51° 26′; the bi-septile of 102° 52′ and the tri-septile of 154° 17′ are gradually becoming more widely used. This is due entirely to the introduction of harmonics which has caused astrologers to become increasingly aware of the nuances of minor aspects. It is also indicative of the greater sophistication of today's astrologers who seek greater understanding of the possibilities inherent in the birth chart. The number seven is the most overtly spiritual number and for this reason there are many references to it in religious documentation. The number seven exemplifies the Life Force inferred by the seven angels of the Chaldeans, the seven archangels of Revelations, the seven thrones and the seven churches, as well as the seven days of the week. The symbolism of the number seven infers that the individual is aware that he has the greatest gift, which is the gift of Life, and is able to embark on a spiritual journey involving growth and development. In the same way, the septiles denote our capacity to be extremely able at something from which we derive immense joy. Astrologers versed in the art of harmonics may often set up fifth and seventh harmonic charts to establish the talents that an individual may have and whether or not they may be deployed and fulfilled as they should.

The septile series can be entered on the aspect grid as follows, 1/7, 2/7 and 3/7.

8. ∠ ⚼ **Semi-Square** and **Sesquiquadrate** 45° and 135°

Having been given the gift of Life, every human being must endeavour to strive constantly to attain equilibrium. The number eight physically embodies the knowledge that as one seeks balance so one must always return to one's origins at the centre of all things. The significance of the division of the 360° circle by 8, the semi-square aspect of 45°, was largely overlooked in the past. With the modern technique of midpoints this aspect has become more prominent. The same yardstick applies to the sesquiquadrate aspect of 135°. As its symbol, ⚼ suggests, it is the sum of a square □ at 90° and a semi-square ∠ at 45° creating a total of 135°. Derived from the number four and the aspects of Manifestation the semi-square and the sesquiquadrate express the concrete world. Inevitably the individual is made thoroughly aware of being part of the panoply of life continuously confronted with the need to justify existence. It is not enough to live or to exist, there must also be purpose. Very often the individual whose chart contains the semi-square or sesqui-quadrate tends to find his purpose thwarted and limited, for how else can one understand the need for such aims? So the individual is taught by the experience of life to respect that which s/he has.

9. **N Novile** 40°

The novile aspect has recently become more noticeable in astrological work, although it is still rarely used. This in itself is synonymous with the meaning of the number nine, for in the Pythagorean understanding nine is the highest number and spiritually the most profound, being the number of Manifested Deity or the God Force in nature. Until recently, the novile has been viewed as somewhat inconse-quential as it can be lost within the context of the trine aspect, for 3 × 3 = 9, or 3 × 40 = 120° the number of the trine aspect. This is particularly so in the ninth harmonic chart. However it is also becoming noted that the novile aspect offers understanding of the subtleties involved in such trine aspects. On their own they are well worth noting for they invariably denote the capacity for an individual to acquire greater spiritual insight and to develop on a higher level of consciousness. This relates markedly to the Kabalistic belief that one should not study or begin to embark on a study of the Kabalah, or spiritual truth, until the age of forty years. Astrologers will sanction this, knowing of the enormous growth period that is within the capacity of every human being from around that age. This concurs with the opposition cycle of the planet Uranus to its natal position between the ages of 40 and 42. Thus the novile aspect serves to indicate that the individual is capable of making considerable advancement in this area should *s/he desire*. In keeping with the quality associated with the trine aspect, it is possible that such a step may rest unacknowledged, being taken for granted or thought too difficult.

10 and 11. 1/10, 1/11 **Decile** and **Undecile**
Decile from 36°
Undecile from 32° 43′

The decile (360° ÷ 10) and the undecile (360 ÷ 11) are not generally used as yet. The symbolism associated with the numbers ten and eleven explains that we are not yet ready to incorporate such aspects into our work. The fact that the aspects based upon the numbers five, seven and nine are increasingly becoming used indicates that the time will come when the decile and undecile will be part of our work. The number ten expresses the idea that the cycle of life is completed and the starting point of another may begin. This means that such an individual would be capable of attaining self-mastery on the human plane and ready to acknowledge a sense of unity that can then be passed to others.

The number 11 together with 22 and 33 are considered the numbers of mastery on the three planes, the physical, mental and spiritual. The number eleven denotes mastery of the physical in the true and pure understanding of the feminine forces in nature including the Mother Earth. Presumably an individual with the undecile prominent or with a powerful eleventh harmonic chart would have the ability to take decisive action where the needs of this planet and its people are concerned.

12. ⚺ **Semi-Sextile** and **Quincunx** 30° ⚻ and 150°

The division of the 360° circle by twelve relates to the natural order of the cosmos, hence the division of the ecliptic into the twelve signs and the division of the birth chart into twelve houses. This number often appears in religious documentation, e.g. the Twelve Tribes of Israel, and the Twelve Disciples. It may be interpreted according to its subdivisions: 6 × 2 or 3 × 4 or 4 + 8, but inevitably the resulting interpretation reads according to the creative union of spirit and nature. As in the case of the decile and the undecile, it is likely that the world is not quite ready to assume certain spiritual responsibilities. In the instance of the semi-sextile this is the responsibility for every human being, for the zodiac comprised of twelve signs means all of mankind. It is inevitable that the semi-sextile aspect is viewed in differing ways according to the individual astrologer, some viewing it as an 'easy' aspect, whereas others view it as 'difficult'. The argument prevails that the signs of the zodiac are not compatible with their immediate neighbour. Perhaps the time will come when such barriers all over the world are dispensed with and each human being and type of personality will be judged according to its humanity. The semi-sextile will mostly reflect a sense of irritation in the chart between the planets involved. As in most instances in our lives, it is those petty irritations which can assume enormous proportions and the semi-sextile may highlight an area which assumes more significance than is its due.

The quincunx aspect tends to occur in the charts of those who are highly strung or especially sensitive in some way. As 5/12 of the 360° circle, 5 × 30° = 150°, the number five reminds us of the capacity to have a particular talent or gift. There is often an accompanying nervous intensity which, if channelled along the lines of the talent shown by the planets in quincunx aspect to one another, can produce remarkable results. Lying in the zodiac 150° from the starting point (0° Aries) are Virgo and Scorpio, thought to be the most complex and difficult of all the twelve signs. With Virgo nervousness is often betrayed by physical symptoms, notably the intestines. Scorpio's nervous intensity is frequently internalized, punctuated with sudden explosions as the soul seeks some sort of release.

Finding the Aspects

It is a very simple matter to determine the aspects in a birth chart, particularly by the Equal House System. Indeed, the advantage of this system is that the planets may be seen according to the 360° circle without any of the distortion that can occur with the Quadrant System. Always work according to the natural order of the signs of the zodiac, in an anti-clockwise direction and, commencing with the Sun, follow planetary order Sun to Pluto as shown in the grids on page 124 and the section, 'The Interplanetary Aspects' on page 123–128.

For example: from the chart on page 111 determine whether Venus and Mars are in aspect. Note that Mars at 28° 24′ Virgo is *applying* (refer to page 115) in the anti-clockwise direction to Venus at 12° 11′ Aquarius. Working from Mars, count to the end of Virgo which is 1° 36′. Then the number of signs to Aquarius, which is four (♎, ♏, ♐, ♑), plus 12° 11′ (of ♒) equals 1° 36′ + 120° (four signs) + 12° 11′ equals 133° 47′ (or 134°) which is within an acceptable orb (2° allowed) of 135° or *sesquiquadrate* ⚼.
(See pages 125 and 126).

Make use of your knowledge of the Triplicities and Quadruplicities to spot trines and squares. The relationships of the signs will help generally.

Aspects are always measured according to their shortest distance from one another.

Aspects are entered on a grid provided on most printed chart forms. The aspects cited are for the chart on page 111. Figure 38 gives the distance of all the planets to the nearest degree. Figure 39 shows the aspects entered in the usual way. Figure 40 is the computerized version. Note that the orb allowance by computer is geared to personal preference and may vary from those given on page 115.

Aspect lines are usually drawn upon an Equal House chart and coloured **red** for contracting ('difficult') aspects and **blue** for expanding ('easy') aspects but this is optional. Minor aspects are shown by dotted lines and coloured appropriately. A

ASPECTS	☉	☽	☿	♀	♂	♃	♄	♅	♆	♇	
☉		32	16	42	92	34	101	177	73	132	☉
☽			16	10	124	2	133	151	105	165	☽
☿				26	108	18	117	167	89	149	☿
♀					134	8	143	141	115	174	♀
♂						126	9	85	19	40	♂
♃							135	149	107	166	♃
♄								76	28	31	♄
♅									104	45	♅
♆										59	♆
♇											♇
Asc.	18	51	34	60	74	52	83	159	55	114	Asc.
M.C.	74	107	90	116	18	108	27	104	1	58	M.C.

Figure 38 Aspect grid A

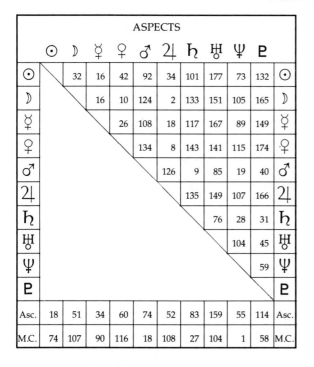

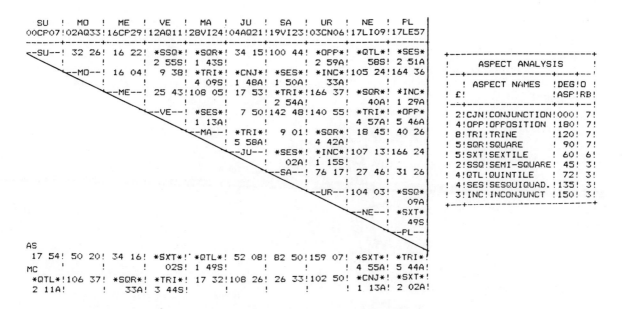

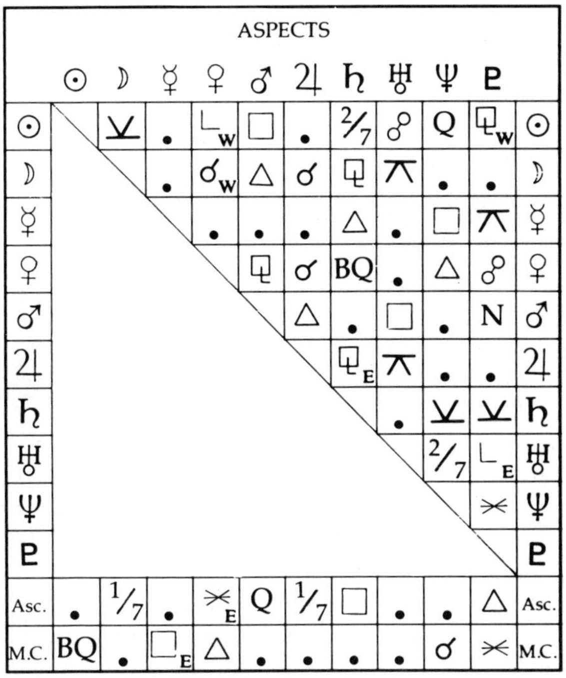

Figure 39 Aspect grid B

```
  SU   !  MO   !  ME   !  VE   !  MA   !  JU   !  SA   !  UR   !  NE   !  PL
00CP07!02AQ33!16CP29!12AQ11!28VI24!04AQ21!19VI23!03CN06!17LI09!17LE57
------+------+------+------+------+------+------+------+------+------
--SU--! 32 26! 16 22! *SSQ*! *SQR*! 34 15!100 44! *OPP*! *QTL*! *SES*
      !      !      ! 2 55S! 1 43S!      !      ! 2 59A!   58S! 2 51A
       --MO--! 16 04!  9 38! *TRI*! *CNJ*! *SES*! *INC*!105 24!164 36
             !      !      ! 4 09S! 1 48A! 1 50A!   33A!      !
              --ME--! 25 43!108 05! 17 53! *TRI*!166 37! *SQR*! *INC*
                    !      !      !      ! 2 54A!      !   40A! 1 29A
                     --VE--! *SES*!  7 50!142 48!140 55! *TRI*! *OPP*
                           ! 1 13A!      !      !      ! 4 57A! 5 46A
                            --MA--! *TRI*!  9 01! *SQR*! 18 45! 40 26
                                  ! 5 58A!      ! 4 42A!      !
                                   --JU--! *SES*! *INC*!107 13!166 24
                                         !   02A! 1 15S!      !
                                          --SA--! 76 17! 27 46! 31 26
                                                !      !      !
                                                 --UR--!104 03! *SSQ*
                                                       !      !   09A
                                                        --NE--! *SXT*
                                                              !   49S
                                                               --PL--
AS
 17 54! 50 20! 34 16! *SXT*! *QTL*! 52 08! 82 50!159 07! *SXT*! *TRI*!
MC    !      !      !   02S! 1 49S!      !      !      ! 4 55A! 5 44A!
 *QTL*!106 37! *SQR*! *TRI*! 17 32!108 26! 26 33!102 50! *CNJ*! *SXT*!
 2 11A!      !   33A! 3 44S!      !      !      !      ! 1 13A! 2 02A!
```

```
+--------------------------+
!      ASPECT ANALYSIS     !
!--+----------------+---+--!
!  ! ASPECT NAMES   !DEG!O !
! £!                !ASP!RB!
!--+----------------+---+--!
! 2!CJN!CONJUNCTION!000! 7!
! 4!OPP!OPPOSITION !180! 7!
! 8!TRI!TRINE      !120! 7!
! 5!SQR!SQUARE     ! 90! 7!
! 5!SXT!SEXTILE    ! 60! 6!
! 2!SSQ!SEMI-SQUARE! 45! 3!
! 4!QTL!QUINTILE   ! 72! 3!
! 4!SES!SESQUIQUAD.!135! 3!
! 3!INC!INCONJUNCT !150! 3!
+--+-----------------------+
```

Figure 40 Computerized Aspect Grid

compass is used to space the aspect lines evenly from the planets. In Chart A (Figure 41), the aspect lines to Venus only have been entered. In Chart B (Figure 42) all aspects have been entered. Quintile and septile aspects are not usually entered but, again, this is optional.

Satellitia

A grouping of three or more planets in one zodiacal sign or house is called a Satellitium (or Stellium). This shows a strong concentration of energy and should be regarded as a dominant feature of the birth chart.

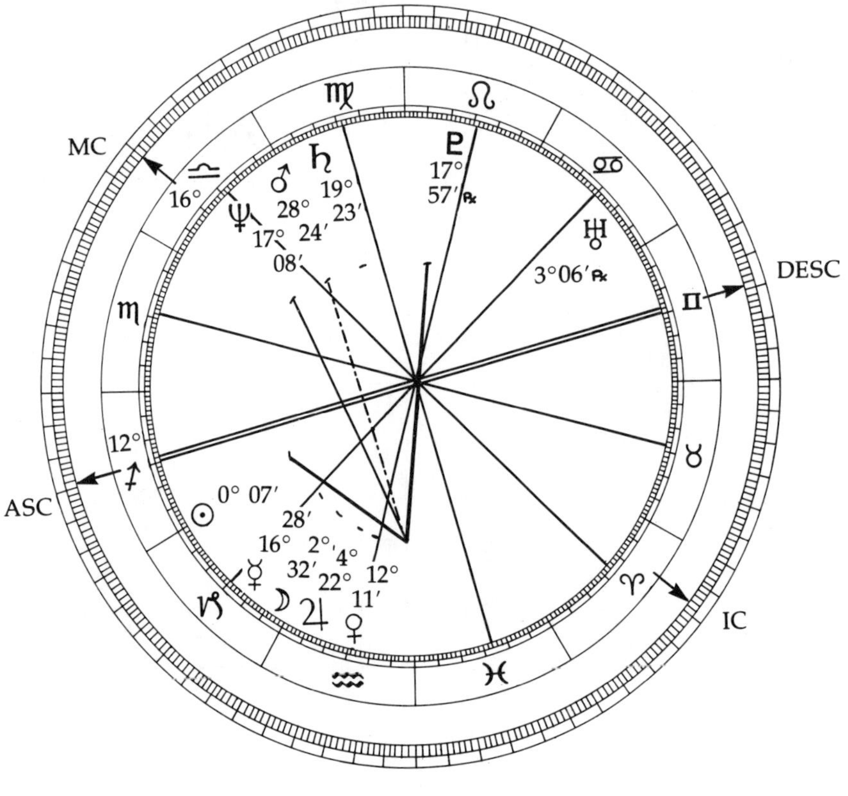

Figure 41 Chart A

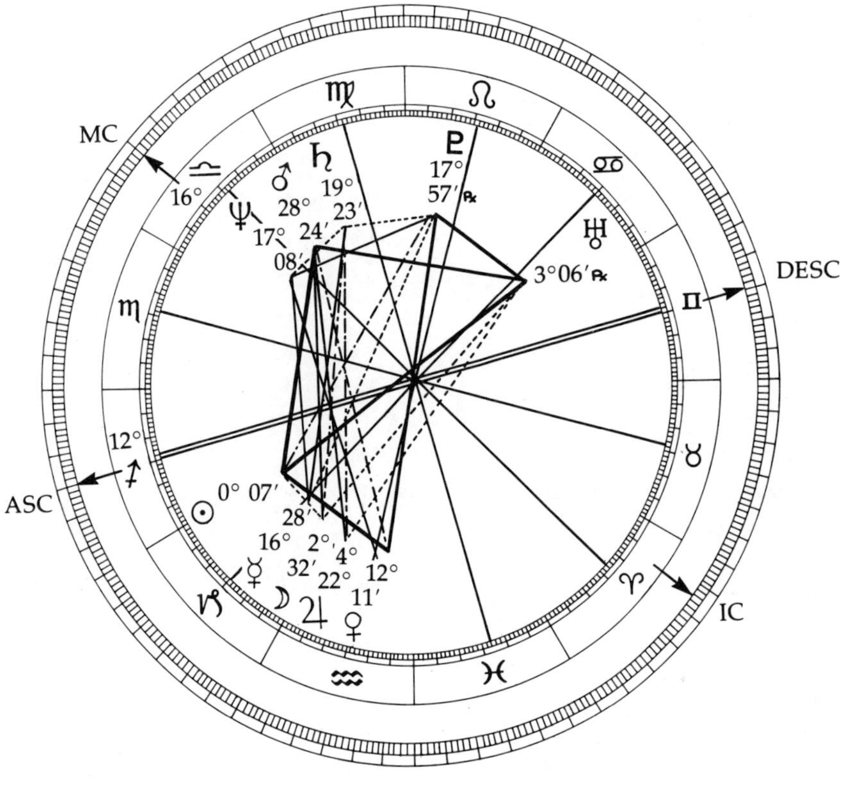

Figure 42 Chart B

Disassociated Aspects

An aspect is said to be disassociated when a planet forms an aspect with another planet that is not in either the same triplicity or quadruplicity, for the ends and the beginnings of the signs may, in a sense, overlap, e.g., Jupiter in the beginning of Aquarius trine Saturn at the end of Virgo. A disassociated square can be helpful in breaking the deadlock of a Dilemma or a disassociated trine can provide the dis-ease that creates the impetus to motivate the Grand trine.

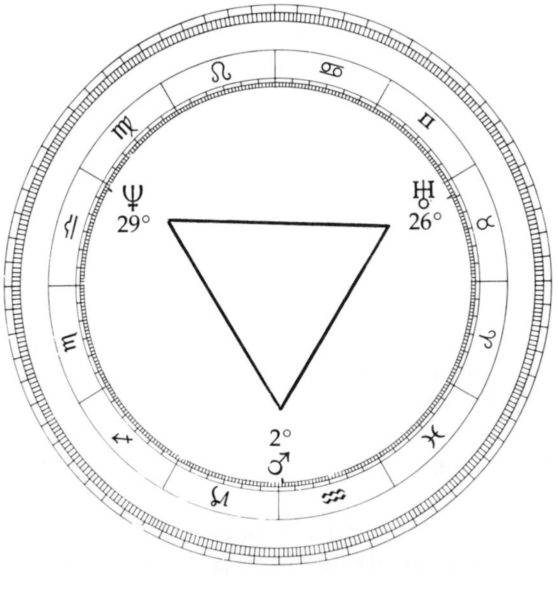

Figure 43 Disassociated Grand Trine in Earth/Air Signs

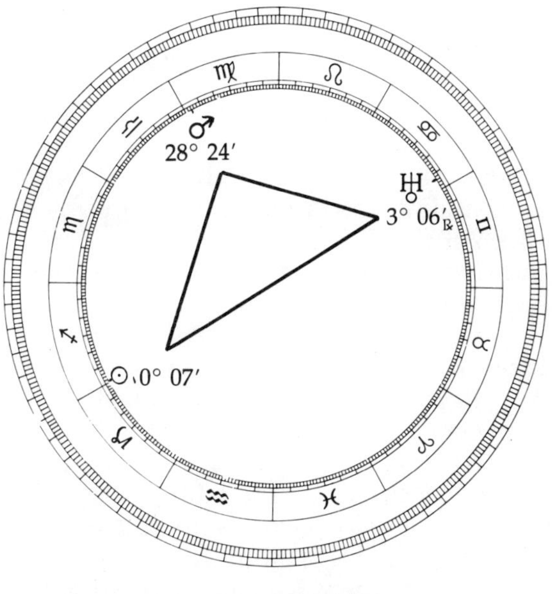

Figure 44 Disassociated T/Square in Cardinal/Mutable Signs *(see also p. 143)*

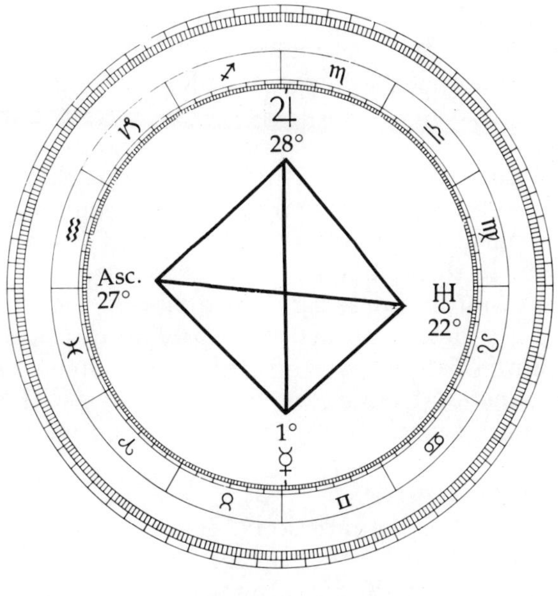

Figure 45 Disassociated Grand Cross in Fixed/Mutable Signs

Chart Forms and Computer Services
It is possible to purchase chart forms that have an aspect grid from astrological book stockists. As each aspect is located, its symbol should be entered on the grid for future reference. Some astrologers note the number of degrees at the same time.

While most of the calculations for the birth chart may be performed on an electronic calculator, it is not possible to use one for finding the aspects. It may be possible, subject to availability, to purchase a 'Visual Aspect Locator' though it is neither, difficult nor too time-consuming to work through the process yourself. It is relatively easy to miss aspects and many astrologers take advantage of the computer services available or purchase their own computer with the appropriate astrological software. Computer software for astrologers is available but does, like all software at the present time, undergo changes according to the new computers being manufactured all the time. Should you feel that computerized data would be helpful, approach a body such as the Astrological Association for up-to-date information. Computer software companies and stockists do advertise in the *Astrological Journal* of this association.

Lack of Aspects
We have seen that the planets are interrelated in a unique system whether they are in aspect or not. The fact that they are in aspect tells us something concerning the *quality* of the relationship between two planetary bodies within that scheme. It follows that when they are not in aspect the same principle must apply. Where there is a lack, there is often a tendency to be more aware of the particular need (see pages 32–33), and the lack of an aspect can often be especially illuminating.

Unaspected Planets
Most credit must be given to Geoffrey Dean for his researches into unaspected planets and lack of aspects in general. Inevitably, as with all such work, criticism has been made on the grounds that an unaspected planet is defined as a planet that lacks major aspects only, with minor aspects included only if within an orb of 1°. The orbs' allowance generally is considered very tight at 5° for major aspects and only 3° between the extra-Saturnian planets. It is thought that the unaspected planet lacks integration with the rest of the scheme of planets and can be seen to operate in isolation. Thus an unaspected Venus can mean an over-emphasis on emotional matters with a driving need to compensate for affection or understanding from others.

The Interplanetary Aspects

The Aspects Involving the Sun

Sun to Moon
Known as the Lights, being the Greater and Lesser Lights. It is automatic to associate the natural parents with these symbols for they are synonymous with the archetypal parental images of the Sun — the father, and the Moon — the mother. The Sun and the Moon correspond to the male and female sides of the psyche common to all human beings. Aspects between these bodies indicate the inner nature in all its rich variety of expression.

The lack of any aspect can reveal the profound need to search for a place or answer to the meaning of the universe in order to function on the most mundane levels of existence.

Sun to Mercury
Since these two bodies are never more than 28° apart and can only form a conjunction or no aspect at all, there is a tendency to diminish their importance. In time to come perhaps this situation will be revised, especially if the higher harmonics are taken into account. Since the Sun denotes our central identity and Mercury denotes that channel through which we comprehend everything, it is only right that due attention is paid. Of course, the signs and houses which these bodies tenant are especially relevant in assessing their quality.

The lack of an aspect clearly shows how significant it is for the individual to understand him or herself before the experience of life can be truly coped with.

Sun to Venus
Only the conjunction, semi-sextile and semi-square can occur, for Venus is never further than 48° from the Sun. As the semi-square indicates the furthest possible distance of these two bodies, it is not

surprising to find how frequently this aspect occurs in the charts of those who have often severe difficulties with their emotional life, finding marriage especially hard to sustain. In common with Sun/Mercury, the signs and houses must be very carefully examined.

Sun to Mars
The ability to confront life and to sustain energy so that it may be directed with purpose can be scrutinized according to the various aspects. Any of the expanding or 'easy' aspects can indicate good health and vitality with the proviso that this is not squandered; the contracting or 'difficult' aspects should not be underestimated for they can reflect the dynamic or challenging quality of personality that can utilize inherent power and creativity to good purposes through the force of individual effort.

Sun to Jupiter
Indicative of the individual capacity to be optimistic and philosophical. There are all shades and manner of expression involved, from the smug, self-satisfied to those who feel fearful of not being able to maintain a sense of hopefulness. Being able to understand one's personality and life-style within the context of the greater framework of society can create difficulties in maintaining self-confidence and the ability to rise above the situations that occur. Bear in mind that the signs Leo and Sagittarius are in natural trine aspect to one another, evocative of the largess of this contact.

Sun to Saturn
Perhaps best described as our Achilles' Heel, for everyone has an area of greatest vulnerability, yet we all cope with it in differing ways. Semi-sextile is often taken unawares that such vulnerability is always there, for it seems to be copeable yet is not. Self-discipline is also apparent, for it often requires much self-control to cope with what are believed to be weaknesses. Later in life with the maturity that comes from experience, extreme sensitivity may well be recognized as meaning emotional strength. Too much or too little discipline by the father may have bearing on the quality of demonstrativeness of the individual.

Sun to Uranus
The demands to adopt the standards of the parents, especially the father, can arouse a sense of rebellion in the child which colours its attitude to life in general. In adulthood it is one's own inner demands of self and of society which must be confronted. For some this means being utterly anti-establishment as in the case of the square or the sesquiquadrate; with quincunx the nervous intensity can create difficulties in which the individual can feel very isolated or alienated from the rest of the world and perhaps it is for this reason that such an individual seeks to attain an original or unusual life-style. The differing aspects show the capacity to be either in or out of step with society or one's generation.

Sun to Neptune
Self-identity comes under scrutiny because its elusive quality creates a fascination in itself. Not knowing who one is, or why one is, can mean perpetual dissatisfaction for some, whereas for others it means a life-long journey into the realms of self-knowledge. Psychic ability is common to all human beings but there are all shades and variations just as with our other senses such as seeing or hearing. To deal with the intangible or to desire involvement with the arts varies from one individual to another; so too does the need to escape, at times, from the reality of life, for we all fear disillusionment.

Sun to Pluto
The intensity of feeling and ability to become totally immersed, or even obsessed at times, with certain matters is part of the human condition. With the trine or the sextile the ability to rid oneself of bad feelings or repressions is decidedly easier and shows the capacity to bounce back from difficulties and begin a new phase in life. Contact with Pluto indicates a need to be fully aware of the meaning of life, for Pluto is the outer-most planet yet discovered. Fears must be endured, accepted and overcome to truly know the joy of life.

The Aspects Involving the Moon

Moon to Mercury
Awareness of own behavioural needs and responsibilities gradually increases through

the sheer fact of being. The trine aspect shows a natural flair for combining the instinctive with the rational, which is so useful for gauging public moods or trends, encouraging the individual to become an historian or journalist, etc. With the square, for instance, the inclination is to dissipate nervous energy and to give way to the conflicts in the immediate environment and those which one creates for oneself.

Moon to Venus
Clearly the emotional response and ability to comprehend one's own and others' feelings would be uppermost with the conjunction or opposition. The arts must be favoured but it is largely dependent upon the signs and houses. We tend to create that which we need and personal happiness must be examined according to individual requirements which may only reveal themselves once the emotional experiences have been gained. So many fear the possibility of being hurt but perhaps it is an experience that is required to shape and mature the psyche, so it must be faced.

Moon to Mars
Humour is the antidote to pain and should never be underestimated in helping to redress the status quo and to deflect likely conflicts especially in the home environment. The capacity to be angry is a normal, natural and healthy outlet for pent-up feelings and it is just as possible to channel this remarkable source of energy into creative and constructive areas as it is to let it be dissipated in negative and destructive urges. A good Saturn would indicate the capacity for determination and perseverance in this instance.

Moon to Jupiter
We all have the power to be happy, to be optimistic and to be generous of spirit but, for one reason or another, we find this area can be threatened. Usually a feeling of benevolence stems from a happy heart and it is possible to look forward to the future with equanimity if one is generally blessed with self-confidence and likeability. It is possible that, as with the square or opposition, there may be an element of greed, or, as with the trine, laziness, or with the conjunction, of self-righteousness. Bear in mind that Jupiter is exalted in Moon-ruled Cancer.

Moon to Saturn
All human beings suffer from a sense of inadequacy and a feeling of insecurity. It is largely dependent upon the individual's self-control and self-discipline whether or not feelings of inadequacy will overrule the existence. The contracting aspects may battle daily with timidity or shyness until a rigidly realistic appraisal of the early conditioning lends perspective which encourages self-discipline. Parental relationships and influences should be carefully and delicately examined.

Moon to Uranus
Invariably all combinations, including Uranus in the fourth house, indicate some form of rebelliousness or cantankerousness in the personality. It is possible that the mother was absent for lengthy periods so that the child adopted a pattern of outrageous behaviour in order to attract attention to itself. The same may be true of the father where Sun/Uranus aspects are concerned. Thus a habit of being deliberately 'different' can be set up. The square shows inner tension which must erupt, often disastrously, resulting in break-downs in relationships of all kinds, but most consistently and conspicuously in emotional involvements. However, in certain instances, there can be signs of genuine intelligence, intuition and even real genius. Perhaps personal problems are the price that must be paid for such gifts.

Moon to Neptune
At some point in time, we all wish to run away from a confrontation with our own selves for we all feel, and are prey to, varying degrees of sensitivity and openness not only to the Unknown but also to the moods and pain of others in our immediate environment and the world at large. The contracting or 'difficult' aspects may allow such feelings to be used in a beneficial manner. The conjunction inclines to reform and a philanthropic nature but also to disillusionment and the knowledge that everyone is gullible in one sense or another. The trines and sextiles must be particularly wary of being duped.

Moon to Pluto
Powerfully combustible with moods that are not always readily seen. Capable of being

disruptive at will, life has a way of being extremely changeful and upsetting. The expanding, 'easy' aspects inevitably enjoy change for its own sake and quickly adapt to new situations. The square seems to be disrupted just at the wrong times which means that new beginnings have to be shaped from very difficult happenings. We never get more than we can actually cope with and those who are subject to the greater difficulties must be stronger and more capable than they might believe.

The Aspects Involving Mercury

Mercury to Venus
Only aspects within 76° can occur, for that is the maximum distance between these two planets. The conjunction occurs relatively frequently and is, therefore, dependent upon the position by sign, house and aspects involving other planetary bodies. For this reason, it is wiser not to overload any interpretation of it. All the aspects involve the blending between the workings of the nervous system and the emotional nature. Clearly any contact must speak of the individual's capacity for conscious awareness and with the quintile aspect this can lend common sense to a fine intellect.

Mercury to Mars
The power of the human mind has still to be fully explored and understood. The contact with Mars shows a ready openness to allow the mind to function freely and forcefully, especially with the trine, sextile and quintile series. With the contracting aspects, the mind and the nervous system can be stretched to their limits, with far less control over tongue, nerves or temper. It is necessary to work according to one's energy resources and to limit concentration to only one area for any length of time. Change is as good as a rest and twice as stimulating.

Mercury to Jupiter
The mind is capable of thinking in very large concepts so that there may be absentmindedness or carelessness where mundane or petty details are concerned. Self-indulgence or mental laziness can occur and a good Saturn would help where mental discipline is concerned. The trine is indicative of generally sound common sense and material success through intellectual endeavours. The capacity to comprehend lofty thoughts and ideals as a natural part of being is likely with sextile and trine. For contracting aspects there may well be the feeling that there is nowhere on Earth where there can be peace for oneself.

Mercury to Saturn
The quality of this contact must be carefully assessed for it is easy to suggest that the individual may be dull-witted when the truth reveals a finely tuned, disciplined and capable mind. It is said that for true success all that is required is persistence and determination. Certainly the mind benefits if trine, sextile, quintile or septile, but there are inevitable problems and difficulties with the remaining aspects. Early education may be pitted with problems and yet the mind which remains open to more knowledge, rather than having been forced to specialize at too early an age, can eventually produce on-going, good work.

Mercury to Uranus
The nervous system is invariably very highly tuned as would be expected with any bright or inventive type of personality. Impatient and eager for new ideas, the trine and sextile can be exceptionally clever. Difficult to contend with in early youth, the square and semi-square improve with the mental discipline that comes with age. Difficulties in communicating thoughts and ideas which may be too 'avant garde' for contemporaries. The tendency can be to disregard the value of own ideas.

Mercury to Neptune
It is all too easy to overload these contacts with profound significance so that the opposition may be accused of drug addiction or alcoholism when it is clear that no artist or writer could possibly function without imagination. We all need to day-dream or fantasize and so long as we are consciously aware that this is what is taking place, such flights of fancy can serve to enhance our lives. The nervous system can be ultra sensitive and especially the square and semi-sextile should take care to maintain a simple regime which promotes a toxin-free system.

Mercury to Pluto
The powerful mind that knows all and sees

all but refuses to accept certain matters which are deemed best left deep in the unconscious mind. Small wonder that the nervous system can come under subversive attack by those very same hidden elements resulting in nervous intensity and verbal explosions. This is particularly true of the contracting aspects. With the trine or sextile, nervous tension finds ready release. Relationships with brothers and sisters are, of course, part of any of the Mercury contacts and in this instance, with Pluto, there may be special difficulties which the child cannot voice to the parents, perhaps jealousy or bullying, etc.

The Aspects Involving Venus

Venus to Mars
Timing and co-ordination varies from one person to another. The actor or the sportsman would have a strong contact between these two bodies, if not by aspects certainly by sign or house, with Venus in the first house or Mars in Taurus for example. In just the same way, the ability to express warmth and emotion differs from one individual to another. With the expanding aspects, clearly it is easier to be open and, therefore, find ready response in others. Differences, and the type of difficulties encountered in emotional relationships, can be understood from the variety of aspects formed.

Venus to Jupiter
It takes confidence to reach out to people and to life in general, and whereas some do so with considerable charm and grace which finds favour and wins approval, others may overdo a good thing or find it extremely difficult. A sense of being able to be at ease with oneself and with others, under any circumstances or in any environment. Clearly the conjunction, or the expanding aspects, would achieve this instinctively, exuding a good deal of natural charm whereas the opposition or square would find it difficult to be at ease or question the feelings and motives of others.

Venus to Saturn
Although Saturn is exalted in Venus-ruled Libra, the connection between these planets, especially where the contracting aspects are concerned, indicates the possible unhappiness and problems which can be encountered in emotional matters. There may be a gross disparity in ages or outlook with the partner, and perhaps some hardship must first be experienced before the fullness of emotional understanding can be gained. A sense of loneliness is probably the most trying burden to bear, particularly during the early part of the life. The self-discipline and determination that such combinations express in artistic charts may also explain the other side of the coin where personal relationships are often found to be so difficult.

Venus to Uranus
Each one of the teeming millions on this planet sees him or herself as an individual. Emotional involvements are formed between two individuals who do not necessarily see life in the same way. Whether the relationship withstands the changes that it is subject to via society, changing times or even fashions in thinking, depends largely upon mutual attractiveness and the capacity to be friends as well as lovers. A disruptive pattern may be more prevalent with the contracting aspects, but is the partner prepared to be amenable?

Venus to Neptune
Since Venus is exalted in Pisces, emphasis must be given to the quality of the artistry of the individual concerned. It is a fact that human beings must suffer some hurt or disillusionment at some stage in their life as part of the life experience, and for some this is especially arduous. Projection of feelings onto the partner, blaming the partner for that which ails self, can be frequent with the conjunction and opposition; disillusionment and distrust, and the propensity to attract scandal with the square or semi-square; deluding self to the reality of the romantic situation with the expanding aspects.

Venus to Pluto
Feelings can sometimes be so intense that it is as if they cannot be borne. They may be discarded, rejected or repressed so that appearance and behaviour may well belie what is really being felt. It is unwise to assume that this contact means obsession. However, infatuation or feeling preoccupied by thoughts of the loved can

dominate all else especially with the conjunction, square or opposition. Although it may well take considerably longer than might be anticipated, sextile, trine and quintiles are more likely to appreciate the eventual benefits that stem from being emotionally stretched.

The Aspects Involving Mars

Mars to Jupiter
The life-style comes under scrutiny for it is bound up with the general qualities of enthusiasm, vitality and purpose, for they are essential to enjoy life to the full. The trine may well inherit the wealth of good health and the kind of background which allows for a great deal of freedom, but s/he may squander such easily gained good fortune. The sextile is usually robust, enjoying good health and can shake off illnesses through philosophical outlook. Clearly a liking for healthy exercise helps. The square may feel confined or too restricted and should seek ways of gaining greater leeway in life without being bombastic. The 'prime' of life would reflect the full value of this contact when success, in its myriad forms, can be attained.

Mars to Saturn
Bear in mind that Mars is exalted in Capricorn, and the conjunction should not be regarded with disfavour as it is extremely powerful and indicative of the capacity of the individual to endure and sustain concentrated effort when used positively. Notoriously the two 'malefics', they are more favourable when in an expanding aspect with one another. The square particularly, seems to embody difficulties with health which may be inherited weaknesses; problems with parents and a way of being which does not find favour with those in authoritative positions. Far better to channel the energies into work which is self-employed, or satisfying in some way, than to risk being at the mercy of another's 'power trip'. The health must be guarded and it is certainly wise to encourage a life-style in which adequate rest and a healthy regime help to eliminate stress or overstrain. Invariably such types are very aware of the pain that life can mean and are often able to give compassionate and helpful advice.

Mars to Uranus
Marked impatience and a feeling that there is never sufficient time governs an often frenetic pace which would continue, were it possible, twenty-four hours a day. Endless curiosity drives the conjunction, sextile and septiles to be inventive and curious about what it is that not only makes people tick but machines to function. A well supported trine, opposition or quincunx could have a quality of genius concerning some things, but it depends on sufficient interest being initially aroused. The square may be accident prone through too much haste and a mind that functions faster than the physical reflexes. Often a dangerous love of speed.

Mars to Neptune
In so many instances in life, self-confidence needs a good deal of humouring. With the trine, it is a rare talent to be able to restore self-confidence through a humorous appraisal of situations; with the opposition there is a feeling of being stretched on the rack of injustice until every weakness in the personality has been experienced. If well supported, this aspect can signify marvellous resilience and an ability to aid others to stand more firmly on their feet. The minor contracting aspects are especially difficult since such an individual would suddenly be knocked sideways for so many differing, and often odd, reasons. Aims in life can be confused, or have an unreal quality, so that disillusionment can void the desire to progress. However, with a strong Mars it is possible to channel the energy into extremely creative and meaningful pursuits.

Mars to Pluto
Two sides of a highly combustible coin on the surface, but there is a need to understand the place that anger and powerful feelings have in the scheme of self-understanding. Pent-up energy or frustration must find a safety valve; otherwise temperamental outbursts for their own sake dissipate vital energy sources. Prone to stress to a high degree, the square and opposition lend a good deal of 'guts' to any map together with the capacity to be a human dynamo. The trine can erupt, but usually this can be beneficial. Quincunx and semi-square are very trying

since there seems to be no let-up from pressure. Periods of solitude and peacefulness are essential for general well-being.

The Aspects Involving Jupiter

Jupiter to Saturn
All of the Jupiter/Saturn aspects are indicative of the overall life pattern, the 'ups' and 'downs' of life. With the conjunction there is always something that tends to mar the best of times, yet even the darkest moments are found to contain eventual benefits, very often in the most unthought of ways. The ability to juggle becomes the main standby of the opposition, for the most expansive periods seem pitted with downfalls, yet so much can be rescued or gained from difficult periods. The trine tends to ride over the bumps with relative equanimity but can be unprepared for difficult periods so that they may seem far worse than they actually are. In common with the trine, the sextile may well find that life is infinitely better from middle age onwards. The ability to recognize that even the most arduous times can be beneficial in one way or another can lead to eventual success with any endeavours; the square, semi-square and quincunx are extremely trying with no apparent cease-fire where trials and tribulations are concerned. Although it can be very wearying, once the ability has been learned to take the swings with the roundabouts, much can be gained especially in terms of gathering human experience.

Jupiter to Uranus
The significance of aspects involving the 'generation planets' depends largely on their prominence in the birth chart, for such aspects will be common to large numbers of people. Strong idealism and originality can inspire qualities of leadership and daring. The trine, sextile, quintile and septile aspects are especially useful in a map with humanitarian leanings, for the ability to think in large terms yet seeing the individual within that context, can be useful in any of the helping professions and indeed in any socio-economic field. It is as if there is a sense of truly belonging to Collective Man. With the square or opposition the need is to find self-confidence and belief in self on the earthly plane, so that the power latent in the personality may be more inclined towards practical, business-like schemes.

Jupiter to Neptune
Certainly the capacity to gain spiritual insight would be apparent, yet in some, perhaps with the square, semi-square, sesquiquadrate and certainly with the quincunx, a nervousness or scepticism concerning the Unknown would reject anything unless supplied with considerable evidence. However, such scepticism may not necessarily apply to tangible matters and so s/he may be especially susceptible to confidence tricks, or part easily with money or material possessions. The trine must indicate charisma, charm of manner, and a persuasiveness that would be hard to deny.

Jupiter to Pluto
Concentration on ideals can mean that aims and desires are pursued relentlessly and, sometimes, even ruthlessly with little regard for others, yet with square or opposition it may be that the individual is sacrificed for the sake of the many. Trine and sextile desire to be free to pursue an unfettered life-style but semi-square or sesquiquadrate may be unable to do so through a fear of living life in such a manner or because the subversive element of past conditioning refuses to allow such inconceivable joy. The ability to be helpful or optimistic could be hindered by many subtle feelings.

The Aspects Involving Saturn

Saturn to Uranus
Since these planets are co-rulers of Aquarius, the inclination is to associate them with practical and scientific endeavours. However pertinent it is to think in terms of the scientific, the reality is that this often masks the denial of the emotional nature. It also reflects the often severe terror that many experience when confronted with modern technology. The square may confound critics by the forcefulness and dedication of manner; the trine may coast along, glad of the benefits

afforded by modern society but able, once galvanized to effort, to contribute mightily to improving those areas for the good of others.

Saturn to Neptune
In artistic charts this contact is seen as immensely valuable, for out of inspiration and a belief in what one is doing can come eventual sanction and favour on a large scale, particularly with the expanding aspects. The square conjures problems where none may have existed. Health factors can weaken a sensitive constitution, imbuing further lack of confidence to pursue own goals. It is especially difficult to maintain an image of self-worth. In some instances it is all too easy to play the victim.

Saturn to Pluto
In some instances, shades of inadequacy are thrown together with repressed feelings making it a perpetual struggle to cope with each day, yet in other maps the capacity for dedicated self-denial can encourage almost magical achievements. With the opposition and, in some instances the conjunction, energy is depleted very rapidly so that periods of intense activity are quickly followed by virtual depletion and creative endeavours are punctuated by periods of inertia. Most members of the helping professions, including those active in psychic fields, recognize that early childhood problems are often needed so that they might have the experience with which they can then counsel others.

The Aspects Involving Uranus, Neptune and Pluto

The aspects between Uranus, Neptune and Pluto express the subtle changes in the differing generations as well as our ability to cope with life as it must be experienced in accord with those shifting cycles. Unless any of these planets are prominent natally, it is wise not to over-endow the meaning gained from their differing aspects. The aspects from Uranus to Neptune and Pluto occur during its 84 year cycle, so that it will only be in opposition once, trine and square twice, etc., in that period. Through the aspects we can see shades and variations of the changes of attitudes to the arts and sciences, and to the manner in which we have the confidence to cope with change and modern technology. Those who were born between 1963 and 1967, when Uranus–Pluto formed a conjunction in Virgo (exact October 1965), are those who are the most affected in adulthood by the enormous changes in the structure of the working life during the 1980s.

Old orders must change, for this is the process by which we transmute consciousness in a continuum of evolution, but does everybody accept such a process with ease or equanimity? For some it can be an unnerving and even terrifying contemplation. It is a usual human characteristic to prefer to maintain and cling to known territory rather than risk the consequences of disruption that change might entail. The furious pace and pressure of modern life is, for many, immensely trying. Some prefer to deny that life does change or that there should be any disruption of the normal status quo. Some welcome change, embracing the benefits of modern technology as if brand new toys, quickly becoming familiar with computer jargon and the delights of the latest software, others know the loneliness and trauma of life in high-rise flats or estates.

When we include the aspects of all three bodies, we can visualize the virtual futility of action against the powerful machinery of society that appalls many people and conjures up Orwellian shadows of nightmare. At the other end of the scale, it is possible to see how powerful the impact of one individual human life can be in helping to reform and shape collective consciousness to provide more freedom and innovative leeway for every individual. In such instances, these 'generation planets', and their aspects, will be especially pertinent in the birth chart.

At the time of the Second World War, Pluto moved into Leo and, in 1942 it was in a 4° orb of sextile with Neptune, just changing sign from Virgo to Libra. Since these planets are such slow-moving bodies, they shall be in sextile aspect until the year 2036. The people born during this virtual 100 year period are those who are most readily capable of accepting the vast changes that are really only just beginning to emerge in the 1980s. It is reasonable to suppose that this sextile aspect is indicative of the lessening of a sense of fear of that which lies within our own selves and society. It shows that the people born within these years will have the opportunity and the power to alter life for the better.

The Aspects Involving the Ascendant

Sun to Ascendant
Outward behaviour does not necessarily reflect the true personality. To aver, 'I am who I am' without any inhibition of self-expression is probably the most difficult task a human being can perform. Lack of aspect expresses little desire to compete for recognition. The rather abrasive, arrogant attitude of square and opposition can mask the need to be accepted for oneself by oneself. Healthy vitality and outlook can prove attractive and marketable attributes for trine and sextile.

Moon to Ascendant
Women are likely to play an important part in the shaping of attitudes and outlook. Family mannerisms or spoonerisms may well be apparent. While the expanding aspects tend to be more openly demonstrative giving rise to a preference for dealing with the public, conjunction and contracting aspects are usually more touchily sensitive. No matter how hard it may be to reconcile feelings and motivations, personal experiences do prove useful in helping others to cope with their problems.

Mercury to Ascendant
To be interested in life and other people encourages the desire to communicate thoughts and ideas and to be receptive to knowledge which fosters perpetual growth. Trine and quintile series can be highly articulate with a facility for the right phrase; sextile and septiles are able to capitalize on such talents; square can sometimes be defensive and carping. The obvious nervousness of quincunx, sesquiquadrate and square will affect speech and behaviour belying real feelings and intentions.

Venus to Ascendant
The desire to know and understand people is a reflection of the need to comprehend self. Tactful, diplomatic relations with others are easily created with trine and quintile series. Special awareness of others' needs as well as the ability to know self very well is shown by sextile, septiles and lack of aspect. Square expresses a greater awareness of one's own needs often emerging as self-consciousness, gaucheness or a tendency to justify actions. With opposition, the partner usually provides motivation taking priority over one's own wishes.

Mars to Ascendant
Because Mars is the ruler of the natural Ascendant, the quality of the ability to be self-assertive and decisive is illustrated by the aspects. Square may appear to be bombastic yet is invariably dynamic and creative, displaying exceptional leadership qualities since the challenge of life is immediately accepted head on. Trine and sextile tend to more easy-going, which probably explains why the health is generally more sound and the individual less prone to accidents. Opposition can be contentious but may also become the victim of others' anger or pugnacity.

Jupiter to Ascendant
The freedom to be oneself, to 'live and let live', derives from an instinctive awareness of life and human behaviour. The expanding aspects tend to be more relaxed about such matters, for their lives tend to be generally fortunate. With conjunction and square an effusive *bonhomie* cannot always disguise a sense of dissatisfaction. Material well-being is often endowed with too much significance. Sextile and trine can attain great success in middle age which, if well handled, will succour and sustain the remainder of the life in style.

Saturn to Ascendant
The tendency to feel overly conscious of feelings and appearance can result in shyness especially with the minor aspects and opposition. The objectivity of conjunction and square may be welcomed by the scientist yet could prove to be a security screen that protects self from personal contact or emotional involvement. Opposition may mean a late marriage or the necessity to assume responsibility for others. Trine and sextile are usually able to enjoy an old age that is healthy, wealthy and worldly wise.

Uranus to Ascendant
Readiness to be part of the maelstrom of life does not always mean preparedness for the unexpected. Conjunction, square and opposition invariably have exceptionally outstanding, charismatic personalities capable of influencing other people. Minor aspects can be very highly strung, erratic, eccentric and very changeable, yet capable of deriving sudden insights that more than compensate for the stresses to the nervous system. Trine and sextile can flow with the tide, often gaining where others seem to fail.

Neptune to Ascendant
The desire to be at peace with oneself and the rest of the world shows itself through compassion for others. Square, semi-square and semi-sextile tend to deliberately seek to know the inner person, for until self is understood there can be no real belief or confidence in what one does, nor true appraisal of others and their problems. Minor aspects reflect subtleties of personality that are only recognized by the selfless and discerning. Trine can be gullible, fabricating fears where none exist. Sextile readily attunes to the needs of others often through having first encountered the meaning of pain.

Pluto to Ascendant
An enigmatic aura can mask the exceptionally powerful personality of the conjunction, square and opposition, which may well be misunderstood and found threatening by others. The psychologist with the disconcerting ability to see into the recesses of another's soul. Quintiles and septiles have a super-awareness of life which may not be appreciated until the latter years. Trine and sextile may have the knack of bouncing back from difficult periods, but contracting aspects tend to need to learn the hard way!

The Aspects Involving the Midheaven

Sun to Midheaven
Pure consciousness of self is the ideal that is sought, for creativity can then be focussed and disciplined to be productive and useful to society. With conjunction and square, the ego can interfere with the creative process since the need for recognition may obscure the true path. Opposition and trine could deny one's individuality, seeking something that might not exist. Minor contracting aspects could seek forms of self-denial, perhaps through lack of control or spates of energy depletion.

Moon to Midheaven
When the feeling nature is nurtured the whole personality radiates dramatic growth. Mother or family may well influence the all-important career direction but, unless the correct choice of career and life-style is made, states of unhappy restlessness can ensue. A ready appraisal of social requirements encourages a public life for conjunction, trine and sextile. The contracting aspects often feel too caught up in dealing with immediate dilemmas, for their path in life tends to be pitted with obstacles mainly stemming from domestic issues.

Mercury to Midheaven
The posing of the questions, *who, what, how and why?* release the individual to assume personal control over his development, but the search for inner truth must not gainsay the right of others to be. Square generally challenges the veracity of social dictates as applied to the individual; minor contracting aspects often encounter nervousness and an inability to articulate thoughts and feelings, especially when dealing with those in authority; trine, sextile and septiles can successfully utilize fluency in career.

Venus to Midheaven
A feeling of ease with self and the rest of the world is paramount. Moral and material worth comes under constant scrutiny to maintain self-respect and regard of others. Contracting aspects cannot side-step the realities of life nor potential disappointment with what can be achieved. Lack of aspect has to understand self before situations can be faced with clarity. Conjunction and trine are attracted to creative areas where temperament and personality problems are more acceptable.

Mars to Midheaven
To become self-reliant and to forge a life-style that is unique requires forcefulness and sustained self-assertiveness as well as the ability to work hard and long towards

particular goals. The independent-spirited conjunction, square and opposition are competitive and contentious, often encountering conflicts with those in authoritative positions. Minor contracting aspects find difficulty in sustaining courage and vitality but opportunities arise for trine and sextile, who can create success through well-directed ambitions.

Jupiter to Midheaven
The greater the personal growth, the larger can be the contribution made to the rest of the world. Growth does not depend upon self-confidence, but trust in the meaning of life. Conjunction, trine and sextile may attain enormous success in the middle years especially if pursuing a career associated with improving the lot of others. Square, opposition, sesquiquadrate and semi-square must guard against over-inflated ideas of what life is meant to produce.

Saturn to Midheaven
Concentration upon goals that take time to mature is nevertheless punctuated by a sense of inadequacy that dares not believe that success could be a reality. Conjunction could reach a plateau in the career or be forced to relinquish aspirations at some stage. Square and opposition tend to fear the future and may seek methods of hindering one's own development, for failure is at least a known quantity. Expanding aspects find that life becomes immeasurably better with maturity, attaining success in later life.

Uranus to Midheaven
Nothing is impossible or beyond the scope of human ingenuity. Conjunction will stride beyond the bounds of conformity to opt for the new and unusual and may change direction completely. Sextile, quintiles and septiles quickly respond to shifting situations, successfully pursuing an independent life regardless of social pressures, unlike the minor contracting aspects. Square and opposition are generally unsuited to employed situations, automatically rebelling against any form of supervision. Trine flows with life, deriving opportunities even in the worst of times.

Neptune to Midheaven
It is not easy to maintain idealism when reality has the habit of disturbing and distorting illusions. For conjunction, self-sacrifice and the willingness to serve others can lift depression when self-confidence is low. Square and opposition tend to feel out-of-step with the rest of the world, wishing for a sense of belonging that seems perpetually denied. Conjunction, trine and sextile have natural leanings towards the arts and mysticism but should beware gullibility. Minor aspects indicate vulnerable sensitivity.

Pluto to Midheaven
A subtle strength that refuses to accept the dictates of others, piercing through sham to expose the reality of one's own and others' purposes. Conjunction allows for direct access to higher development, acknowledging the compulsion to fulfil a particular mission in life. Development is subject to dramatic phases for conjunction, square and opposition. Minor contracting aspects find difficulty in maintaining their tenuous hold on fundamentals. Trine and sextile rapidly gain insight into situations to their advantage.

Chapter 7
Interpretation and Consultation

Interpretation is the most fascinatingly enjoyable yet infuriatingly frustrating part of all astrological work. It is the essence and object of astrology, challenging and confounding not only the new-comer to astrology but also the professional consultant of many years standing. The reason interpretation is difficult is because it employs the creative function. In exactly the same way that the artist and the writer must learn their craft and be prepared to face the agony of the empty canvas or the blank page, so the astrologer must conjure up his inner resources to confront both himself and the person in the birth chart. The astrologer must allow self-expression to flow freely. Although the fact that every chart contains the Sun shows that everyone has the potential to be creative, the most naturally creative among us will suffer the frustration of not always being able to express oneself easily. For many students it is comforting to find that they are not alone in finding it difficult to satisfactorily mix and mingle the basic principles to formulate correct deductions.

Astrology's principles of the signs, houses, planets and aspects may be learned by rote but they cannot be put to use until they are felt by heart, mind and spirit. Books and teachers can supply only hints, clues and techniques, for, in common with any creative field, the actual process of interpretation cannot be taught. They are meant as guides until sufficient confidence is acquired to depend upon the only tools that are really needed, your ephemeris and yourself. Far more will be gained through personal observation and experience than by attempting to emulate another's thoughts. The best method of learning is to work closely with friends and family members who are willing to share their intimate experiences.

Interpreting a birth chart can seem rather like a fun game at first, but as more knowledge is accumulated there comes an inevitable stage when the pattern of interweaving lines and symbols means absolutely nothing. Congratulations! You have reached the first of many 'brick walls'! This syndrome seems to occur as a means of giving the mind time to assimilate the information that has been acquired and space in which to allow the next stage in development to take place. To allow for this process it is wisest to put your studies aside temporarily. Enthusiasm will return as quickly as it vanished. It is often surprising how much more mature your ability to interpret will be; that is, until the next 'brick wall' is encountered! No matter how able or advanced you may become, this syndrome is bound to re-occur. Understand and work with the process rather than believing that your interpretative capabilities are inadequate.

Astrological analysis should be termed astrological synthesis, for analysis involves the dissection of the factors in a birth chart in a systematic way. Its value is that nothing is omitted. Synthesis of the information to create a true representation of a complex human being undoubtedly presents most difficulty for newcomers. Knowing where to start and how to sustain a firm picture of the total personality are the major stumbling blocks. They can be mastered.

The Card System outlined on pages 25 and 120 will have helped you to become more reliant on the symbols to evoke their meaning from the knowledge you have already aquired during your study of them. In effect, they are helping to train your mind to develop its intuitive function in order to save time, effort and to promote accuracy. In a process akin to that of the computer which is programmed to sort through its memory banks, to locate a relevant piece of information, the intuition often unerringly knows more than the conscious mind. In any field, those who are able to employ their intuitive resources freely have a creative flair that raises the quality of their work above the average. This is certainly true of the astrologer. It is surprisingly easy to develop the intuition.

While calculation may be the least popular word in the newcomer's vocabulary, the setting up of the birth chart should be understood as a ritual of self-preparation for the ensuing interpretation. The resources of one's total self should be concentrated upon the chart and, as each detail is entered upon it, either speak aloud your thoughts and impressions into a cassette recorder or make handwritten notes. As well as helping to train the intuitive function, this will aid fluency of the spoken and written word, for the astrologer must be able to communicate his findings. Use the Four Angles of the chart to focus your mind and spirit (see page 23). Having completed the chart, spend sufficient time to drink in its wholeness, then put it away. Most practising astrologers set up the chart well in advance of a consultation, knowing full well the value of allowing the chart to 'percolate'. The mind needs time to do its work.

Create a starting point for yourself by stripping the chart down to its barest essentials. Having concentrated your attention on the whole chart return to the Four Angles. Examine them simply according to the Quadruplicities, Cardinal, Fixed and Mutable (see page 34) for this will show both the impact of reality as well as the fundamental dynamism of the personality. While the Placidus House System provides an immediately identifiable Cross of Matter (see page 42), the Equal House System illustrates the unequal distances between the Ascendant and Midheaven during the course of the day. Any aspect occurring between these points of reference is more obvious by Equal House. In Chart A (Figure 46), Cardinal signs on the Asc/Desc

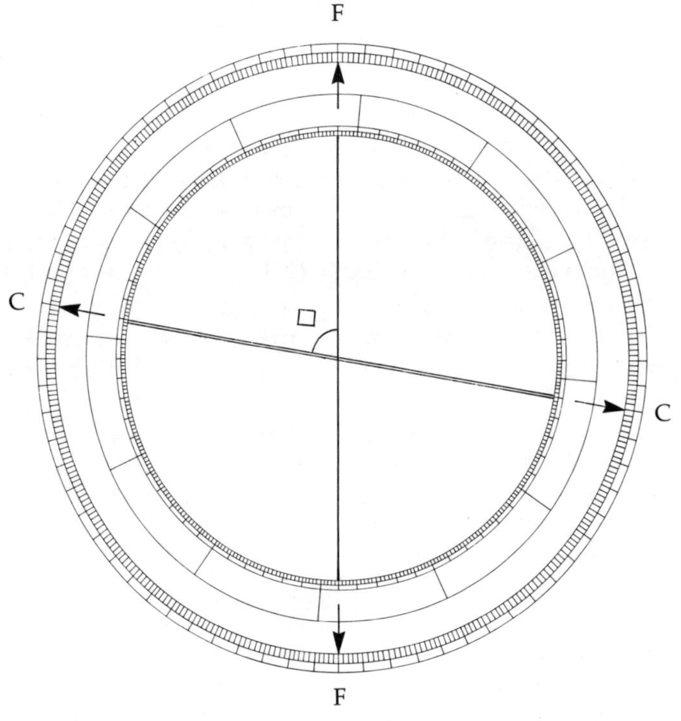

Figure 46 Chart A

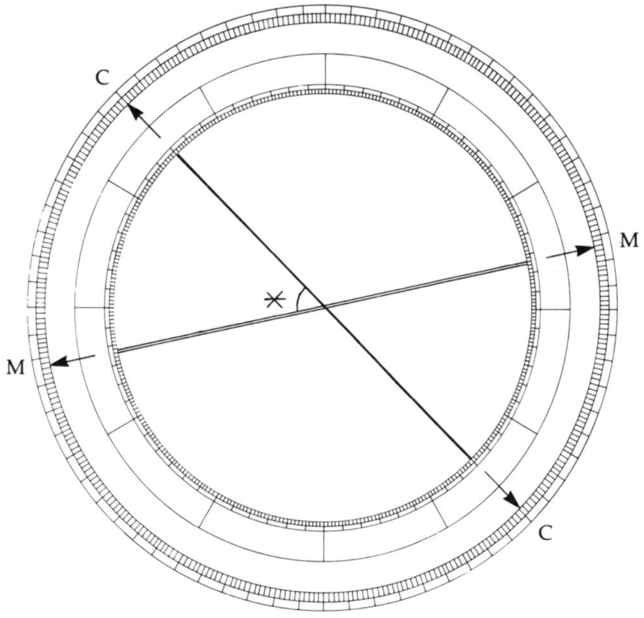

Figure 47 Chart B

axis Squaring Fixed signs on the MC/IC axis are reflective of an individual who is in the habit (F) of viewing life as a challenge (SQ) that must be confronted (C). Constant attempts (C) will be made to shrug off (SQ) the conditioning of the past (F) in order to establish oneself (MC/IC) as a complete individual. Great strength of character is displayed (C, SQ, F) but health problems (Asc Squared) are likely to create obstacles (SQ) in promoting ambitions and a way of being (MC) that are not always welcomed or understood by loved ones (IC, SQ, Desc).

Example Chart B (Figure 47), with its Mutable signs on the Asc/Desc axis in Sextile aspect to the Cardinal signs on the MC/IC axis, represents the skeleton of the birth chart for 'Kate'. Used as the main example throughout *The Astrology Workbook* you will have gradually become familiar with its features. The same birth chart is used for the consultation in the final section of the chapter. You may wish to test yourself to discover how much information

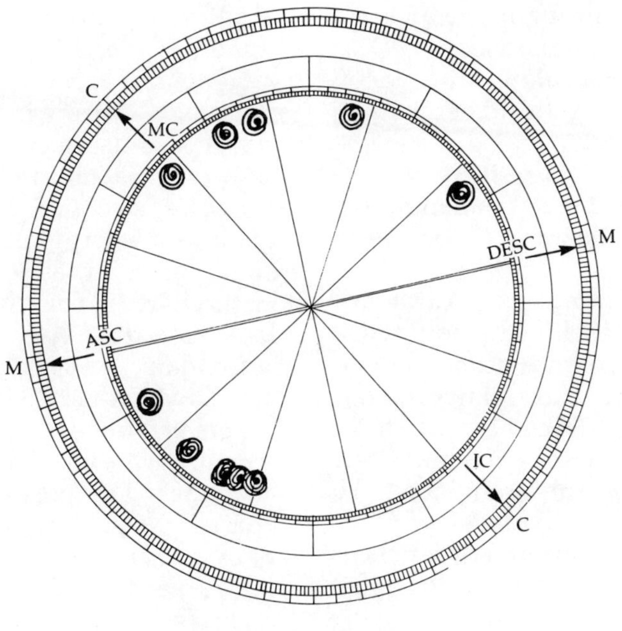

Figure 48 Chart C

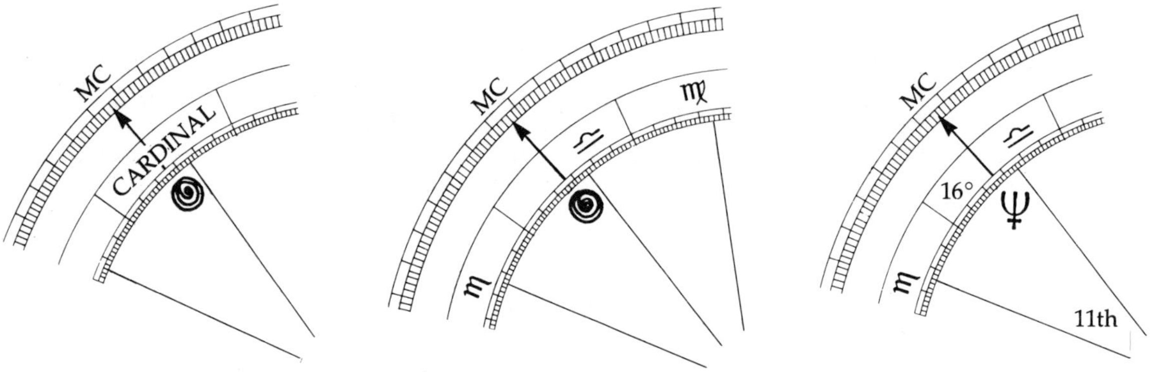

Figure 49 Interpreting the planetary positions: three steps

you can gain from Chart B before referring to the opening paragraph of 'An Astrological Consultation with Kate' on page 148.

Having examined the dynamism of the individual via the Four Angles and their Quadruplicities, it is helpful to think of the ten planets as globules of pure energy. Chart C proved useful both as a starting point to analysis as well as to Kate's Consultation. The globule of energy that is most prominent will be that which is Angular (see page 115), for this has immediate bearing on the fundamental dynamism of the personality. It can be tackled in stages, as for example in Kate's chart. Step One: *Conjunct the Cardinal MC* showing how great the priority for self-understanding is. Step Two: *Conjunct the Libran MC* indicating how much will be gained through experiences with and through other people. Step Three: *Neptune in Libra Conjunct the 11th House MC*, revealing the deep significance of her search, to aid others with all the compassion of her being. First she must gather sufficient experience of life through periods of doubt, unhappiness, loneliness and disillusionment, but also, sublime joy and love.

To interpret a birth chart the astrologer must find within himself, common sense (Earth), fluency of communication (Air), intuition (Fire) and, most importantly, compassion (Water). Seen in its most positive light the birth chart depicts the ultimate potential of the individual. To enable this potential to develop it is necessary to work for it through experiences that are both positive and negative. How much the individual is capable of being stretched by such experiences depends upon the overall quality of the chart. The angular Neptune in Kate's chart speaks of the calibre of her personality. She must encounter a rich experience that stretches her mental (Air sign/11th house), emotional (Libra/Venus ruled) and spiritual (Neptune) resources. She is meant to become especially aware of issues beyond the personal (Neptune/11th house are Generation factors).

Energy tends to ebb and flow, and since the planets represent energy, everything concerning them may be interpreted from a negative and a positive point of view. This means that every feature of the birth chart will both receive and emit. The next most obvious feature of Kate's chart is the concentration of planets that lie in the 2nd house and athwart the 3rd house cusp. Thus the value that she places upon herself (2nd) is bound to colour her attitude of mind (3rd); equally, anything said to her by anyone, but especially by teachers, brothers or sisters (3rd) will have bearing on her sense of inner security (2nd). The zodiacal sign of a Satellitium of planets is likely to prove a stronger feature of the overall quality of energy expression than the Sun sign. However, as with *every* particle of the birth chart, it *must* be viewed through the lens of the **Ascending** sign. As the Ascendant is Sagittarius, the Satellitium in Aquarius with MC Libra, great awareness of others is shown as well as a decidedly anti-establishment and often rebellious character. The position of the Ruler of the chart by sign and house should now be known. As Jupiter is part of the Satellitium in Aquarius, the above information is endorsed and shown to be an especially dominant factor in Kate's personality.

It is wise to make written notes of all your findings. There is no one method of doing this. Since it is a matter of personal preference, the best method is your own which you will develop in time. Eventually you could become so proficient that, like many professional astrologers, you dispense with it altogether.

It is helpful to make orderly, well-constructed notes so that any section might easily be referred to. Use A4 size paper which can be turned sideways and headed as follows:

Significator	**Deduction**	**Category**
Disassociated T/SQUARE CARD/MUTABLE 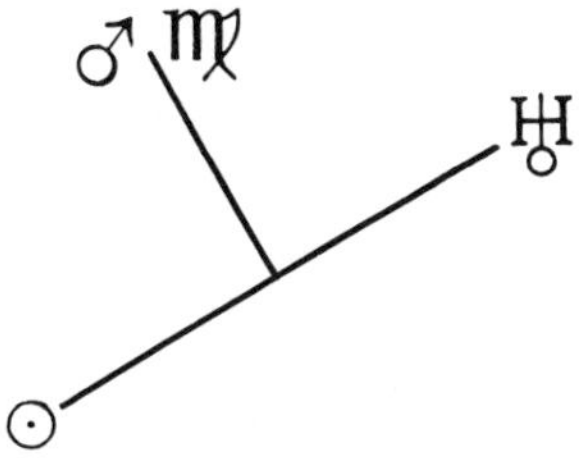	Takes self and goals very seriously. Demands/expects high standards of behaviour from others but more so from self. Extremely ambitious yet may fear consequences of responsibility and capabilities unless self-engineered/instigated. However, may be reluctant to admit this until maturity/experience gained. Hardworking but will switch off completely if hurt, betrayed or exploited in business or personal life. Allows self to be exploited, then complains when situation becomes unsatisfactory, yet it has occurred because of liability to work below level of competence. Perhaps fears own power.	PERSONALITY RELATIONSHIPS CAREER PERSONALITY GENERAL TRAITS

Obviously there is far more that could be included since every planet in the T/Square connects with a personal planet: the Sun in the 1st house, Mars in Mercury-ruled Virgo in 10th (re: Sun in Capricorn), Uranus in Mutual Reception with the Moon. The factors surrounding the T/Square are likely to be seen in virtually everything that Kate does. Bear in mind that notes are meant to provide a starting point for all on-going statements.

If a planet is part of a chart feature such as a Satellitium, T/Square or, as in the case of Kate's Mars and Saturn which are both in the 10th house although not actually in conjunction, they should always be considered together. This also applies to planets that are in Mutual Reception with one another. For example, Moon and Uranus or Mercury and Saturn in Kate's chart.

A planet is more powerful when it occurs before an angle rather than after it, as if 'leaning into' the angle. This also applies to the houses and a planet before the house cusp would be more pertinent to the following house than that which it might seem to occupy. There is no example of this

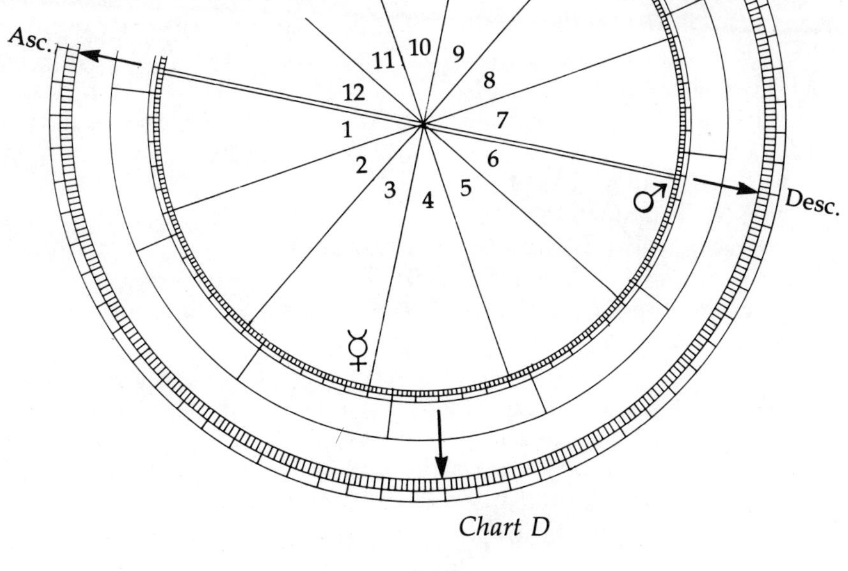

Chart D

in Kate's chart but you can observe that Venus conjunct the 3rd house cusp must have particular relevance to that house. Since Venus is part of a Satellitium, all the planets concerned, including Moon and Jupiter, will colour the quality of the 3rd house. In Chart D (Figure 45), Mercury is 'leaning into' the 4th house and Mars conjunct the Descendant into the 7th. The factors surrounding the 3rd and 6th houses in each instance should also be taken into account.

Rulerships

Having examined the main features of the birth chart, as in Kate's chart — the angular Neptune, ruler Jupiter, Satellitium in Aquarius and T/Square — the individual planets must then be explored thoroughly by sign, house and aspect with the other planetary bodies. The simplest method is to examine each planet in its natural order from the Sun to Pluto. Alternatively, it may well be found illuminating to 'unveil' the globules of energy in Chart C one by one in order of their relevance within the context of the birth chart itself.

Until confidence is gained, it may be preferable to use the Generation planets as sole rulers:

Uranus as the sole ruler of **Aquarius** and the 11th house

Neptune as the sole ruler of **Pisces** and the 12th house

Pluto as the sole ruler of **Scorpio** and the 8th house

The associated rulerships will help to determine the strength of the individual planets. In Kate's chart, Uranus is both the ruler of the Satellitium in Aquarius 2nd involving chart ruler Jupiter and the natural ruler of the 11th house (re: Neptune conjunct MC). Thus Uranus would be the globule of energy to be 'unveiled' following Jupiter. Uranus is in the 7th. Venus is natural ruler of the 7th and Libra (re: Neptune) and is part of the Satellitium *2nd*/3rd in Aquarius. Although not actually in aspect with one another, they clearly represent dominating facets of Kate's personality.

Serving as a reminder that there are no 'empty' houses (even when untenanted by a planet and helping to integrate the various features of the chart) is the examination of the rulers of the house cusps, or *dispositors* (see page 45). In some of the older astrological books phrases such as, 'the Lord of the Twelfth is in the Ninth' refer to the planet that is the natural ruler of the sign on the cusp of the 12th, which will be posited in the 9th house. In Kate's chart, the ruler of the 12th with its Scorpio cusp is Pluto which is in the 9th house. Because Jupiter is the chart ruler, its natural 9th house becomes the most prominent of all the houses in the chart. Since Pluto is in Leo referring immediately to the Sun (Leo's natural ruler), it is possible to see that Kate would tend to keep personal feelings and any hurts to herself.

Compiling an Astrological Analysis

Once the many details of the birth chart have been examined and collated, the process of synthesizing the information into a cohesive whole begins. Unless you have the opportunity to experience a thorough examination of your character by a competent astrologer, you are unlikely to discover much guidance concerning what constitutes a good astrological analysis. That there is no set method of presenting an analysis may appear to be a serious drawback at first, but this is really as it should be. No artist wishes to be told how and where to apply his paint, otherwise the result could be akin to 'painting by numbers'. Each astrologer has to learn to dig deeply into his own resources of self-expression. It is often said that it is possible to learn as much about the astrologer as the subject from the resulting analysis.

Presentation of an Astrological Analysis

There are three ways of presenting an analysis: (i) a written analysis, (ii) a cassette recording, (iii) a personal consultation with the option of being taped on cassette.

(i) *Written analyses.* If studying for the examinations held annually by the Mayo School of Astrology, or the Faculty of Astrological Studies, becoming well versed in written work is advisable. It is not necessary to follow any prescribed order. Sift, sort and mingle the information so that it may be easily and clearly read. A written analysis may be compiled according to personal preference. It could, perhaps, be presented in the form of a personal letter, a book with separate sections headed 'Personality Traits', 'Career', etc., or in any way you prefer. Whichever method you choose, the analysis should clearly show how privileged you feel to have access to the subject's innermost being. The chart itself will describe how the information should be given. A highly-strung, sensitive type of personality obviously needs to be handled gently and with great tact. A person whose birth chart speaks of their love of honesty will naturally respect your honesty and integrity as an astrologer.

If possible the work should be neatly typed on one side of the paper, then housed in an attractive folder. Most importantly, due deference must be given to what is written. Every word will have meaning for the subject of the analysis, so do not be afraid to give full explanations of what you mean. Should you feel that certain characteristics could apply to virtually anyone, do not be afraid to say so. We are all members of the human race. It is often the smaller details, that might possibly be dismissed, that may well bring your interpretation vividly to life. The most expert psychologist admits that little is understood concerning human behaviour so do not be perturbed should certain quirks of character appear that are new to you. Freely admit this and, no doubt, the subject of the analysis will enjoy explaining them to you! The study of human nature is endlessly fascinating and each chart will teach you more.

On either the carbon copy or a photocopy of the original, keep a record of the astrological correlatives by entering them in either the right or left hand margins alongside relevant statements. This is useful for any future work with that particular chart or possible research.

The disadvantage of written work is the time factor. It can take a full week to compile and present a written analysis. However, it may not be possible to expect a fee commensurate with the time and effort involved. It is for this reason that today's professionals can, unfortunately, rarely undertake written work.

(ii) *Cassette Recordings.* Obviously a verbal facility is important if the work is to be recorded on cassette, but again, the quality of the individual astrologer should come across freely. Warmth and compassion in the voice is more welcome to the listener than perfectly enunciated tones. A good cassette recorder with a 'Pause' switch is helpful since this does not interfere with the general recording too much. This manner of working is extremely useful for those unable to be present at a personal consultation.

The disadvantage of a cassette recording, in common with written work, is that there is no immediate feedback.

(iii) *Personal Consultation.* The taping of a personal consultation is an option that some astrologers and clients take up. It can prove impossible to tape a consultation even when using the very best equipment. Although defying the rational, it is a situation that may have to be accepted. In the main, this is a popular and satisfying method of working for both astrologer and client, for there is plenty of opportunity to freely discuss particular issues.

Giving Advice

Strictly speaking, unless qualified to do so, an astrologer should not give advice. Certainly, advice should not be offered unless the client has requested it. Because astrology offers an over-view of the personality and the current situation within the context of the life-span, through judicious usage of Progressions and Transits the astrologer is in a privileged position in which he is able to give positive impetus to the manner in which the next stage in the life may unfold. A positive and optimistic approach can often inspire and encourage a client to cope with sometimes very difficult situations. Should it arise that you are confronted with problems beyond your understanding and capabilities, have no compunction in referring the client to someone who can help. During a consultation it might arise that the client would benefit from some other therapy. The astrologer is often able to specify the type that would be most useful or least helpful. A list of practitioners in all areas of the healing and helping professions should be kept for such contingencies. Indeed, the astrologer often acts as a 'way station' giving confidence to do further work on oneself.

While it may be hard not to give advice or to pass judgement, it is all too easy to precipitate happenings. This will not happen if you treasure that person who has only reached a particular stage along the pathway to wholeness. *See* the person in the chart and *listen* to what they say. It is no fallacy that, 'the person will speak their chart'.

Dealing with a Client's Expectations
It is not necessary or wise to attempt to singlehandedly prove the case for astrology, yet it is important to define what you believe astrology to be at the outset. Many people misunderstand what astrology is or what an astrologer can do. It is helpful to clarify your feelings, stating what you can and cannot do before the consultation or undertaking a written or taped analysis. It can happen that someone believes that an astrologer should be able to divulge the most extraordinary details having *the* answer to life, particularly *their* life! An astrologer is not a wizard. There are no magical panaceas or passports to happiness. An astrologer cannot change circumstances or make anything happen. To behave as a responsible human being means that you do not undertake to make decisions for someone else, but encourage them to assume responsibility for their own lives so that they can exert more control over themselves and their own actions through the agency of greater self-understanding.

Children's Charts
The value of knowing how to encourage the development of an individual's full potential cannot be denied, but whether it is appropriate for a parent to have intimate knowledge of their child's personality is debatable and, therefore, a matter that should be most carefully considered. Examination of babies' and children's charts, has proved extremely valuable particularly where there was reason for guidance and further understanding. Not many astrologers will undertake such work for there are so many factors to be considered. It also necessitates examination of the parents' charts for parental influences cannot be separated from the development of a child.

The Astrologer in Consultation
Inevitably, there is a 'right' time to begin the process of self-discovery. When this occurs, or what triggers off this need, will vary considerably from one person to another. Asking 'why do you wish to see me?' will not necessarily reveal the purpose of the consultation, for the client may not be aware of the real reason. Thus it can occur that a consultation takes a different direction than was at first apparent. It is not unusual to find clients who have a tendency to listen only to information that interests them, shutting off from certain facts that they prefer not to think about or face up to. Here may well be encountered the delicate dividing line between what constitutes an astrological consultation and a counselling session. A growing number of astrologers are seeking additional qualifications as psychological counsellors or therapists for this reason.

An astrologer's role is to shed light, thereby introducing the Soul to the Self so that the personality may be seen at its most positive. Verbalizing the potential can encourage the individual to help himself to concur with the Soul's promptings to actualize that potential. Not surprisingly, many astrologers suffer a form of stage fright before tackling analysis of a new chart. This is a healthy and natural part of the process showing how important the work and the life involved are.

It takes years of study and experience to become a good astrologer. Openly admit that you are a student and allow the client to help you. While absolute accuracy is desirable, there will be no slur upon you, your astrology or astrology itself if you are, at times, in error. Indeed, being fallible can sometimes prove an excellent way of relaxing the client and allowing him the opportunity to be more open about himself. There are, at least, two opportunities for observing this in the section called 'An Astrological Consultation with Kate' which is the transcript of the actual consultation.

An Astrological Consultation with Kate

Kate was keen to find out more about herself, expressing most interest in the problems she has encountered with her family.

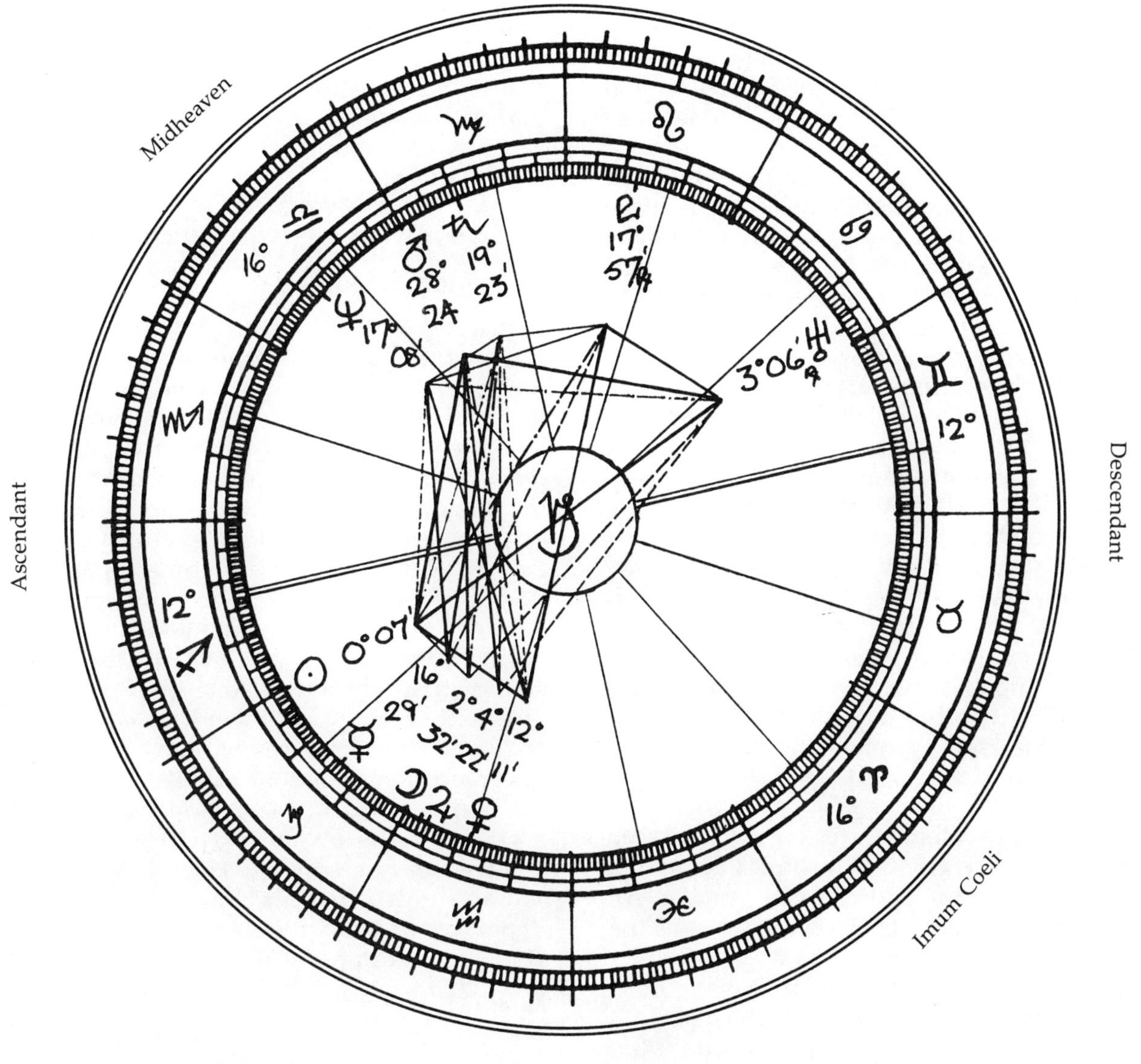

The Sun is in Capricorn
The Moon is in Aquarius
Mercury is in Capricorn
Venus is in Aquarius
Mars is in Virgo
Jupiter is in Aquarius

Saturn is in Virgo
Uranus is in Cancer
Neptune is in Libra
Pluto is in Leo
The Ascendant is Sagittarius
The Midheaven is Libra

This is a map of the
Heavens as seen from the
exact place of birth
HULL: YORKSHIRE
at the exact moment of
birth *6.58 am GMT*
22nd December 1949

Figure 51 The natal horoscope chart of 'Kate'

MC
(CARDINAL)

ASC — DESC
(MUTABLE)

IC
ASC ✶ MC

ASC/DESC
MUTABLE SIGNS

MC/IC
CARDINAL SIGNS

DESC/7TH CUSP
♊

ASC ♐ (FIRE)

MC ♎ (AIR)

✶

Astrologer:
Just from looking at the Angles of the chart, we can gain an overall impression of your energy seen as dynamic force. Underlying everything there is a sense of rightness about you being here on this planet, and a sense of knowing the full measure of your own worth as an individual. When you reach out to other people the quandary begins for they do not always understand your feelings and intentions. Because they reflect back to you the question of what it is you mean, the emphasis and responsibility for your actions is then thrown on you, so it is that you then can doubt your own self and sense of self worth. Most of the time your energy flows very freely and delightfully, with a ready eagerness to move outwards and meet life in the happy, hopeful way associated with a Sagittarius Ascendant. Your Libran Midheaven shows a strong commitment to others, that feeling of, 'I need to belong, to be part of the world', allied with the need to relate and to understand who you are within that context.

For the moment, if we look at the planets in terms of globules of energy rather than individually, one's eye immediately goes straight to the globule of energy that is Angular conjunct the Midheaven. It is the most significant factor in the birth chart for it reflects your whole attitude and outlook on life showing the way you view yourself. Libra on the Midheaven shows you are a people person who must inevitably give of yourself. This is endorsed when we see that the planet conjunct the Midheaven is Neptune, for there is that element of self-sacrifice, a sense of seeing life perhaps not as it is or people as they are, but the way you would like them to be. There is the need for you to make a commitment in your life that has to do with helping and aiding other people, and if you don't do that, then you deny your own self. You would actually be happy in either the healing or the creative professions. It is an 11th house Midheaven so you would prefer

something that has an unusual yet personalized approach rather than working as part of a group. It has to be you who does it, and possibly influences the group. Because the planet in question is a Generation planet, it shows that you have to make a bigger commitment than you might have thought.

Kate:
Yes. I've felt that but haven't been able to do much about it yet.

Astrologer:
It is meant to take a fair amount of time to discover what it is you have to do, for it requires a rich life experience before you can be ready to do whatever it is. It is so easy for you to be disillusioned by what you have encountered in life generally. Nevertheless you have to overcome that in order to ultimately do what you have to do. Just knowing you were born when the Sun was in Capricorn shows that you are likely to be a proverbial late developer. This is endorsed in other areas of your chart. There are altogether four planets across the 2nd and 3rd houses, showing the great emphasis on the way in which you use your personality. How you are as an individual is much more important to you in the earlier part of your life. Finding out who you are.

Kate:
Yes, it has always bothered me. Sometimes it seems to be so selfish.

Astrologer:
As you mature and come into the Jupiter period of your life, which won't be until you are forty-five or so, the early knowledge you have gained will come to have its proper place and meaning. It truly will all be seen to be worthwhile in the end.

Kate:
That's good to know and a relief to find it will all be for a purpose.

Astrologer:
Your chart shows that there are transition periods. The early part with its very profound experience, followed by the period when you are reaching

STRONG ♍/♏
♆ IN LAST QUADRANT

☉ ♃/♄
ASC △ ♇

8TH 10TH
♂ ~ ♇

SATELLITUM
2ND/3RD

♐ ASC
RULING PLANET
♃

5 PLANETS ♍/♏
IN FIRST QUADRANT

out into the world, and then as you come into your forties you will reach back to your origins, take hold in a very different way and make positive use of it.

With the Angular planet in the Aquarian house and three planets in Aquarius, the note that is going to be sung has to be very strongly Aquarian. Whatever other signs are apparent in the chart, this is going to be the most prominent sign of all.

Kate:
Yes I feel that. Much more Aquarian than Capricorn.

Astrologer:
Taken as a Generation sign you would feel part of your generation and yet, being strongly Aquarian determinedly out of step with it.

Kate:
(laughs) Determinedly out of step. Sounds good.

Astrologer:
There's a sort of definitive quality of rebellion about you. The anti-establishment sign, Sagittarius on the Ascendant, and three planets in Aquarius conjures up a picture of a lady who has to go against the establishment by nature. Yet this globule of energy in the first house is the Sun in Capricorn, so perhaps we can say that she makes the establishment work for herself?

Kate:
That phrase was popular during my college days and I always identified with it.

Astrologer:
Even if we don't look at the Capricorn Sun, with three planets in the 2nd house and two in the 10th, there would be a strong need to be very much down to earth, on this planet, dealing with the here and now. It also shows how vital it is to have a tangible sense of security. There has to be evidence of 'I am who I am'. Possessions and surroundings would necessarily reflect your personality and be part of you. You would have to own your own property and to decorate it according to your own particular taste. No matter how rebellious or anti-establishment you may appear to be, it would also be extremely difficult for you to cope with being unemployed for any length of time because you would be denying your sense of self-worth in terms of society.

Kate:
Oh that's interesting. It doesn't matter whether I always get paid for what I do as long as I can recognize value in it, that's fine.

Astrologer:
Then it's perfectly all right.

Kate:
I do take care of my possessions you know. I very much need physical grounding. I know this.

Astrologer:
I can imagine your house. It would have to be very unusual and at the same time beautiful with a great sense of peace. You like to see your possessions around you and look after them, seeing that everything is orderly and well cared for, because this makes you feel good.

Kate:
Yes, it's true. In the past even with rented accommodation the first thing I always did was to redecorate the room I was living in. You know what I mean, it had to be mine. I had to put my own stamp on it. Have my things on the wall. Very important.

Astrologer:
Visible evidence of your own…

Kate:
Of me, yes.

Astrologer:
…being. It's interesting isn't it, some people don't bother and when someone says to you, 'Why do you set so much store on possessions?', as if it were a terrible thing…

Kate:
Terribly materialistic…

Astrologer:
They don't understand the need for those things.

Kate:
And it was a need in me, wasn't it?

Astrologer:
Yes, because your sense of security is not supposed to come from others, but from yourself. That's why the challenges have been set up for you. Aries on the I.C, at gut level, it is you who must take the commitment for you. You have to be your own person, which is sometimes a terrible responsibility. Having pretty things around you is a reflection of you. You have a delightful chart so why shouldn't you have a delightful home. I mean if people don't...

[margin: ♈ I.C. RULER OF ♈, ♂ WITH ♄ IN ♍ 10TH]

Kate:
If they don't like it, it doesn't matter.

Astrologer:
It doesn't matter one jot. It gives you a sense of peace when you go into your home. It is almost like a form of religion. By having a peaceful environment and a place where you can withdraw from the world, you gain a greater sense of faith in yourself and a greater sense of self-confidence. *Then* you can help others.

[margin: ♓ CUSP 4TH]

[margin: ♃ TRADITIONAL RULER OF ♓ IS CHART RULER]

Kate:
That's right. And if I don't get that, I just feel too harrassed.

Astrologer:
Yes, you must have a room that is only yours that you can withdraw to.

Kate:
Absolutely, yes.

Astrologer:
I mean a lock on the door, if necessary, where you can just...

Kate:
I haven't needed locks on doors but I have needed, as you say, a room for peace and withdrawal and then I can go out and help others. If I haven't got that, I'm useless.

[margin: ♓ ASSOCIATED WITH 12TH, ♏ CUSP 12TH ♇ IN 9TH (♃ IS NATURAL RULER OF 9TH+12TH]

Astrologer:
Then life becomes an absolute burden and you get easily drained, your energy drains very quickly. You are subtly sensitive. When Neptune is in a prominent position, it shows you can suffer, literally, the sins and feelings of the world, and as Pisces is on the 4th cusp, it comes right home to you. Scorpio on the 12th cusp shows how you bury it all deep within you. It all gets internalized. It's very private, so that unless you can withdraw and restore your sense of peaceful stillness...

Kate:
I used to cry a lot as a child, you see.

Astrologer:
I can imagine. But nobody would know how you feel.

[margin: ♏ CUSP 12TH ♈ IC ♇ IN 9TH]

[margin: ♆ ☍ IC]

Kate:
But you can't go on doing that because people immediately brush you aside. They don't want to know, I mean...

Astrologer:
It's too much feeling.

Kate:
It's too much feeling, it's too weak, and to be of any strength and help, you just can't show that to people. So...

[margin: ♊ DESC NATURAL RULER OF ♊, ☿ IN ♑ NATURAL RULER OF 7TH ♀ ♒ ON 3RD (☿) CUSP]

Astrologer:
Especially when the Moon is part of this cluster in Aquarius, it is as if you're not supposed to show those kind of feelings, or let them out so easily. One of these planets is Venus, ruler of the Midheaven, which is on the cusp of the 3rd house of communication. So what people say would have an enormous influence on your thinking and your image of yourself. The 3rd house also concerns brothers and sisters.

Kate:
I have two sisters who were enormously important in my young life.

Astrologer:
... and anything they say could bring you down as quick as a flash.

[margin: ☽ ♐ ♅ ☉ ♀ ♀ ☍ ♇]

Kate:
They were brilliant, talented, and I felt very out of it all.

Astrologer:
I can imagine how you were as a child. Were you the middle one?

Kate:
I was the youngest. There were four years between the middle one and myself, and only two years between them. They went everywhere together and I was left on my own rather a lot.

Astrologer:
Yes, that Aquarian sense of alienation and feeling of not belonging.

Kate:
When you are little you don't want to be alienated. It's not nice. But in all honesty I usually had a girlfriend who was a neighbour. For many years I had a friend called Jenny and she lived in the house next door, and before that I had a friend called Anne who lived down the lane.

Astrologer:
And you remember them so well?

Kate:
Oh yes, very important.

Astrologer:
It still gives you a good feeling?

Kate:
Oh yes.

Astrologer:
There is a strong emphasis on the family image but it is especially your self-image that is very, very important. Who you are, how you behave and what you do. So there is the element of prestige attached to your sense of self-worth. If anybody says the right thing, you swell with pride. By the same token if they say the wrong thing you can be quickly, easily deflated. You are very self-aware. Because Sagittarius is on the Ascendant anything to do with Jupiter and the 9th house will be significant. Thus, any planet which is in the 9th house says a great deal about you. In this instance it is Pluto in Leo. You have to be self-seeking. And how do you go about that? You do it intensely, and take things very much to heart. But you do not confide your thoughts and feelings about yourself to anyone. It is all kept very much tucked away. So it is not a question of judging other people's behaviour, for your strongly Aquarian nature says that they can behave in a very free way, in fact, in any way that they want. But the same rules do not apply to your own behaviour. That's another matter entirely! How you behave comes under close scrutiny, constantly analysed. Again it's very much something that nobody would realize that you do. No-one would think that you would go to such lengths. Do you see that you have five planets all in this area? The Sun, Moon, Mercury, as well as Jupiter, the ruler of the chart, and Venus, the ruler of the Midheaven. It really isn't possible for you to avoid a rich life experience. It would have to start when you were very young. You would be thrown in at the deep end from the beginning to befit you for the work that you have to come. Notice the aspects, the oppositions — from the Sun to Uranus and Venus to Pluto. You would have to be stretched before you could get to grips with who and what you are. In the Sun opposition Uranus, we can see how diametrically opposed you were, and still are, to the basic established practices of your family.

Kate:
Yes, oh that has been a theme of my life for many years.

Astrologer:
The Moon, Aquarius and Sun opposition Uranus show that your family attempted to put you into a particular mould, to stick labels on you and say you must behave in a certain way, and all while this child has been constantly anti whatever they said.

Kate:
That's it! Whatever they said. Yes, I'm afraid so...

Astrologer:
And they never tried reverse psychology on you?

Kate:
No (laughs).

Astrologer:
Your father is very much the archetypal male figure, the male chauvinist type who is very, very aware of his existence ordered in a

certain way. Outsiders may not see it as ordered, but he does.

Kate:
His career, was very much laid down.

Astrologer:
Very career-orientated, Sun Capricorn, isn't it?

Kate:
Yes, he was, yes.

☽ ♒
⚻ ♅ exact
☉ ⚺ ☽
☽ + fixed sign + house
Sat ♒

Astrologer:
You have a mother who demanded that her child behave in a certain way. Perhaps she was too busy to look after you herself and placed you with other people. But the child feels alienated and interprets her behaviour as 'you don't want me', thereby setting up a pattern of rebellious behaviour in order to be noticed.

Kate:
That's right, yes.

☽ part of satellitium
☉ ⚺ ☽ ☌ ♅ ⚻ ♇
∟ ♀ (☌ ♇)

Astrologer:
It is an escalating pattern: the child becomes more demanding because she feels her needs are greater. She says nobody is paying any attention to me, so I'll make them pay attention to me.

☽ part of Sat.

Kate:
Yes, it was like that. I suppose my mum thought my sisters would take care of me or I'd develop other friends, you see. But yes, my mum didn't have much time for me.

Strong ♒/♅

Astrologer:
Were you an afterthought?

Kate:
Well, I wasn't a boy.

☉/♑ representing father
☽/♋ representing mother

Astrologer:
Oh, because they'd had two girls already. I see. Sun Capricorn opposition Uranus, you opposed your father's wishes. And with Uranus Cancer, you opposed your mother's wishes. Neither of them wanted a girl.

Kate:
No, they didn't.

☿ ⚻ ♇
♀ cusp 3rd (♊) ☌ ♇
☉ representing self

Astrologer:
And your sisters didn't want a girl either. I think you must have spent quite a long time wishing you were a boy yourself.

☉ 1st
Asc ♃
☽ △ ♂
☽ □ ♄
♋ cusp 8th

Kate:
Oh, I did. I was good at being a tomboy. I could climb trees and was very athletic. That side was encouraged. The bit that did get attention. June and Susan were pretty little girls, and when I look at photographs of myself as a kid, my mother never brought out the pretty little girl in me. There's a grip stuck in my hair like this. My clothes were all... my femininity as a child was...

Cardinal T/square

Astrologer:
It's sad how families can make us deny our own self, but through it, and perhaps because of it, you will find it. You become so much more aware. In a way they do you a favour, but it still doesn't stop the hurt does it?

Kate:
No, and you know there was a lot of hurt as a kid, a lot.

☉ ⚺ ☽
General statement

Astrologer:
I think that half the time they don't realize what they are doing. It's so painful isn't it? When I look back over my own childhood and think of myself growing up, I feel sorry for the child that I was, do you feel like that?

Kate:
Yes I can picture myself.

♆ ☌ MC 11th
♅ N. ruler of 11th in 7th ♋
ruler of 7th (♊ cusp), ☿ in ♍
☉ ♍ Q ♆
Asc Q ♂

Astrologer:
Such an unhappy growing up. But I think this is very typical of the soul who is capable of making a large contribution to life. You are bound to experience more tribulations than most. When you're growing up nobody tells you that, you don't know about that. If someone had said you need all those experiences to shape your personality and that it will eventually prove useful, it probably would have made it easier for you to cope.

Kate:
Yes, it would. It does now.

☽/♋
Fixed signs/houses

Astrologer:
As children we are conditioned by so many negative values; all absorbed by the unconscious. Perhaps we can

redress the situation by throwing a few positive values into the pot. It is a pity more parents do not realize this. So what we'll do now is to throw a few good notes in, in the hope that they take root as well.

Kate:
I think that's important, I think that's good.

Astrologer:
It is a pity that we aren't taught about the meaning of life as children.

Kate:
I can see that if parents had a chart of their child you could help encourage them intead of destroying them with negativity.

Astrologer:
So now we can see why you are a natural born rebel.

Kate:
Yes, too much so.

Astrologer:
Sometimes you're bolshi when you needn't be, so that you can actually destroy some things before they've even got a chance to see whether they have any value for you. Part of an inbuilt rejection.

Kate:
Very true, that inbuilt rejection.

Astrologer:
It is a kind of scepticism that accepts rejection as a norm. The conditioning has always been that you are supposed to adopt their standards but they've never given you a chance to adopt them gently. It's always, 'Do it!'. You have a preoccupied mother. With the Sun in the 1st, an impatient father. They did not have the time to give you, and so you have had to quickly establish a standpoint in which the onus has been firmly placed on you to control the situation. Perhaps a little tolerance on your part could give you a little more chance of adapting more easily to things. That is tolerance of yourself as well as others. Aquarius is a fixed sign, so you really can be very dogmatic, you know.

Kate:
Very dangerous.

Astrologer:
It is that, 'Don't tell me what I should know, I'll tell you!'

Kate:
About this rejection for its own sake, it's very true, and it has to be watched, I think.

Astrologer:
If Peter were to say to you, let's get a place of our own and get married, you would say, 'I don't want to do that!'

Kate:
That's right!

Astrologer:
And then, if in the next breath, he said, I don't want us to get married, you would say, 'Why not?'

Kate:
(laughs)

Astrologer:
It really is a fear of being left by yourself. The fear of being thrown on your own resources. Yet that is the path you have chosen. You demanded a life where you can be free and unfettered and yet when you're given the opportunity to be free and unfettered, you refuse to accept it.

Kate:
Is it a defence mechanism? I mean being the fifth member of the family, you are thrown on your own resources much of the time.

Astrologer:
That's why I asked if you were the middle child, because the attention usually passes more to the first-born and then to the youngest. The one in the middle tends to have the least attention.

Kate:
Up to about the age of twelve I think I was the one who was left rather. My sister, Susan, felt like that as a teenager. It is just a defence mechanism, 'Oh, they're leaving me on my own.' So when they *do* want to include me I am going to say, 'No, I don't want to.'

Astrologer:
Well, you have no experience of being drawn into being together so you prefer to do that which you know and understand, which is to say, 'Well I know it's awful and painful to be on my own, but at least I know what it feels like.'

Kate:
That's right.

Astrologer:
There's an automatic rejection that perpetuates itself; your family get into the habit of thinking you want to be on your own.

Kate:
And it did in the family.

Astrologer:
In the first four most vital years of your life this whole patterning was set up.* Right from birth your father would have been too busy with his career to spend much time with you, and this you would have felt keenly.

* The degree numbers of the planets, Ascendant and Midheaven may be used to represent significant years in the life, commencing with 0°00′ at birth. Kate's Sun at 0°07′ indicates the period immediately following birth, and the Moon at 2°31′ and Jupiter at 4°22′, the early conditioning.

Kate:
There was a wonderful time when my dad and I were both ill at the same time. He had two weeks off work, and you know we were playing games during the day and cards. It was bliss, absolute bliss.

Astrologer:
I don't suppose he realized. With Sun Capricorn you are very much your father's daughter. The need for father and a strong father figure is so profound. Of course the father/daughter relationship is so important. The conditioning you received regarding your father is bound to translate as your emotional response to the kind of man you will attract and be attracted by.

You are strongly nurturing and want to care and give love. Laughter and the company of other people is important to you, so you may well find more demonstrativeness and warmth among friends where it doesn't seem to be so forthcoming from the family. On the surface, it would seem that you find platonic friendship easier and that an emotional relationship might be short-lived, simply because the emotions would prove hard to handle over a long period.

Kate:
I started off with platonic boyfriends and used to get very upset because they would see my friends as attractive but not me. Then, when I was still at school, I did have a relationship which was very intense. It lasted about five years, so I can't say that it was shortlived.

Astrologer:
I'll say not. I would think that he would have been pretty unusual and intelligent. It wouldn't have lasted if he didn't fit that bill...

Kate:
He was a Pisces.

Astrologer:
Oh, that's interesting, especially with your Neptune on the Midheaven in Libra.

Kate:
He was a musician and I thought he was wildly romantic. He used to write me yards of poetry. What happened was that I went to University and he couldn't incorporate the fact that I was meeting other people there, but that was so important to me at that time. I thought well, if you can't take this then I'm not going to take you. He was pretty hurtful in other ways, but it's over now.

Astrologer:
Perhaps, but there is this factor that people don't always credit you for the sensitivity that you have. You don't always show your feelings.

Kate:
No, I've found it wiser not to.

Astrologer:
I know what you mean. But you see how prominent Neptune is. You

♆☌MC
♇ IN 9TH
HE ♃ RULER
OF CHART
AND NATURAL
RULER 9TH

♇ CUSP 9TH

♆

would have to be in love with the man. The romantic side of the relationship must be really strong. If it isn't there then you couldn't possibly be involved with any man. You are part of an era when promiscuity is more accepted, but you couldn't be like that, even though you are such a truly unusual and rebellious type, because the romantic side has to be so strong.

Kate:
Very idealized.

Astrologer:
Yes. You also tend to inflate the importance of the other person, seeing them in a romantic guise so that you can gull yourself into believing they are all kinds of things. That they are absolute saints when they are absolute...

Kate:
That's right, that was Jeremy. He's married now with two children, but I'm glad I didn't stay with him. You know, we weren't right for each other. I had to go through quite a... I mean after Jeremy, I had about three other relationships in my twenties.

☉ ♍/♄ 10TH
PREFERS
HONOURABLE,
LASTING
RELATIONSHIPS
EVEN THOUGH
♀ ♒

Astrologer:
That's not a lot compared to...

Kate:
Other people, no. One thing I used to hate was that if my emotional life wasn't running right, I couldn't get on with other things. That was terrible.

♀ ⚹ ♂

Astrologer:
But that is such a typically feminine attitude.

Kate:
You know, I felt terribly weak about that. Like other people have to get on with it. When I was just gone twenty-six I had split up with somebody, I was devastated. I spent three months in a cellar unable to go out.

♓ CUSP 4TH

♆ ☌ MC

Astrologer:
That's bad!

Kate:
I mean it was a flat in a cellar, and I'd have people round about once a fortnight. To come round and see me.

♍ 12TH
♇ IN ♎
☉ 1ST

I'd go out, and do a bit... but I just couldn't face the world. It was absolutely terrible. I never wanted to be like that again.

Astrologer:
Did he let you down? Or was it just...?

Kate:
It was my projection of him. What I thought we were going to be.

Astrologer:
Old Neptune, again?

Kate:
Yes. He was the wizard. You know, he was Mr Magic that one.

Astrologer:
It is really unbelievable, isn't it? But it just goes to prove what an essentially very, very feminine lady you are.

♆ ☌ MC
☽ IN 2ND
(EXALTED ♂)
PART OF SAT. 2ND

T/SQ
♂ ⬧ ♇♋
☉ ♍ ☽ ♐

Kate:
I'm beginning to recognize that now. That's why I say, as a child, it was really not wanted.

Astrologer:
Yes. This is why you had to have that kind of childhood so that you could go full circle and come to respect and adore your own femininity. To revel in it. We're very funny, we human beings, unless you actually have it taken away from you then...

Kate:
You're not going to appreciate it, no.

Astrologer:
If you look at the opposition aspects between Venus and Pluto, you can see that it creates a kind of bowl of planets on the left-hand, or Eastern side, of the chart. We can say that a focal point is created of the sum total of all the energy contained in that bowl, emerging in the sign Taurus in the 6th house. In other words to express your energy on its purest level, so that you can use it as fully as you should, you must have some sort of regular employment. Whether you work for yourself or not, you must have an income of your own. It is back to security, to a sense of self-worth, anything which places you on a level

AGAIN
STRONG EMPHASIS
ON ♉/2ND
NOTE 6TH IS
NATURALLY
RULED BY ♀
WHICH IS IN 2ND

where you feel that you are making a contribution to society. But the Taurean factor here is that your image of yourself must be seen to be a profoundly beautiful one. Most of the time you can't handle it. You can't hold on to it. Nobody told you when you were a child that the qualities which you have are good. The initial impact of Capricorn always seems to indicate that the first part of the life is pitted with obstacles, problems and tribulations. Everybody takes it all so seriously. There's just not enough laughter and fun. Up at the top of the chart you have Mars and Saturn in Virgo in the 10th house. Mars is the ruler of the 1st house, Saturn the ruler of Capricorn, so I ask, where is the laughter? There are no gales of laughter or giggles.

Kate:
It just sort of sinks instead.

Astrologer:
Yet you have a naturally effusive nature.

Kate:
Which I could find with my school chums, but not with my family.

Astrologer:
And so you go outside the family environment.

Kate:
I was very interested in what you were saying about this energy coming out in my work and the thing about me valuing the work myself. Valuing what I have. In the past I used to see that as arrogance, but it is not arrogance. I was on a far too superficial level about it. I can hear you say that and understand it now.

Astrologer:
Yes, because you have to ground yourself.

Kate:
Yes, whereas if somebody had spoken to me earlier about it, when I was younger, about being beautiful, I would only see it as a sort of glossy kind of beautiful, and I wouldn't have...

Astrologer:
You would have wondered what they were talking about.

Kate:
Yes, but that makes more sense to me now.

Astrologer:
Yes you are now actually looking at it. The ruler of the 6th house is Venus in Aquarius here on the 3rd house cusp and it goes literally opposite Pluto expressing this sort of intense kind of rejection of self.

Kate:
Yes, absolutely bang on.

Astrologer:
So that it's as if you have to go to the full extent of touching self-worthlessness, finding family, men, friends and even neighbours who would make you feel like you have no right to live. So that you would touch bottom.

Kate:
And I sought them out in a way, to do that to me, didn't I?

Astrologer:
Yes, instead of seeking the kind of partner who would teach you self-respect, you seek one who would rob you of your sense of femininity.

Kate:
But he did that to this feminine, this rejection of femininity, this deep rejection of femininity...

Astrologer:
Which comes from when you were little.

Kate:
Yes.

Astrologer:
Once you have touched the extremes you can come to appreciate the positive values of what you have. Which you will do as you get older so that you will come to see that your femininity is your strength, your power. It is from your femininity that you truly function...

Your ruling planet, Jupiter is closely allied with the Moon. It has been said that Moon-Jupiter combinations have the feeling of being able to touch God. There is a sense of being able to understand life on a very broad scale. Of being able to take a very broad image of life which actually makes it more difficult to see things in personal terms.

Kate:
I can feel at peace in a landscape, but find it more difficult to find peace in myself.

Astrologer:
Understanding humanity on the large scale is relatively easy for you.

Kate:
Well, I've been interested in the scope astrology has to link the outer planets' movement with sociological changes. Now that's something that…

Astrologer:
That would appeal to you…

Kate:
It does. I've always been interested in that.

Astrologer:
You could really home-in to the feeling of a whole generation, but to see *yourself* within the context of the generation would be much more difficult. It is almost as if the price you pay for your sociological understanding, or socio-conscience, is not being able to necessarily cope with your own things on a petty level. They are too small. You are bigger than that and that is why it gets you down sometimes. That is, it did! You've reached an age now where you are starting to get it together anyway, and as you get older, you will find that life will just get better and better.

Kate:
Oh very noticeably since I've been thirty.

Astrologer:
The Saturn Return* at that age would have been like a godsend for you. Society says that we are over the hill at thirty, but astrologers know better. You are just beginning.

Kate:
It's great, isn't it?

Astrologer:
Marvellous, because it is much the best way round. Having the tough breaks in the first part and looking forward to using that knowledge in the second part. But this is what you agreed to do. This is the contract you made when you came to be born. You said, 'Oh sure, I can handle all that. That's nothing! But when you come to live it you realize, and think, 'What have I done? I chose this? I must have been mad!' Later on, we come to see the sense of it all and are glad for all those awful experiences. For they shape our personalities. Very often, the tougher the innings, the greater can be the eventual contribution to life.

We ought to look at your health. In your case it is tied very closely to your personality.

There is a tendency for you to dissipate your own energy, to allow your nerves and emotional upsets to drag your health down. You would have to be very careful because you have been given a very, very strong constitution, and the tendency is for you to actually abuse your own good health by taking liberties with it.

Kate:
I know I do.

Astrologer:
You have the potential to have a nice, ripe, old age and if you want to enjoy that, you'll have to wake up to what you are doing to yourself. Actually, humour is a great restorer of the status quo, of health and of self-confidence. It is actually easy for you to break the whole problem. Just through laughter and exercising your usually delightful sense of humour.

You have a very highly tuned type of personality. Very highly strung which is also synonymous with being touchy, and easily irritable, but it is also why you have this finely developed sense of

* The planet Saturn 'returns' to the same degree occupied at birth after approximately 29½ years, when it completes a full orbit. There are many such astrological cycles coincident with life crises periods but their study is beyond the scope of this book.

consciousness. Why you are so very aware. Perhaps it is the price that has to be paid? So many minor aspects like this raise the quality of the chart. The whole nature is much more subtle, and more prone to sudden states of anxiety that come upon you almost as if from nowhere.

Kate:
Yes, it does happen like that.

Astrologer:
You get a sudden rush of nervousness right through you whole system, and have to hold on to something in order to feel, 'Am I still here? What is happening to me?'

Kate:
It's very true, and the suddenness of it is one of the features.

Astrologer:
Uranus/Aquarius, yes. If you know that you are prone to that, what you can do is make use of your best outlet which we now know to be Taurus and actually hold on to something tangible. Do some gardening, some clay modelling and literally hold on to the earth. You'll find that when you do, all that incredible electrical energy is suddenly earthed and given tremendous power. That's how flashes of inspiration can come to you quite out of the blue.

Kate:
While I'm doing things, yes.

Astrologer:
Everything comes suddenly. If you become ill for instance, you're probably alright one day and the next...

Kate:
That's true. I was suddenly whisked off to hospital on an emergency.

Astrologer:
By the same token, you have to find ways of restoring your energy. It doesn't fuse, it is as if somebody has switched on a fire in a room and forgotten all about it. Suddenly the energy which should have been able to be used has been burnt off somewhere else. It has just gone. So you have to learn to mentally go through your inner house, and switch off where it is not required. If necessary you must earth it. Then tremendous energy comes through. But sometimes it can be too much for you to take and you go all shaky.

Kate:
Yes, I do go all shaky.

Astrologer:
Thinking about your overall Life Pattern... Just when you think you're managing to create a nice little status quo for yourself, something happens to disturb you. Invariably it is outside you, an external factor or occurrence. Even if you haven't done anything, there is yet another eruption which throws you out of gear. You aren't allowed to escape or even opt out of it for five minutes — someone will come to the door! It just goes on and on. I think that it is a pattern that would be very trying to live with.

Kate:
Yes, I think it is. But then again, I wonder if it's not a good thing in some ways. In that without it, I could get too withdrawn.

Astrologer:
These things occur so that you do not opt out of the challenge of life. It is also very typical of you to get some benefit out of the worst times. You have a very bright mind but it's also a very practical mind. Very sound. You can go through periods when so many things keep cropping up that you could say, 'I'm tearing my hair out', but in truth you are actually sorting everything out in a very practical way, finding solutions to those things. By saying that the 6th house is the best outlet for your energy, we can see that you are a born organizer. You may not be able to organize yourself, but that doesn't really have anything to do with it. You can organize anything and anybody.

You are the large thinker and you should get somebody else to deal with the bits and pieces of your life that bore you or you find difficult to deal with. You can go into a company and organize that. Whereas in your home you wouldn't find things unless they were carefully labelled and in their proper place.

Kate:
Well, in our household I am always the one who is asked where something is. I do have visual memories of where I last saw it. We don't have a place for everything and everything in its place, but ask Kate and she'll probably know where it is. If I've seen it, I'll remember it.

Astrologer:
A very practical memory that serves you well. You've also got good powers of concentration.

Kate:
I wanted to ask you about work and about employing people. I've only had people working for me on two or three occasions in the past. The nice thing is thay have all remained very friendly with me and I think they enjoyed working with me. They worked well, and I've been wondering whether this is partly the Capricorn thing. Do you think it is?

Astrologer:
You should be in an executive position. The 'Boss'. I don't think you are at the moment, are you?

Kate:
But I was told Mars in Virgo means me being the secretary.

Astrologer:
No, not when you look at the *quality* of your Mars. You have an excellent Mars, very strong.

It is in its house of exaltation in the 10th. You have Sun square Mars and any textbook will tell you that Sun square Mars is far too bolshi and too arrogant to cope with working for other people for any length of time. You are far too ambitious. Forgive me, but I think you have been looking at Virgo in the wrong light. Virgo isn't subservient to anything or anybody unless it wants to be. Sun square Mars doesn't want to be subservient to anyone. For you to remain a secretary would be an absolute waste. You need it, perhaps, to learn the skills, to gain experience, but certainly not as a permanent situation.

Kate:
One thing I liked about my father was that he worked his way up through the ranks, so to speak...

Astrologer:
Now that's the meaning of Sun square Mars, the self-made person!

Kate:
Right. If he ever asked somebody to do something, he could always do the job himself. In the pits that means a lot of physical work. I admired that in him.

Astrologer:
What did he do?

Kate:
Like my grandfather, his father, he started as a miner. He worked hard at evening class, got his Inspectorate and he ended up as an Area General Manager.

Astrologer:
What, from being a miner? My word, I admire that man.

Kate:
Yes, so do I.

Astrologer:
You are very much his daughter, you know. Sun Capricorn. You've got that spirit, that ability to pioneer your way through. Now you are older you understand why the man had to work so hard when you were a little one. He was ambitious too. Good luck to him. Definitely, a father to be proud of. Did he go in the war? Did he fight?

Kate:
No.

Astrologer:
Ah, because he was in the mines; they were important, weren't they? But there's that resentment that he wasn't able to fight. You know, he would have liked to have done that and he felt a kind of, a form of guilt which you have in you. That's why you're so self-critical. You see how it works? But then that's the self-seeking. Also the striving for perfection, that demand upon yourself, and you are very, very

☿ MR ♄

demanding upon yourself. Much more so than most people. But then you don't succeed unless… It is only as you get older that you start to understand that you can't have one thing without the other.

☿ ♃ 2d

Kate:
I'm so glad. I feel better about this family thing. Talking about it today, I feel so much better.

Astrologer:
That's good. Then it's worth going through all this, isn't it? Everything you've ever been through. It's all worthwhile. You see the emphasis on Mother Earth here? All these planets in the 2nd house, 10th house strong Capricorn… the emphasis on Taurus. Even the Moon is in the Taurus house of exaltation. Clearly you are meant to have a good grounding in earthly experience in order to measure up to the full force of your being.

Kate:
I've never thought like that, but it makes sense to me.

Astrologer:
Your ruling planet, Jupiter, is also nicely earthed. In fact, traditional authorities say that the best position for Jupiter is either in the 10th or the 2nd House, and look where yours is, in the 2nd. So you have the capacity to make a profoundly good life-style for yourself. Just as your father did. You have to make obstacles and difficulties work *for* you. Maybe you could be a 'troubleshooter'. You know what I mean, going into a company and re-organizing everything.

CARDINAL FACTORS SHOW THAT T/SQ CAN BE MADE TO WORK FOR RATHER THAN AGAINST SELF

Kate:
I've done that on occasions. That's another thing about enjoying being older, because now I feel I can demand more responsibility. When you are younger, people won't give it to you. But when you get beyond a certain age, then yes, then they listen to you.

Astrologer:
Make it work for you. You could found your own business doing that.

Kate:
I had my own business you know… I left University at twenty-four in 1974 with a Psychology degree… it's like an 'A' level, you've got to do research to do anything any good. That was the time of the oil crisis and there was no more money for research. During my years at college, I supplemented my grant doing stalls at a local market. So I came out, no job, no research and kept on with the stalls. In September of that year, a friend who lived above a shop told me that the shop was coming up vacant. 'How about it?' she said, 'It's only got a limited life because of the local council,' but it was fantastically cheap. I didn't have any capital. The bank loaned me £1200 to do this with. I had the shop for just over a year, and then the Council took it back.

Astrologer:
What did you do in the shop?

Kate:
Fabrics and oriental rugs were my aspirations, but second-hand clothes were my bread and butter. I sold bits of pine furniture — anything I could buy and sell at a small profit. You know, turn it over quickly. That was one of the occasions when I had people working for me. I had a boy and a girl who came in on Saturdays to help do the shop; they were always there. They loved it. I know they loved it, and it was a time when, absolutely, my work was my life. At that time I had no involvement with anybody, and I was travelling around a lot buying the stuff.

Astrologer:
Happy as a lark!

Kate:
Absolutely! I really enjoyed it. So my sister said, when the shop folded, 'Buy a house, Kate, or a flat and sell it in a few years. That's how you'll get your capital for your business.'

♀ ♂ 3RD PART OF SAT ♅ (26269) ✳ ASCe BQ ♄

Astrologer:
Interesting. Good thing you did do that because you will end up with some capital, once the house is sold.

Kate:
And you see, that's Susan! And so all

this talk about me as a child, and how I suffered as a child, she cares really.

Astrologer:
With Venus conjunct Jupiter here, you must be able to learn from them.

Kate:
And I do. I mean I like women. They help me enormously.

Astrologer:
Yes, you are right. Women are your best teachers. But you have to go through losing your femininity, to regain it, so that you can really appreciate it.

Kate:
I still like climbing.

Astrologer:
Just going off in some hills and climbing around? I can't sit for long on a beach; it irritates me. Are you like that?

Kate:
Yes, I get bored.

Astrologer:
Yes, you are too much of a live wire. You can't sit still for any length of time. That's why you get a lot of nervous intensity, and why you must be careful that you don't take it for granted. You have a very healthy chart. Plenty of ambition... but then again you see you are too modest about your own capabilities, which is something you have to learn to get over. You shall have to re-programme yourself. When there's a strong emphasis on fixity in the chart, fixed signs and planets in fixed houses, there is a tendency to be more prone to habits and conditioning. But did you know that you can also re-programme yourself?

Kate:
I'm going to try. I think I've started to do it, albeit unconsciously.

Astrologer:
You have very little Water in your chart. It doesn't mean to say that when you have little Water you don't have emotional feelings. On the contrary, the problem lies in expressing your feelings. It shows that you don't have enough outlet for emotional expression. And if you don't find an outlet for all this emotional intensity and your highly-strung, highly-tuned nature, then it can become very hard work. It internalizes and then you can make yourself ill that way, and your energy depletes so that you have no desire to go out and fight the good fight. Your energy is sapped. Gone! If you look at your Mars/Saturn in Virgo. It is very difficult. I think it is one of the most difficult positions because your expectation of yourself is so high that you feel you can never hope to attain...

Kate:
I'm getting a lot better than I was. I mean I had trouble at school handing essays and things in because they were never good enough. I mean I wanted to write books for every essay. Not enough research. Very critical.

Astrologer:
Well you take yourself so seriously that everything you must do has to be done absolutely perfectly. But it does get better as you get older.

Kate:
Why was it, as a child I couldn't laugh at myself?

Astrologer:
It's this seriousness. Look at Mercury in Capricorn. There's nothing more powerful than the power of thought. It governs everything. You see it is 'earthed' in an earth sign, Capricorn, and in an earth house, the 2nd. Unless you understood what was going on... you would tend to be very pragmatic. Everything as one plus two equals three. Unless it equalled three and came out as you expected it to, because of all the Virgo, then you would toss it to one side. Dismiss it.

Kate:
Don't want to know. Yes, that's true.

Astrologer:
And you would concentrate. You had a very old mind on young shoulders. You were a very old, adult child. And if you weren't taught to play as a child...

Kate:
I was hard on my family and myself, whereas with my friends I could relax. When you were talking about the globules of energy, you said these two planets are in the 10th, and you said something about great family pride, or the importance of the appearance of the family to the world.

Astrologer:
It's very important.

Kate:
I mean I've never had that said. It was, terribly important.

Astrologer:
Who you are, your image of yourself in the family, is profoundly important.

Kate:
Yes, my sisters, as I say, were elder, and they'd sing these duets together at the church and at school. That was wonderful...

Astrologer:
They didn't have a trio?

Kate:
I was always June or Susan's sister.

Astrologer:
You weren't Kate?

Kate:
No, and I went through this whole thing of getting people to know my name. It's interesting, this thing about where the 'I' comes in.

Astrologer:
But if you think there's that sense of not necessarily belonging to them and feeling alienated so that you become rebellious, yet there is also this 'But they're my family.' Anybody who threatened your family or the image ... Lord help them! The standard of belief of who you were, this is where the modesty comes in. This thing of the high expectations has been with you since you were little. You felt that you were a special family.

Kate:
Yes, we did think that.

Astrologer:
You belonged. And here's a man, your father, who clawed his way from nothing. He must be a special man to do that, because most people aren't able to. So there's that sense of pride that he had in himself which is instilled in you. You are his daughter. Whether June and Susan are very much his daughters or not is beside the point.

Kate:
Oh they are. They are. I thought that was common. I thought everybody was the same about families. I thought you can criticize your family, and I can criticize mine, but don't you dare...

Astrologer:
Say anything about mine and I'll punch you on the nose!

Kate:
I thought that was a common thing to humanity.

Astrologer:
No, I don't think so. Some people just take their families for granted. You see yours as special. When Prince Charles was growing up apparently he was quite surprised to find out that people were bowing and scraping to his mother. He couldn't understand what they were doing. Why are they going out backwards? Because his mother wasn't a queen when he was very small. Suddenly she became queen and had to be different. She was all mumsy before by all accounts. As far as he was concerned she was just an ordinary mother. Suddenly she had to go out to work and was treated differently, and he wasn't allowed to go with her. It must have been quite a blow. But you see, it puts it into perspective.

Kate:
It does help.

Astrologer:
You have, in a sense, to be more of a daughter to your father. Your father is very important in your chart, yet your mother is shown as a very bright lady...

Kate:
Oh, she was. She won a scholarship to Oxford, which at her time was really something.

Astrologer:
Really?

Kate:
She was adopted. She thinks she had quite wealthy real parents, and was adopted into a very poor family. So when she won this scholarship, at the time I think it meant they paid the fees, and your own parents had to pay for your board...

Astrologer:
And they couldn't afford it...

Kate:
And they couldn't afford it!

Astrologer:
And they couldn't get a grant or anything?

Kate:
They didn't exist at those times. So she went to Teacher Training College. She was brilliant I think, at one time.

Astrologer:
But this is what you have from her. The flashes of the old genius here in your mother which you have inherited from her, yet which you tend to reject. Perhaps it is shades of the way your mother had to reject her own brilliance. You have a very fine brain which you tend to put down.

Kate:
That was the pattern that was established when I was at school, in that I had no trouble keeping up with my contempories in the class, but I attributed it to the fact that I had two elder sisters. Because when you are trying to keep up with them, you're never as good as they are, you know.

Astrologer:
No, because they were obviously years ahead of you, nothing to do with brain power.

Kate:
But the fact that you are as good as most of your contemporaries doesn't register, you know. So what! I wanted to be as good as... so I got into this way, and I never had much trouble at school.

Astrologer:
No, especially on your own merits you could achieve any kind of academic credit that you wanted, but because of Venus here, you see yourself in competition with your sisters. As you get older you'll come to appreciate what you've got.

Kate:
I think I am doing that more now, since I've been studying again. These past few years I've been enjoying it more as well.

Astrologer:
Studying for its own sake, not for academic kudos.

Kate:
Yes, absolutely. Which I never had much time for anyway.

Astrologer:
Also, with strong Aquarian on the 3rd cusp, is that need to keep your mind wide open, and if anything tried to force it to specialize, you would reject that too, because it was again like discipline. Anything that tried to, like authority tried to stamp on you, you would immediately push the reject button every time.

Kate:
What about this arrogance? Not 'competing' because, as a kid, my mother wanted to make us all compete against each other. When I was a teenager I really wanted to reject this competitive thing. Yet, in doing so, wasn't that arrogant in thinking that I could compete if I wanted to?

Astrologer:
You are naturally competitive. When you have a natural inclination for something, you don't really have to do it, do you? What are you out to prove? Having proved it to yourself, there's no point in proving it to anyone else.

Kate:
Well, why not though?

Astrologer:
Because that's your life lesson. It is about yourself. Proving what you can do to your own satisfaction.

Kate:
Yes, but it's still arrogance, isn't it? If you just set yourself up as your own arbiter?

Astrologer:
But that's what it is all about.

Kate:
I know, I know.

Astrologer:
In the final analysis, having to go through all that guff of being in competition with other people. Here you are with that old modesty rubbish that's been browbeaten into you. Yet there is this other side of your coin which says 'I am who I am, blow you, people.' There is the fact that you need that touch of abrasiveness in order to stand up and say 'I am an individual, I am different from the rest of you!' You have this quality of being part of humanity, yet at the same time standing out very much as an individual. It's a kind of dichotomy isn't it? They don't cancel one another out. You are both. Supposing you were in a group and someone identified you with that group rather than as an individual, you would be furious. Am I right?

Kate:
Yes, there was a lot of that.

Astrologer:
Supposing the group were geared to being wholly competitive, you would back off because you don't want to be like them. That's individuality surely?

Kate:
There are times when I think it is productive, and when I think, you know...

Astrologer:
It is all shades and in betweens. There is nothing perfectly clear cut, is there? Let me try to explain what I mean. Madam Blavatsky, who founded the Theosophical movement, is supposed to have said that an astrologer should find seven interpretations for anything in the chart. That must have some relationship, I think, with the Seven Naked Eye Planets that the old astrologers used. Presumably, since we have discovered another three planets, we ought to be able to find ten reasons or interpretations. Certainly the three should be more sophisticated. Just as an astrologer can look at an aspect or a planet from differing views, so you use that quality of energy, or a facet of your personality in different ways at different times.

Let's take, for example, Sun square Mars which is notoriously ambitious, but in your chart with Sun Capricorn and Mars Virgo it can also be fearful. That's shown in the way that you fluctuate between thoughts of, 'I am the boss. No, I'm not, I'm the secretary!' Then, 'Wait a minute, I don't want to be a secretary. But I don't want to be a boss either! Then who am I?'

Kate:
It's true, yes. At different times, all those things.

Astrologer:
It can be from moment to moment. Look what has just happened. You have been offered an executive position with a fabulous salary, and you have suddenly been confronted with the thought that you will have to be answerable to another person yet again. 'They call me an executive, but I shall be working for *them*.' And you reject the job. Then someone says, 'Hey Kate, what about setting up your own business...' 'Er...who, me? I'm not ready for that.' Then you just might remember that you already have run your own business, and did it without realizing that that's what you were doing, and loved every minute of it!

We have had a look at your Sun square Mars but let's imagine that you have Sun trine Mars in an easy, expanding aspect. You would automatically be the boss, or the secretary and perfectly happy because you had accepted that position.

But it is square and it has to be. You obviously needed this particular quality of being able to accept challenge in order to become the person you are. Without it, you cannot achieve all that you are meant to. It is not meant to be clear cut. We can see that because it is a square aspect not in the same quadruplicity, Libra/ Capricorn but what is called *disassociated* in a Cardinal (Libra) and a Mutable (Virgo) sign, it is not so easy to fathom. The whole nature of it is more obscure and, in the long run, better for being more subtle. It shows that you are capable of working in any situation, under any circumstances and can adapt to those working conditions as and when you feel you need to. Yet you are still in command of yourself. Still the individual, and you are welcomed in companies for your unique quality.

MUTABLE ASC/DESC ♍ MUTABLE FOCAL POINT OF ENERGY THROUGH 6TH

Kate:
Because I do work hard.

☉ □ ♂ ♍ STRONG EARTH AND FIXITY

Astrologer:
But that's the talent that you have; nobody would ever say that you're trading on anything. You are just a naturally delightful lady and nobody really sees the driving force. The trouble with you is that you are so anxious to please. You want to be well-liked, and why not? The thing is people like you anyway, you don't have to prove it. Underlying that is that sense of, 'Well, either they like me or they don't,' but the fact is they do like you. But they don't necessarily see the ambition, nor the power of your personality because you do it very low key, soft pedal, until suddenly they realize that you've taken over anyway.

Asc ✶ ♀E
MC △ ♀

MC □ ☽E

♐ Asc ♎ MC
SAT. ♏ ☽ ♀

♀ △ (MC ☌ ♆)

The session with Kate comes to a close because of the time factor, but the work on the chart has only just begun. There will be other sessions, and time for Kate to grow closer to who she is. At any future stage in her development Kate can compare the person she feels she is becoming with her own blueprint, her birth chart.

Appendix: The Legend of Prometheus

The seeker after truth will encounter considerable difficulty in tracing the growth and development of the myths and legends of antiquity for he will constantly be met by differing opinions among various authorities. The myths and legends appear to be attempts by early man to seek explanations for the complexity of the majestic vista of the heavens and as a means of understanding nature. Nevertheless they are evocative of archetypal images associated with feelings and behavioural traits unique to man. It is clear that the myths cannot be separated from association with the planets and fixed stars. One of the best known stories is that of the seven daughters of Atlas who, pursued by Orion, were transformed for their own safety into the star cluster known as the Pleiades.

The Titans were a race of giants who reigned supreme until deposed by Zeus, later to be called Jupiter by the Romans. The Titans were overthrown by the Olympian gods and thrust into Tartarus, an abyss far below Hades, which later became the place of punishment for all sinners. Whether Prometheus remained a captive on Mount Caucasus or, like his fellow Titans was eventually incarcerated in Hades is not clear. The seven Titans correspond with the Seven Naked Eye Planets 'deposed' by the twelve Olympian gods who have their links with the twelve signs of the Zodiac. The rulerships of the signs by the planets show that the Divine Gifts originating with the Titans would pass naturally to one or other of the Olympian gods. Thus the Gift of Fire, Healing, rulership of astronomy and knowledge of music and the discovery of the lyre passed from Prometheus to Hermes who was known by the Romans as Mercury. In qualifying the archetypal energies and attributes associated with the *planet*, Mercury, the gods, Hermes (Mercury) and Prometheus are one. Interestingly, Prometheus is not always acknowledged as being a Titan[1] and certainly his fall from grace was different to the demise of the other Titans, Hermes was the only one of the Olympian gods to elect himself as a god. In both instances the similarity arises indicating that quality in man that differentiates him from the animals, the Gift of Mind and, therefore, Choice.

That Hermes leads Herakles (or Hercules) to Hades in order to release Prometheus gives the impression that they are separate entities and there is no reason why they cannot be seen as such. Nevertheless, they are facets of the same archetypal force. In *De Natura Deorum,* Cicero explains that there were really five Mercurys, one of whom killed Argus and fled to Egypt where he gave the Egyptians their laws and letters and became known as Thoth.[2]

Authorities vary concerning the order and detail of the Twelve Labours of Hercules. Some maintain that Cerberus is 'tamed', 'mastered' or actually 'slain' but this really involves an exercise in semantics for the inference is the same, that of conquering those particular dark areas of the psyche. It is possible to encounter references showing that it is Cerberus and not Prometheus who is led from Hades to the earth and light. The rescue of Prometheus may sometimes be found in another Labour, the Golden Apples of the Hesperides. Poor Prometheus is variously torn by an 'eagle', a 'vulture' or a 'griffon-vulture'; presumably depending on translations of original documents. It truly does not matter since it is the meaning of the legend that is important. 'If the ancient myth of Prometheus is to help us onward, we must make Herculean efforts to cleanse away the mire of the senses, and the dust of the lower mind, so that Mercury, the mind, may reflect only the image of the god that dwells within.'[3]

1. Robert Graves, *Greek Myths,* page 48 (Cassell, 1955)
2. Frances A. Yates, *Giordano Bruno and the Hermetic Tradition,* page 2 (Routledge and Kegan Paul 1978)
3. Bessie Leo, *Rays of Truth,* page 222 (Fowler 1909)

General Information

Astrological Teaching Bodies (Supply SAE when sending for prospectus)

Advisory Panel For Astrological Education 42 Lillian Road, Barnes, London SW13	Local Teachers, classes including Evening Institutes.
The Company of Astrologers (see The Astrological Lodge)	Evening courses, weekend seminars.
Pamela Crane College of Horoscopy 63 The Street, Ospringe, Faversham, Kent	Correspondence courses.
Faculty of Astrological Studies BCM Box 7470, London WC1N 3XX	Correspondence courses, classes, seminars, Consultants' List.
The Mayo School of Astrology 8 Stoggy Lane, Plympton, Plymouth, Devon	Correspondence courses Consultants' Register.
The Jill Moore School of Astrology Victorian Arcade, Torwood Street, Torquay, Devon	Seminars, workshops.
The White Eagle School of Astrology New Lands, Liss, Hampshire	Correspondence courses, London lectures.

Inner London Education Authority (ILEA)

See *Floodlight* Magazine (published August) for details of Evening Institutes and classes.

Local Education Authorities
Should sufficient interest be shown some authorities will create a class when none exists already. Contact Advisory Panel for Astrological Education for advice and likelihood of local teacher

Astrological Societies (Supply SAE when sending for details)

The Astrological Association Bay Villa, Plymouth Road, Totnes, Devon	London meetings, quarterly *Journal* annual conference, research and *Correlation*, journal of research into astrology.
Astrological Counselling Forum 21 Greystone Gardens, Kenton, Middlesex	Referral list of astrologers with counselling training.
Astrological Lodge of London 6 Queen Square, Bloomsbury, London WC1	Weekly meetings, class for beginners, *Astrology* quarterly.
The Astrological Society 5 Stanton Avenue, Didsbury, Manchester	Weekly meetings, weekend seminars.

There are many local groups in existence throughout Great Britain. Contact can often be made via The Astrological Association or The Faculty of Astrological Studies.

Recommended Reading and Bibliography

Chapter 1
John Addey, *Astrology Reborn* (Astrological Association Publication, 1973)

Lyall Watson, *Supernature* (Coronet, 1974)

G.L. Playfair & S. Hill, *The Cycles of Heaven* (Pan, 1979)

J.A. West & J.G. Toonder, *The Case for Astrology* (Macdonald, 1970)

Geoffrey Dean, *Recent Advances in Astrology* (Astrological Association, 1977)

Arthur Koestler, *The Sleepwalkers* (Hutchinson, 1968)

Nicholas Campion, *An Introduction to the History of Astrology* (Inst. for the Study of Cycles in World Affairs, 1982)

Manly Palmer Hall, *The Story of Astrology* (David McKay, 1943)

Chapter 2

Charles E.O. Carter, *The Principles of Astrology* (Theosophical Society, 1971)

Charles E.O. Carter, *Essays on the Foundations of Astrology* (Theosophical Society, 1978)

Jeff Mayo, *The Astrologer's Astronomical Handbook* (Fowler, 1976)

Iain Nicolson, *Astronomy* (Arrow, 1977)

Carl G. Jung, *Man and his Symbols* (Dell, 1964)

Violet Shelley, *Symbols and the Self* (A.R.E. Press, 1971)

Chapter 3

Isabelle M. Pagan, *Signs of the Zodiac Analysed* (Theosophical Society, 1969)

Joan Hodgson, *Astrology, the Sacred Science* (White Eagle, 1978)

Linda Goodman, *Sun Signs* (Harrap, 1976)

Stephen Arroyo, *Astrology, Psychology and the Four Elements* (C.R.C.S., 1975)

Charles E.O. Carter, *The Zodiac and the Soul* (Theosophical Soc., 1972)

Chapter 4

John Filbey, *Natal Charting* (Aquarian, 1981)

Ralph William Holden, *The Elements of House Division* (Fowler, 1977)
Jeff Mayo, *The Astrologer's Astronomical Handbook* (Fowler, 1976)
Derek Howse, *Greenwich Time* (Oxford University Press, 1980)
Dane Rudhyar, *The Astrological Houses* (Doubleday, 1972)

Chapter 5

Alan Leo, *Art of Synthesis* (Fowler, 1975)
Joan Hodgson, *Astrology, the Sacred Science* (White Eagle, 1978)
Liz Greene, *Saturn* (Aquarian, 1977)
Bessie Leo, *Rays of Truth* (Fowler, 1909)

Chapter 6

Charles E.O. Carter, *The Astrological Aspects* (Theosophical Soc., 1975)

Chapter 7

Margaret E. Hone, *The Modern Textbook of Astrology* (Fowler, 1973)
Derek and Julia Parker, *The Compleat Astrologer* (Mitchell Beazley, 1984)
Nicholas De Vore, *Encyclopaedia of Astrology* (Philosophical Library, 1947)
Charles E.O. Carter, *An Encyclopaedia of Psychological Astrology* (Theosophical, 1972)
Alan Oken, *Alan Oken's Complete Astrology* (Bantam, 1980)
Lovell, Spencer Jones, Newell, Moore and Kopal, *The New Space Encyclopaedia* (Artemis, 1973)
Alister Hardy, *The Biology of God* (Jonathan Cape, 1975)
R.A. Schwaller de Lubicz, *Nature Word* (Lindisfarne Press, 1982)
Ralph Waldo Trine, *In Tune with the Infinite* (Bell & Hyman, 1981)

Index

Of further interest . . .

THE CHINESE ASTROLOGY WORKBOOK

How to Calculate and Interpret Chinese Horoscopes

DEREK WALTERS

There is far more to Chinese astrology than the personality types of Rat, Tiger, Monkey, etc. Traditional Chinese astrology is used, in fact, far more for divinatory purposes than for character analysis, and this practical guide therefore follows this bias.

With the aid of a glossary and numerous worksheets and charts, THE CHINESE ASTROLOGY WORKBOOK takes the student into the fascinating world of Chinese astrology: the intricacies of the Chinese calendar; both planetary and Purple Crepe Myrtle astrology (that based on the stars of the Great Bear); the Five Elements, vital to Chinese philosophy as well as their astrology; the Chinese interpretation of the five planets and its fundamental differences from the Western view; constructing and interpreting the final horoscope — all are explained clearly and methodically so that even the complete novice can grasp easily the concepts of Chinese astrology. These include:

stems and branches

the Five Elements and planets

personality profiles

the rulers of the Purple Palace

twenty-eight lunar mansions

imaginary planets